Student Practice Workbook
Grade 6

create.mheducation.com

McGraw Hill create®

Copyright 2022 by McGraw-Hill Education. All rights reserved.

Printed in the United States of America. Except as permitted under the United States Copyright Act of 1976, no part of this publication may be reproduced or distributed in any form or by any means, or stored in a database or retrieval system, without prior written permission of the publisher.

This McGraw-Hill Create text may include materials submitted to McGraw-Hill for publication by the instructor of this course. The instructor is solely responsible for the editorial content of such materials. Instructors retain copyright of these additional materials.

ISBN-13: 9781309127148

ISBN-10: 130912714X

Contents

WONDERS PRACTICE BOOK GRADE 6 STUDENT EDITION 1

Credits..... 405

Wonders

Practice Book

Grade 6

McGraw Hill

Contents

UNIT 1

Week 1

Grammar Sentences and Fragments 1
Grammar Sentence Types 2
Grammar Mechanics 3
Grammar Proofreading 4
Grammar Test: Sentence Types 5
Spelling Pretest/Posttest: Short Vowels 6
Phonics/Spelling Word Sort 7
Spelling Word Meaning 8
Spelling Proofreading 9
Phonics/Spelling Review 10
Vocabulary Content Words 11
Vocabulary High-Frequency Words 12

Week 2

Grammar Subjects 13
Grammar Predicates 14
Grammar Mechanics 15
Grammar Proofreading 16
Grammar Test: Subjects and Predicates 17
Spelling Pretest/Posttest: Long Vowels 18
Phonics/Spelling Word Sort 19
Spelling Word Meaning 20
Spelling Proofreading 21
Phonics/Spelling Review 22
Vocabulary Strategy Dictionary
    and Glossary 23
Vocabulary Strategy Metaphor
    and Simile 24

Week 3

Grammar Conjunctions and
    Compound Sentences 25
Grammar Compound Subjects
    and Predicates 26
Grammar Mechanics 27
Grammar Proofreading 28
Grammar Test: Sentence Combining 29
Spelling Pretest/Posttest:
    Frequently Misspelled Words 30
Phonics/Spelling Word Sort 31
Spelling Word Meaning 32
Spelling Proofreading 33
Phonics/Spelling Review 34
Vocabulary Related Words 35
Vocabulary High-Frequency Words 36

Week 4

Grammar Clauses 37
Grammar Complex Sentences 38
Grammar Mechanics 39
Grammar Proofreading 40
Grammar Test: Complex Sentences 41
Spelling Pretest/Posttest:
    r-Controlled Vowels 42
Phonics/Spelling Word Sort 43
Spelling Word Meaning 44
Spelling Proofreading 45
Phonics/Spelling Review 46
Vocabulary Strategy Context Clues 47
Vocabulary Strategy Context Clues 48

Week 5

Grammar Run-On Sentences 49
Grammar Comma Splices 50
Grammar Mechanics 51
Grammar Proofreading 52
Grammar Test: Run-On Sentences
    and Comma Splices 53
Spelling Pretest/Posttest: Compound
    Words 54
Phonics/Spelling Word Sort 55
Spelling Word Meaning 56
Spelling Proofreading 57
Phonics/Spelling Review 58
Vocabulary Related Words 59
Vocabulary Strategy Root Words 60

iii

UNIT 2

Week 1

Grammar Common and Proper Nouns 61
Grammar Concrete and Abstract Nouns 62
Grammar Mechanics 63
Grammar Proofreading 64
Grammar Test: Kinds of Nouns 65
Spelling Pretest/Posttest:
   Irregular Plurals 66
Phonics/Spelling Word Sort 67
Spelling Word Meaning 68
Spelling Proofreading 69
Phonics/Spelling Review 70
Vocabulary Content Words 71
Vocabulary Spiral Review 72

Week 2

Grammar Singular and Plural Nouns 73
Grammar Changes to Make Plurals 74
Grammar Mechanics 75
Grammar Proofreading 76
Grammar Test: Singular and Plural Nouns .. 77
Spelling Pretest/Posttest: Inflectional
   Endings 78
Phonics/Spelling Word Sort 79
Spelling Word Meaning 80
Spelling Proofreading 81
Phonics/Spelling Review 82
Vocabulary Strategy Word Origins 83
Vocabulary Strategy Greek and
   Latin Prefixes 84

Week 3

Grammar More Plural Nouns
   and Collective Nouns 85
Grammar Irregular Plural Nouns 86
Grammar Mechanics 87
Grammar Proofreading 88
Grammar Test: More Plural Nouns 89
Spelling Pretest/Posttest:
   Closed Syllables 90
Phonics/Spelling Word Sort 91
Spelling Word Meaning 92
Spelling Proofreading 93
Phonics/Spelling Review 94
Vocabulary Related Words 95
Vocabulary Spiral Review 96

Week 4

Grammar Possessive Nouns 97
Grammar Plural Possessive Nouns 98
Grammar Mechanics 99
Grammar Proofreading 100
Grammar Test: Possessive Nouns 101
Spelling Pretest/Posttest:
   Open Syllables 102
Phonics/Spelling Word Sort 103
Spelling Word Meaning 104
Spelling Proofreading 105
Phonics/Spelling Review 106
Vocabulary Strategy Thesaurus 107
Vocabulary Strategy Connotations and
   Denotations 108

Week 5

Grammar Appositives 109
Grammar Essential and Nonessential
   Appositives 110
Grammar Mechanics 111
Grammar Proofreading 112
Grammar Test: Appositives 113
Spelling Pretest/Posttest:
   Consonant + *le* Syllables 114

Phonics/Spelling Word Sort 115
Spelling Word Meaning 116
Spelling Proofreading 117
Phonics/Spelling Review 118
Vocabulary Related Words 119
Vocabulary Strategy Personification 120

UNIT 3

Week 1

Grammar Action Verbs 121
Grammar Direct Objects and
  Indirect Objects 122
Grammar Mechanics 123
Grammar Proofreading 124
Grammar Test: Action Verbs and Objects...125
Spelling Pretest/Posttest:
  Vowel Team Syllables 126
Phonics/Spelling Word Sort 127
Spelling Word Meaning 128
Spelling Proofreading 129
Phonics/Spelling Review 130
Vocabulary Related Words 131
Vocabulary Spiral Review 132

Week 2

Grammar Verb Tenses 133
Grammar Subject-Verb Agreement 134
Grammar Mechanics 135
Grammar Proofreading 136
Grammar Test: Verb Tenses 137
Spelling Pretest/Posttest:
  r-Controlled Vowel Syllables 138
Phonics/Spelling Word Sort 139
Spelling Word Meaning 140
Spelling Proofreading 141
Phonics/Spelling Review 142
Vocabulary Strategy Word
  Relationships 143
Vocabulary Strategy Paragraph Clues 144

Week 3

Grammar Main and Helping Verbs 145
Grammar Perfect Tenses and
  Progressive Forms 146
Grammar Mechanics 147
Grammar Proofreading 148
Grammar Test: Main and Helping Verbs ... 149
Spelling Pretest/Posttest:
  Frequently Misspelled Words 150
Phonics/Spelling Word Sort 151
Spelling Word Meaning 152
Spelling Proofreading 153
Phonics/Spelling Review 154
Vocabulary Related Words 155
Vocabulary Spiral Review 156

Week 4

Grammar Linking Verbs 157
Grammar Predicate Nouns
  and Adjectives 158
Grammar Mechanics 159
Grammar Proofreading 160
Grammar Test: Linking Verbs 161
Spelling Pretest/Posttest: Prefixes 162
Phonics/Spelling Word Sort 163
Spelling Word Meaning 164
Spelling Proofreading 165
Phonics/Spelling Review 166
Vocabulary Strategy Greek and
  Latin Roots 167
Vocabulary Strategy Prefixes and
  Suffixes 168

Week 5

Grammar Irregular Verbs 169
Grammar Special Spellings 170
Grammar Mechanics 171
Grammar Proofreading 172
Grammar Test: Irregular Verbs 173
Spelling Pretest/Posttest:
  Suffixes -ion and -tion 174
Phonics/Spelling Word Sort 175
Spelling Word Meaning 176
Spelling Proofreading 177
Phonics/Spelling Review 178
Vocabulary Content Words 179
Vocabulary Strategy Synonyms and
  Antonyms 180

v

UNIT 4

Week 1

Grammar Pronouns and Antecedents	181
Grammar Pronouns and Antecedents	182
Grammar Mechanics	183
Grammar Proofreading	184
Grammar Test: Pronouns and Antecedents	185
Spelling Pretest/Posttest: More Words with *-ion*	186
Phonics/Spelling Word Sort	187
Spelling Word Meaning	188
Spelling Proofreading	189
Phonics/Spelling Review	190
Vocabulary Content Words	191
Vocabulary Spiral Review	192

Week 2

Grammar Kinds of Pronouns	193
Grammar Subject and Object Pronouns	194
Grammar Mechanics	195
Grammar Proofreading	196
Grammar Test: Kinds of Pronouns	197
Spelling Pretest/Posttest: Vowel Alternation	198
Phonics/Spelling Word Sort	199
Spelling Word Meaning	200
Spelling Proofreading	201
Phonics/Spelling Review	202
Vocabulary Strategy Exaggeration and Hyperbole	203
Vocabulary Strategy Idioms	204

Week 3

Grammar Possessive Pronouns	205
Grammar Possessive Pronouns	206
Grammar Mechanics	207
Grammar Proofreading	208
Grammar Test: Possessive Pronouns	209
Spelling Pretest/Posttest: Prefixes and Suffixes	210
Phonics/Spelling Word Sort	211
Spelling Word Meaning	212
Spelling Proofreading	213
Phonics/Spelling Review	214
Vocabulary Related Words	215
Vocabulary Spiral Review	216

Week 4

Grammar Pronoun-Verb Agreement	217
Grammar Contractions	218
Grammar Mechanics	219
Grammar Proofreading	220
Grammar Test: Pronoun-Verb Agreement	221
Spelling Pretest/Posttest: Greek and Latin Prefixes	222
Phonics/Spelling Word Sort	223
Spelling Word Meaning	224
Spelling Proofreading	225
Phonics/Spelling Review	226
Vocabulary Strategy Sound Devices	227
Vocabulary Strategy Homophones	228

Week 5

Grammar More Pronouns	229
Grammar More Pronouns	230
Grammar Mechanics	231
Grammar Proofreading	232
Grammar Test: More Pronouns	233
Spelling Pretest/Posttest: Consonant Alternation	234
Phonics/Spelling Word Sort	235
Spelling Word Meaning	236
Spelling Proofreading	237
Phonics/Spelling Review	238
Vocabulary Related Words	239
Vocabulary Strategy Figurative Language	240

UNIT 5

Week 1

Grammar Adjectives	241
Grammar Order of Adjectives	242
Grammar Mechanics	243
Grammar Proofreading	244
Grammar Test: Adjectives	245
Spelling Pretest/Posttest: Homophones	246
Phonics/Spelling Word Sort	247
Spelling Word Meaning	248
Spelling Proofreading	249
Phonics/Spelling Review	250
Vocabulary Related Words	251
Vocabulary Spiral Review	252

Week 2

Grammar Articles	253
Grammar Demonstrative Adjectives	254
Grammar Mechanics	255
Grammar Proofreading	256
Grammar Test: Articles and Demonstrative Adjectives	257
Spelling Pretest/Posttest: Words from Around the World	258
Phonics/Spelling Word Sort	259
Spelling Word Meaning	260
Spelling Proofreading	261
Phonics/Spelling Review	262
Vocabulary Strategy Homographs	263
Vocabulary Strategy Context Clues	264

Week 3

Grammar Comparative Adjectives	265
Grammar Superlative Adjectives	266
Grammar Mechanics	267
Grammar Proofreading	268
Grammar Test: Adjectives That Compare	269
Spelling Pretest/Posttest: Latin Roots	270
Phonics/Spelling Word Sort	271
Spelling Word Meaning	272
Spelling Proofreading	273
Phonics/Spelling Review	274
Vocabulary Related Words	275
Vocabulary Spiral Review	276

Week 4

Grammar Comparing with *More*	277
Grammar Comparing with *Most*	278
Grammar Mechanics	279
Grammar Proofreading	280
Grammar Test: Comparing with *More* and *Most*	281
Spelling Pretest/Posttest: Greek Roots	282
Phonics/Spelling Word Sort	283
Spelling Word Meaning	284
Spelling Proofreading	285
Phonics/Spelling Review	286
Vocabulary Strategy Puns and Humor	287
Vocabulary Strategy Adages and Proverbs	288

Week 5

Grammar Comparing with *Good*	289
Grammar Comparing with *Bad*	290
Grammar Mechanics	291
Grammar Proofreading	292
Grammar Test: Comparing with *Good* and *Bad*	293
Spelling Pretest/Posttest: Suffixes *-ive*, *-age*, and *-ize*	294
Phonics/Spelling Word Sort	295
Spelling Word Meaning	296
Spelling Proofreading	297
Phonics/Spelling Review	298
Vocabulary Content Words	299
Vocabulary Strategy Connotations and Denotations	300

UNIT 6

Week 1

- **Grammar** Adverbs 301
- **Grammar** Intensifiers 302
- **Grammar** Mechanics 303
- **Grammar** Proofreading 304
- **Grammar** Test: Adverbs 305
- **Spelling** Pretest/Posttest:
  Suffixes -*ible* and -*able* 306
- **Phonics/Spelling** Word Sort 307
- **Spelling** Word Meaning 308
- **Spelling** Proofreading 309
- **Phonics/Spelling** Review 310
- **Vocabulary** Content Words 311
- **Vocabulary** Spiral Review 312

Week 2

- **Grammar** Adverbs That Compare 313
- **Grammar** Superlative Adverbs 314
- **Grammar** Mechanics 315
- **Grammar** Proofreading 316
- **Grammar** Test: Adverbs That Compare 317
- **Spelling** Pretest/Posttest: Suffixes -*ance*,
  -*ence*, -*ant*, and -*ent* 318
- **Phonics/Spelling** Word Sort 319
- **Spelling** Word Meaning 320
- **Spelling** Proofreading 321
- **Phonics/Spelling** Review 322
- **Vocabulary Strategy** Greek and
  Latin Affixes 323
- **Vocabulary Strategy** Latin Roots 324

Week 3

- **Grammar** Negatives 325
- **Grammar** Double Negatives 326
- **Grammar** Mechanics 327
- **Grammar** Proofreading 328
- **Grammar** Test: Negatives 329
- **Spelling** Pretest/Posttest:
  Greek Suffixes 330
- **Phonics/Spelling** Word Sort 331
- **Spelling** Word Meaning 332
- **Spelling** Proofreading 333
- **Phonics/Spelling** Review 334
- **Vocabulary** Related Words 335
- **Vocabulary** Spiral Review 336

Week 4

- **Grammar** Prepositions 337
- **Grammar** Prepositional Phrases 338
- **Grammar** Mechanics 339
- **Grammar** Proofreading 340
- **Grammar** Test: Prepositions 341
- **Spelling** Pretest/Posttest: Absorbed
  Prefixes 342
- **Phonics/Spelling** Word Sort 343
- **Spelling** Word Meaning 344
- **Spelling** Proofreading 345
- **Phonics/Spelling** Review 346
- **Vocabulary Strategy** Literal and
  Figurative Language 347
- **Vocabulary Strategy** Greek Roots 348

Week 5

- **Grammar** Combining Sentences 349
- **Grammar** Combining Sentences 350
- **Grammar** Mechanics 351
- **Grammar** Proofreading 352
- **Grammar** Test: Sentence Combining 353
- **Spelling** Pretest/Posttest:
  Words from Mythology 354
- **Phonics/Spelling** Word Sort 355
- **Spelling** Word Meaning 356
- **Spelling** Proofreading 357
- **Phonics/Spelling** Review 358
- **Vocabulary** Related Words 359
- **Vocabulary Strategy** Figurative
  Language 360

Handwriting 361

Grammar • Sentences and Fragments

Name _____

> - A **sentence** is a group of words that expresses a complete thought.
> - Every sentence begins with a **capital letter** and ends with an **end punctuation mark**: *I like to visit the beach.*
> - A **sentence fragment** does not express a complete thought: *To the beach.*

Read each sentence or phrase. If it is a sentence, write *S* on the line. If it is a fragment, write *F* on the line. Add words to each fragment to make it express a complete thought. Write the new sentences on the line.

1. The students wanted to buy a necktie for their teacher, Mr. Porter.

   _____

2. Mr. Porter always wears an unusual tie on Fridays.

   _____

3. Collected money for the tie.

   _____

4. Wanted something colorful and humorous.

   _____

5. Sophie and Max went shopping at a store that sells vintage clothing.

   _____

6. Max a wide, colorful tie from the 1970s.

   _____

In your writer's notebook, write about a time when you were surprised. Check your work to make sure each sentence expresses a complete thought and ends with the correct punctuation.

Grammar • Sentence Types

Name _____

> - A **declarative sentence** is a statement: *The cat slept on the chair.*
> - An **imperative sentence** gives a command: *Make your bed in the morning.*
> - An **interrogative sentence** asks a question: *What is your favorite book?*
> - An **exclamatory sentence** expresses excitement: *You are a great swimmer!*

Write whether each sentence makes a statement, gives a command, asks a question, or expresses excitement. Then write whether the sentence is declarative, imperative, interrogative, or exclamatory.

1. Tennis, badminton, table tennis, and racquetball are types of racquet sports. _____

2. Another name for table tennis is ping-pong. _____

3. Which racquet sport do you enjoy most? _____

4. Tell me more about badminton. _____

5. It sounds like great fun! _____

Reading/Writing Connection

Reread this paragraph from "The Monster in the Mountain." Underline one question. Circle the end punctuation of the question. Then explain why you think the author used this question in the paragraph.

> It was quiet for now, but I knew it was only sleeping. Frequent tremors and small earthquakes prove that this monster is not dead. Did the others standing there with me know about the danger beneath their feet?

_____

_____

2 Grade 6 • Unit 1 • Week 1

Grammar • Mechanics: **End Punctuation**

Name _____

- Every sentence begins with a capital letter.
- A statement ends with a period.
- A command ends with a period or an exclamation point.
- A question ends with a question mark.
- An exclamation ends with an exclamation point.
- An exclamation point can set off an **interjection**—a word that expresses strong emotion: *Careful! The soup is very hot.*

Rewrite each incorrect sentence, correcting the capitalization and end punctuation mark. If the sentence is correct, write *correct*.

1. let's buy the ingredients we need to make a tossed salad?

   _____

2. We will need lettuce, cucumber, radishes, carrots, and tomatoes.

   _____

3. please chop all the vegetables and toss them together?

   _____

4. how do you like our tossed salad.

   _____

5. Wow. I think it's great!

   _____

In your writer's notebook, write about a favorite food. Use sensory details to describe the ingredients and the taste of your food. Make sure you have used complete sentences and correct end punctuation.

Grammar • Proofreading

Name _____

- A **sentence** expresses a complete thought. A **fragment** does not express a complete thought.
- Sentences begin with a **capital letter** and end with an **end punctuation mark**.
- **Declarative** sentences end with a period.
- **Imperative** sentences end with a period or an exclamation point.
- **Interrogative** sentences end with a question mark.
- **Exclamatory** sentences end with an exclamation point.

Rewrite the passage. Correct the fragments so that they form complete sentences. Correct all capitalization and add correct punctuation marks.

HANDWRITING CONNECTION

Be sure to write legibly. Use proper spaces between words.

1. Hooray our school's dance team. Is competing in the state dance competition.

   _____

2. the dancers perform in four different categories?

   _____

3. I love to watch the dancing

   _____

4. are you going to go watch the dance team and cheer for them.

   _____

5. sign up for the bus in the school office

   _____

4 Grade 6 • Unit 1 • Week 1

English: Grammar • Apply

Name _____

What was your favorite reading selection or other text you read this week? Write a paragraph describing what you learned from it or why you enjoyed it. When you're done, exchange your writing with a partner. Proofread your partner's writing. Remember to apply the grammar you have learned this week.

Spelling • **Short Vowels**

Name _____

Fold back the paper along the dotted line. Use the blanks to write each word as it is read aloud. When you finish the test, unfold the paper. Use the list at the right to correct any spelling mistakes.

1. _____
2. _____
3. _____
4. _____
5. _____
6. _____
7. _____
8. _____
9. _____
10. _____
11. _____
12. _____
13. _____
14. _____
15. _____
16. _____
17. _____
18. _____
19. _____
20. _____

Review Words
21. _____
22. _____
23. _____

Challenge Words
24. _____
25. _____

1. gram
2. clash
3. dense
4. dread
5. prank
6. strict
7. drill
8. swan
9. prod
10. shrunk
11. scuff
12. clutch
13. threat
14. dwell
15. fund
16. text
17. rank
18. brink
19. mock
20. plaid
21. stuff
22. batch
23. sense
24. guest
25. cleanse

6 Grade 6 • Unit 1 • Week 1

Name _____

Phonics/Spelling • Word Sort

Short vowel sounds can be spelled in different ways.

- *Pl**ai**d* and *t**a**ck* each have the short *a* sound.
- *Dw**e**ll* and *h**ea**d* each have the short *e* sound.
- *Sw**a**n* and *r**o**ck* each have the short *o* sound.

Read each spelling word out loud. Listen carefully to each short vowel sound.

SPELLING TIP

The short *i* sound is usually spelled using the vowel *i* (*thin, wind, string*). Similarly, the short *u* sound is usually spelled using the vowel *u* (*lucky, bus, fund*).

Read the words in the box. Write the spelling words that contain the matching short vowel sound.

gram	prank	prod	threat	rank
clash	strict	shrunk	dwell	brink
dense	drill	scuff	fund	mock
dread	swan	clutch	text	plaid

short *a*, as in *cap*	short *e*, as in *pen*	short *i*, as in *pin*	short *o*, as in *hot* (spelled *a* or *o*)	short *u*, as in *but*

Look through this week's selections for more words to sort. Create a word sort for a partner in your writer's notebook.

Spelling • Word Meaning

Name _____

gram	prank	prod	threat	rank
clash	strict	shrunk	dwell	brink
dense	drill	scuff	fund	mock
dread	swan	clutch	text	plaid

A. Write the spelling word that matches each definition below.

1. thick, heavy, _____
2. live, reside, _____
3. verge, threshold, _____
4. laugh at, make fun of, _____
5. trick, joke, _____
6. grip, clench, _____
7. nudge, urge, _____
8. practice, exercise, _____
9. severe, stern, _____

B. Write the spelling word that best completes each sentence.

10. Please don't _____ your new shoes!
11. What is the _____ of that soldier?
12. The doll's red pants and orange shirt _____.
13. This social studies _____ is really interesting!
14. Can we start a _____ to build a new library?
15. I _____ playing my flute in front of an audience.
16. The band wore matching _____ shirts.
17. A _____ is a smaller amount than a kilogram.
18. What animal is a _____ to hummingbirds?
19. The _____ swimming on the lake is pure white.
20. My shirt has _____, and it no longer fits me.

8 Grade 6 • Unit 1 • Week 1

Spelling · Proofreading

Name _____

Six words are misspelled in the paragraphs below. Underline each misspelled word. Then write the words correctly on the lines.

    Mr. Bond was sick on Monday, so a substitute teacher took over our class. He wore a striped shirt under his tailored jacket with a clip-on plaide bowtie. Didn't he realize that stripes and plaide claesh? No one in the class dared to mocke him!

    The substitute teacher was really quite strect. When the fire alarm sounded, no one dared to make a sound as we lined up. During the fire drell, I saw him cluch the stack of tests to his chest. When we returned to the classroom, he passed out our tests. It was so quiet, you could hear a pin drop!

1. _____ 3. _____ 5. _____

2. _____ 4. _____ 6. _____

Writing Connection   Write about an experience you've had in school. Use at least four words from the spelling list.

_____
_____
_____
_____
_____
_____
_____
_____
_____
_____

Phonics/Spelling • **Review**

Name _____

> **Remember**
>
> Short vowel sounds can have multiple spelling patterns. Short *a* can be spelled with the letters *a* or *ai* (*back*, *plaid*). Short *e* can be spelled with *e* and *ea* (*bed*, *bread*). Short *o* can be spelled with *o* or *a* (*top*, *want*).

Circle the spelling word in each row that rhymes with the word in bold type. Write the spelling word on the line.

#	**bold**				
1.	**instead**	dread	deed	done	_____
2.	**shrill**	pail	drill	mail	_____
3.	**bunk**	rink	shrunk	shrink	_____
4.	**cash**	crush	clash	brush	_____
5.	**on**	come	been	swan	_____
6.	**rough**	tuft	scuff	tucked	_____
7.	**swell**	dwelt	dwell	drill	_____
8.	**lamb**	him	came	gram	_____
9.	**much**	clutch	match	itch	_____
10.	**zinc**	brick	brink	branch	_____
11.	**frank**	prank	pink	shrink	_____
12.	**met**	beat	feet	threat	_____
13.	**sod**	wade	prod	does	_____
14.	**picked**	strict	packed	poked	_____
15.	**tense**	vent	dense	depth	_____
16.	**shrank**	shrink	rank	wreck	_____
17.	**knock**	knuckle	mock	knick	_____
18.	**vexed**	trick	text	sect	_____
19.	**stunned**	fiend	friend	fund	_____
20.	**add**	raid	plaid	made	_____

10 Grade 6 • Unit 1 • Week 1

Vocabulary • Content Words

Name _____

> **Content words** are words that are specific to a field of study. For example, words like *eruption, ash,* and *volcanic* are science content words.
>
> Authors use content words to explain a concept or idea. Sometimes you can figure out what a content word means by using context clues. You can also use a dictionary to help you find the meaning of unfamiliar content words.

Go on a word hunt with a partner through "The Monster in the Mountain." Find as many content words related to volcanoes as you can. Write them in the chart.

CONNECT TO CONTENT

"The Monster in the Mountain" gives facts about Mount Vesuvius in Italy. The author describes the volcano through personal stories and uses content words that help you understand this science topic.

Circle two words that you were able to figure out the meaning of by using context clues. Write the words and what they mean on the lines.

_____
_____
_____
_____
_____

Grade 6 • Unit 1 • Week 1   **11**

Name _____

Vocabulary • High-Frequency Words

High-frequency words are the most common words in the English language. Many do not contain regular sound and spelling patterns, but they are found so often in texts that readers can easily recognize them. Below are some examples of high-frequency words. Read them aloud as quickly and accurately as you can.

homes	today	mountain	around	every
skin	time	elephant	buildings	earth
lion	close	fingers	think	down
about	miles	dry	once	shook

Read this excerpt from "The Monster in the Mountain." Underline the high-frequency words listed in the box. Underline each word only once.

> Every time I see this volcano up close, I think about how it had roared like a lion back in 1944. The trembling earth shook buildings for miles around, and streams of scalding lava flowed down the sides. Like glowing red fingers, they stretched out to crush defenseless homes below. It must have been terrifying to witness in person. Today, the lava that once cascaded down the mountain is hard and dry. It looks a bit like the skin of an elephant.

Reading/Writing Connection Imagine a volcano erupted in your community. Describe how you would prepare for this event. Use and underline at least five high-frequency words from the box in your writing.

_____
_____
_____
_____

Grade 6 • Unit 1 • Week 1

Grammar · **Subjects**

Name _____

> - The **complete subject** includes all the words that tell what or whom the sentence is about.
>
>   *The playful kitten pounced on the toy.*
>
> - The **simple subject** is the main word or words in the complete subject.
>
>   *The playful kitten pounced on the toy.*
>
> - A **subject** often performs the action of a sentence.

Read each sentence. Write the complete subject on the line provided below each example. Circle the simple subject.

1. The home soccer team was on the field before the game.

   _____

2. Clouds looked dark and ominous in the sky above.

   _____

3. Loyal soccer fans filled the stands of the Emerson Eagles' stadium.

   _____

4. Cold rain suddenly splashed on the metal bleachers.

   _____

5. We wondered whether the game would be canceled.

   _____

6. A lightning bolt lit up the sky!

   _____

   In your writers notebook, write about a game or sport you like to play. Explain the rules of the game. Reread your work to make sure you use complete sentences.

Grammar • **Predicates**

Name _____

- The **complete predicate** includes all the words that tell what the subject is or does.

    Claude Monet <u>painted water lilies at his home in Giverny, France.</u>

- The **simple predicate** is the main word or words in the complete predicate.

    Claude Monet <u>painted</u> water lilies at his home in Giverny, France.

- A **simple predicate** is a verb. It names actions or states of being.

Read each sentence. Write the complete predicate on the line provided below each example. Circle the simple predicate.

1. James and Maria visited the Art Institute of Chicago while in the city.

    _____

2. They especially enjoyed the Impressionist paintings.

    _____

3. The Art Institute is home to a famous collection of Impressionist art.

    _____

4. The museum houses paintings by Cassatt, Renoir, Monet, Degas, and many others.

    _____

5. Maria likes the works by American artist Mary Cassatt best.

    _____

6. James prefers the paintings of the French painter Claude Monet.

    _____

Use these sentences as a model. In your notebook, write about your favorite subject at school. Reread your work. Circle four simple predicates and underline the complete predicates.

14 Grade 6 • Unit 1 • Week 2

Grammar • Mechanics: **Sentence Fragments**

Name _____

- A **sentence** expresses a complete thought.

    I like to play basketball with my friends after school.

- A complete thought needs both a subject and predicate.

- A sentence that does not have both a subject and predicate is incomplete. It is a sentence fragment: *friends after school*

Below are fragments of sentences. Write *predicate* or *subject* to identify each fragment.

1. Many people. _____

2. Is Yellowstone National Park. _____

3. Visits his grandmother in Poland. _____

4. My friend Lilly. _____

5. Spend a day at the beach. _____

Reading/Writing Connection

Read this excerpt from "Donna O'Meara: The Volcano Lady." Circle the simple subject and underline the predicate of each sentence. Then write a paragraph about a place you would like to visit. Edit your work for sentence fragments.

> From their home, Donna and Steve run Volcano Watch International. (VWI) The O'Mearas' organization is dedicated to understanding how Earth's active volcanoes work. VWI uses photos and video to educate people about the dangers of volcanoes.

_____

_____

_____

_____

Grammar • Proofreading

Name _____

- The **complete subject** includes all the words that tell what or whom the subject is about. The **simple subject** is the main word or words in the complete subject.
- The **complete predicate** includes all the words that tell what the subject is or does. The **simple predicate** is the main word or words in the complete predicate.
- A sentence that does not have both a subject and predicate is incomplete. It is a sentence fragment.

Rewrite the passage. Combine the subjects and predicates so they form complete sentences.

This Saturday. Is our school's Fall Festival. One booth. Has fun games for young children. My class. Is in charge of the craft booth. We. Will provide paper, string, and branches for leaf mobiles. The festival. Will feature entertainment, also. Singers and a magician. Will perform each hour. Everyone. Is excited about the Fall Festival!

_____
_____
_____
_____

Connect to Community

Talk with a parent or another trusted adult about his or her favorite hobby. Ask questions to learn more about his or her interests. Then write a paragraph about the conversation.

_____
_____
_____
_____

English: Grammar • **Apply**

Name _____

COLLABORATE What was your favorite reading selection or other text you read this week? Write a paragraph describing what you learned from it or why you enjoyed it. When you're done, exchange your writing with a partner. Proofread your partner's writing. Remember to apply the grammar you have learned this week.

Spelling • Long Vowels

Name _____

Fold back the paper along the dotted line. Use the blanks to write each word as it is read aloud. When you finish the test, unfold the paper. Use the list at the right to correct any spelling mistakes.

1. _____
2. _____
3. _____
4. _____
5. _____
6. _____
7. _____
8. _____
9. _____
10. _____
11. _____
12. _____
13. _____
14. _____
15. _____
16. _____
17. _____
18. _____
19. _____
20. _____

Review Words
21. _____
22. _____
23. _____

Challenge Words
24. _____
25. _____

1. slope
2. acute
3. remote
4. bathe
5. gaze
6. rhyme
7. keen
8. tile
9. fuse
10. bleach
11. loan
12. tote
13. foal
14. foe
15. coax
16. bleak
17. continue
18. pave
19. meek
20. shrine
21. gram
22. dread
23. shrunk
24. trait
25. capsule

18 Grade 6 • Unit 1 • Week 2

Phonics/Spelling • Word Sort

Name _____

Long vowel sounds can have different spellings.
- Long *a*, or /ā/: st<u>ay</u>, pr<u>ey</u>, tr<u>ai</u>n, br<u>ea</u>k, f<u>a</u>k<u>e</u>
- Long *e*, or /ē/: fr<u>ee</u>, m<u>ea</u>n, f<u>ie</u>ld, athl<u>e</u>t<u>e</u>, <u>ei</u>ther
- Long *i*, or /ī/: sl<u>igh</u>t, f<u>i</u>nd, tr<u>y</u>, ins<u>i</u>d<u>e</u>
- Long *o*, or /ō/: g<u>o</u>, sl<u>o</u>p<u>e</u>, gr<u>ow</u>, l<u>oa</u>n

When a word ends with a silent e, as in *athlete*, the vowel before the consonant will have a long sound. This is called a **vowel-consonant-e (VCe)** pattern. The VCe pattern must stay in the same syllable: *ath/lete*.

Decoding Words

Divide the word *inside* into syllables: *in/side*. Blend the sounds of the first syllable, *in-*. Use what you know about syllable types. Blend the sounds of the next syllable, *-side*. Now say the syllables together to decode the word.

Read the words in the box. Write the spelling words that contain the same long vowel pattern.

slope	gaze	fuse	foal	continue
acute	rhyme	bleach	foe	pave
remote	keen	loan	coax	meek
bathe	tile	tote	bleak	shrine

vowel-consonant -*e* pattern, as in *hope*

1. _____
2. _____
3. _____
4. _____
5. _____
6. _____
7. _____
8. _____
9. _____
10. _____

two-vowel pattern, as in *peak* or *clue*

11. _____
12. _____
13. _____
14. _____
15. _____
16. _____
17. _____
18. _____
19. _____

unique long vowel pattern

20. _____

Look through this week's readings for more words to sort. Create a word sort in your writer's notebook.

Spelling • Word Meaning

Name _____

slope	gaze	fuse	foal	continue
acute	rhyme	bleach	foe	pave
remote	keen	loan	coax	meek
bathe	tile	tote	bleak	shrine

A. Write the spelling word that belongs with each group.

1. wash, cleanse, _____
2. enemy, opponent, _____
3. stare, watch, _____
4. urge, nudge, _____
5. barren, bare, _____

B. Write the spelling word that matches each definition.

6. sacred place _____
7. material used on a floor and roof _____
8. device used to set off an explosive _____
9. enthusiastic and eager _____
10. shy or timid _____
11. to resume _____
12. severe pain _____
13. having the same final sound _____
14. large handbag _____
15. hard-to-reach place _____
16. to lighten in color _____
17. a borrowed amount of money _____
18. to cover a street _____
19. steep incline _____
20. young horse _____

20   Grade 6 • Unit 1 • Week 2

Spelling • Proofreading

Name _____

Six misspelled words are in the paragraphs below. Underline each misspelled word. Then write the words correctly on the lines.

My dad and his friends have a kean interest in hiking and enjoy traveling to remoate locations to experience the outdoors. While other people might think that a rocky, wind-swept mountain is bleek, they look forward to the challenge of climbing it!

As my dad and his buddies make their ascent, they encounter a steep and treacherous sloape. But the reward is great once they reach the mountaintop. They gaiz in wonder at the hills, valleys, rivers, and lakes in the distance. On the way down, they bath in a cold mountain stream, and that takes the most courage of all!

1. _____ 2. _____ 3. _____

4. _____ 5. _____ 6. _____

Writing Connection — Write about what it might be like to hike up a mountain. Use at least four words from the spelling list.

_____
_____
_____
_____
_____
_____
_____
_____
_____
_____
_____

Phonics/Spelling · Review

Name _____

> **Remember**
>
> A vowel-consonant-e (VCe) spelling pattern usually produces a long vowel sound (*vote, bite*), but long vowel sounds can be spelled in other ways. Long *e* can be spelled *ee* or *ea* (*heel, wheat*). Long *o* can be spelled *oe* or *oa* (*toe, boat*). Long *i* can be spelled *y* (*fry, type*). Long *u* can be spelled *ue* (*blue*).

Circle the spelling word in each row that rhymes with the word in bold type. Write the spelling word on the line.

1. **style**	still	bail	tile	_____
2. **hope**	slop	slope	road	_____
3. **speech**	bleach	ouch	reached	_____
4. **own**	code	loan	load	_____
5. **bowl**	maul	foal	cow	_____
6. **jokes**	tux	coax	fax	_____
7. **sinew**	continue	flute	broom	_____
8. **float**	toad	tote	bow	_____
9. **waive**	have	pave	sieve	_____
10. **lathe**	wave	bathe	hath	_____
11. **raise**	gaze	has	rose	_____
12. **peak**	meek	pack	make	_____
13. **seek**	woke	peck	bleak	_____
14. **scene**	been	keen	fiend	_____
15. **time**	him	find	rhyme	_____
16. **whine**	grin	shrine	wind	_____
17. **lute**	acute	cut	feud	_____
18. **tow**	foe	all	cow	_____
19. **views**	news	fuse	us	_____
20. **coat**	load	soap	remote	_____

22   Grade 6 · Unit 1 · Week 2

Vocabulary Strategy • Dictionary and Glossary

Name _____

You can use a **dictionary,** or the **glossary** at the end of a nonfiction text, to find the meaning of an unfamiliar word. Use the **guide words** at the top of the page. Your word, called an **entry word,** will appear alphabetically between these words. It will be divided into **syllables.**

Each entry contains the word's **pronunciation,** its **part of speech,** and one or more numbered **definitions.** You might also find an example sentence that uses the word. The word's **origin,** or the language it comes from, is often shown as well.

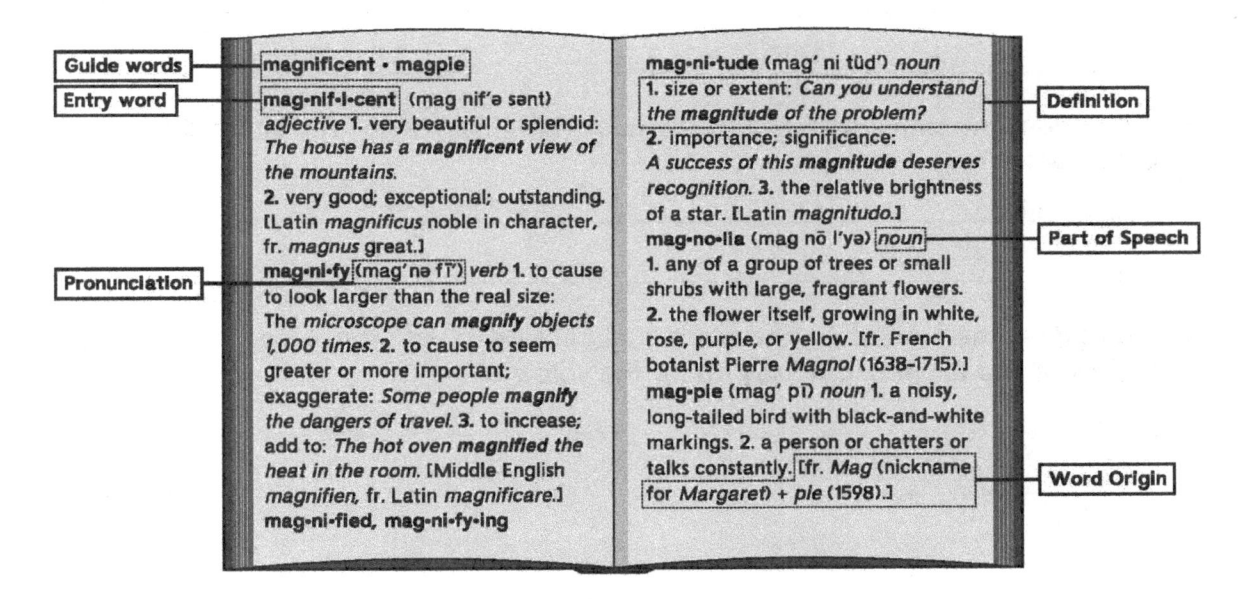

Guide words — magnificent • magpie

Entry word — **mag·nif·i·cent** (mag nif′ə sənt) *adjective* **1.** very beautiful or splendid: *The house has a magnificent view of the mountains.* **2.** very good; exceptional; outstanding. [Latin *magnificus* noble in character, fr. *magnus* great.]

Pronunciation — **mag·ni·fy** (mag′ nə fī′) *verb* **1.** to cause to look larger than the real size: *The microscope can magnify objects 1,000 times.* **2.** to cause to seem greater or more important; exaggerate: *Some people magnify the dangers of travel.* **3.** to increase; add to: *The hot oven magnified the heat in the room.* [Middle English *magnifien,* fr. Latin *magnificare.*] **mag·ni·fied, mag·ni·fy·ing**

mag·ni·tude (mag′ ni tūd′) *noun* **1.** size or extent: *Can you understand the magnitude of the problem?* ← **Definition** **2.** importance; significance: *A success of this magnitude deserves recognition.* **3.** the relative brightness of a star. [Latin *magnitudo.*]

mag·no·lia (mag nō l′yə) *noun* ← **Part of Speech** **1.** any of a group of trees or small shrubs with large, fragrant flowers. **2.** the flower itself, growing in white, rose, purple, or yellow. [fr. French botanist Pierre *Magnol* (1638–1715).]

mag·pie (mag′ pī) *noun* **1.** a noisy, long-tailed bird with black-and-white markings. **2.** a person or chatters or talks constantly. [fr. *Mag* (nickname for *Margaret*) + *pie* (1598).] ← **Word Origin**

Use the dictionary entries to answer the following questions.

1. What is the origin of the word *magnolia*? _____

2. Which entry word is a word that describes a noun? _____

3. Which entry word has the fewest syllables? _____

4. Which word means the same thing as *extent*? _____

5. Identify the definition of *magnify* that is used in this sentence: *Hailey always magnified her problems in her head.*

_____

Vocabulary Strategy • **Metaphor and Simile**

Name _____

**Read each metaphor and simile from "Mount St. Helens."
Answer the questions about each of the following comparisons.**

1. In the simile "Like a sleeping giant, Mount St. Helens lay still," how is Mount St. Helens like a giant before the eruption?

   _____

   _____

2. In the simile "Trees were blown down like matchsticks," what force causes the trees to fall, and what does the simile tell you about it?

   _____

   _____

3. What does the simile "After that, the quakes hit like waves" say about the earthquakes?

   _____

   _____

4. What does the metaphor "the giant could not sleep with the strong shakes of the earth below" say about the volcano?

   _____

   _____

Grammar • **Conjunctions and Compound Sentences**

Name _____

- A **conjunction** joins words or groups of words. *And* adds information; *but* shows contrast; *or* gives a choice.
- A **compound sentence** is two simple sentences that have been combined with a comma and a conjunction.
  There is a concert this weekend, and we would like to go.
- Use a semicolon to separate two parts of a compound sentence not separated by a conjunction.
  There is a concert this weekend; I need to buy tickets.

A. For each compound sentence that is joined by a conjunction, write the conjunction and what the conjunction does. If a semicolon joins the compound sentence, circle the semicolon.

1. Emily and her grandfather eat dinner together once a week, and they sometimes go out to a restaurant. _____

2. This week they could go to their favorite Japanese restaurant, or they could try a new Mexican place. _____

3. Emily could not decide, but her grandfather chose a Japanese dinner.

   _____

4. Grandfather wanted to take the bus; Emily preferred to walk to the restaurant.

   _____

B. Combine the two simple sentences on the lines below. Use the punctuation and conjunction shown in parentheses.

5. Emily wanted sushi. Her grandfather ordered teriyaki. (comma + *and*)

   _____

6. Emily ordered two kinds of sushi. They both were delicious! (semicolon)

   _____

In your writer's notebook, write a paragraph about a room at your school. Use compound sentences to add details to your writing. After you finish, check your work.

Grammar • Compound Subjects and Predicates

Name _____

- A **compound subject** has two or more subjects with the same predicate.
  <u>Lauren</u> <u>and</u> <u>Amy</u> take acting classes once a week.
- A **compound predicate** has two or more predicates with the same subject.
  They will <u>sing</u> <u>and</u> <u>dance</u> in a musical at the end of the year.
- Combine subjects or predicates using *and, or,* or *but,* or the words *either/or* or *neither/nor.*

Write an S if the sentence has a compound subject. Write a P if the sentence has a compound predicate. Write each compound subject or predicate on the line. Then circle word or words that combine the subjects or predicates.

1. Omar got a new puppy and named her Daisy.
   _____

2. Daisy and Omar enjoy playing outside together in good weather.
   _____

3. Neither Omar nor Daisy likes to be outside in the rain.
   _____

4. They either play inside or sleep during a rainstorm.
   _____

Reading/Writing Connection

Read the excerpt from "Cow Music." Circle each compound subject and underline each compound predicate. Then write two sentences of your own using compound subjects and predicates.

> I spun around and saw a tall kid playing a beat-up old saxophone in the clearing. His music was fantastic, and he didn't dress the way I figured a country kid would. Where were the muddy dungarees and plaid bandana?

_____

_____

_____

26 Grade 6 • Unit 1 • Week 3

Grammar • Mechanics: **Punctuating Compound Sentences**

Name _____

> - Use a comma before a coordinating conjunction in a compound sentence.
>   *My sister plays soccer, and she is on a tournament team.*
> - Use a semicolon to separate two parts of a compound sentence when they are not joined by a conjunction.
>   *The team plays in different towns; some towns are a long drive away.*
> - Do not use a comma to separate compound subjects or compound predicates joined by *and* or *or.*
>   *Monika and Lexi have scored the most goals.*

A. Combine each set of sentences to make a compound sentence. Use a comma and a conjunction or a semicolon as shown in parentheses.

1. My brother goes to Valley High School. He is involved in many activities. (semicolon)

   _____

2. Josh is in the Math Club. He is also on the track team. (comma + and)

   _____

3. You can usually find him on the track after school. He will be in the library. (comma + or)

   _____

B. Combine the subjects or predicates. Write the new sentence.

4. Shannon runs hurdles. Shannon throws the discus.

   _____

5. Demetrius plays in the school band. Demetrius sings in the choir.

   _____

6. Band performances keep Demetrius busy. Choir concerts keep Demetrius busy.

   _____

Write about your favorite season. Use compound and simple sentences in your writing. Then check that your punctuation is correct.

Grammar • **Proofreading**

Name _____

- Compound sentences must have a subject in each section.
- Use a comma before a conjunction in a compound sentence.
    We can make dinner at home, or we can go to a restaurant.
- If two parts of a compound sentence are not joined by a conjunction, use a semicolon to separate the parts.
    Today I went to the library; I borrowed two books.
- Do not use a comma to combine compound subjects or predicates.
    The deer ran and leapt through the valley.

Correct all capitalization and punctuation mistakes. Combine sentences with a conjunction to form compound sentences. Use conjunctions to combine subjects or predicates.

HANDWRITING CONNECTION

As you write, make sure that your sentences are written legibly.

1. the Maya and the Inca civilizations had many things in common. they also had many differences. _____

2. both civilizations grew crops. both civilizations developed sophisticated irrigation systems. _____

3. the Inca are known as great builders. the Maya are known as great builders.

4. The Incan culture lasted less than 200 years. The Mayan culture lasted more than 1000 years. _____

5. The Maya developed a written language. The Inca did not.

English: Grammar • **Apply**

Name _____

What was your favorite reading selection or other text you read this week? Write a paragraph describing what you learned from it or why you enjoyed it. When you're done, exchange your writing with a partner. Proofread your partner's writing. Remember to apply the grammar you have learned this week.

_____
_____
_____
_____
_____
_____
_____
_____
_____
_____
_____
_____
_____
_____

Spelling • Frequently Misspelled Words

Name _____

Fold back the paper along the dotted line. Use the blanks to write each word as it is read aloud. When you finish the test, unfold the paper. Use the list at the right to correct any spelling mistakes.

1. _____ 1. accuse
2. _____ 2. affect
3. _____ 3. beautiful
4. _____ 4. bought
5. _____ 5. busy
6. _____ 6. caught
7. _____ 7. different
8. _____ 8. done
9. _____ 9. effect
10. _____ 10. embarrass
11. _____ 11. especially
12. _____ 12. except
13. _____ 13. excuse
14. _____ 14. library
15. _____ 15. minute
16. _____ 16. nickel
17. _____ 17. probably
18. _____ 18. their
19. _____ 19. there
20. _____ 20. they're

Review Words
21. _____ 21. trait
22. _____ 22. remote
23. _____ 23. bathe

Challenge Words
24. _____ 24. recommend
25. _____ 25. separate

30 Grade 6 • Unit 1 • Week 3

Phonics/Spelling • Word Sort

Name _____

Some words are often misspelled because of irregular spelling patterns or confusion with similar sounding words.

- **do, due**
  Do you want to meet at the library after school?
  *Our science project is **due** this Friday.*

SPELLING TIP

Memory tricks can help you spell words that sound the same.
- The word *here* is in the word *there*, which refers to a location.
- *I=my*, helps you remember that *their* shows possession.
- *They're* is a contraction that stands for *they* and *are*.

Read the words in the box. Write the spelling words that contain the matching pattern.

accuse	busy	effect	excuse	probably
affect	caught	embarrass	library	their
beautiful	different	especially	minute	there
bought	done	except	nickel	they're

double consonants

1. _____
2. _____
3. _____
4. _____
5. _____
6. _____

similar-sounding words

7. _____
8. _____
9. _____

unique phonics patterns

10. _____
11. _____
12. _____
13. _____
14. _____
15. _____
16. _____
17. _____
18. _____
19. _____
20. _____

Look through this week's readings for more frequently misspelled words to sort. Create a word sort for a partner in your writer's notebook.

Spelling • Word Meaning

Name _____

accuse	busy	effect	excuse	probably
affect	caught	embarrass	library	their
beautiful	different	especially	minute	there
bought	done	except	nickel	they're

A. Write the spelling word that is an antonym, or opposite, of each word.

1. ugly _____ 4. similar _____

2. sold _____ 5. freed _____

3. inactive _____

B. Write the spelling word that best completes each sentence.

6. Will the teacher _____ the group of cheating on the test?

7. I'll be ready to go in a _____.

8. You need one more _____ to pay for the pencil.

9. _____ going to the Grand Canyon during spring break.

10. Kobe and Lea went to the _____ to do research.

11. She will _____ feel better by tomorrow.

12. I want to have _____ teacher for art class.

13. Keisha _____ likes fish tacos and rice for lunch.

14. Can we go _____ on Saturday?

15. The change in the law will _____ people who ride bikes.

16. He likes all sports _____ for football.

17. Will you _____ me while I do my homework?

18. One _____ of the drought was a rise in food prices.

19. Jake can't play until his work is _____.

20. Did I _____ you when I mentioned your name in my speech?

Spelling • Proofreading

Name _____

Three misspelled words are in each paragraph below. Underline each one. Then write the words correctly on the lines.

    Have you ever wondered what efect the Internet has had on the way students learn? Before the Internet was invented, people would go to there local libary and take out books to research and write a report.

    Today, it takes only a minit to go on the Internet and find reliable websites for research purposes. The Internet is especialy convenient for locating information when you're too buzy to go to the library.

1. _____ 2. _____ 3. _____

4. _____ 5. _____ 6. _____

Writing Connection — Write about the tools you use to research and write reports. Use four or more words from the spelling list.

_____
_____
_____
_____
_____
_____
_____
_____
_____
_____

Phonics/Spelling • Review

Name _____

> **Remember**
>
> Some words are often misspelled because they have unusual spelling patterns. For example, the first syllable of the word *beautiful* features a long *u* sound spelled *eau*. The word *done* has a VCe spelling pattern, but the vowel sound is a short *u* instead of a long *o*.
>
> Some words are misspelled because they sound similar to other words. The words *their, there,* and *they're* have different meanings and spellings, but they are pronounced the same way. Check a dictionary to confirm your spelling.

accuse	busy	effect	excuse	probably
affect	caught	embarrass	library	their
beautiful	different	especially	minute	there
bought	done	except	nickel	they're

Fill in the missing letters of each word to form a spelling word. Then write the spelling word on the line.

1. b ____ ____ utiful _____
2. c ____ ____ ght _____
3. ef ____ e ____ t _____
4. e ____ ____ use _____
5. lib ____ ____ ry _____
6. embar ____ as ____ _____
7. dif ____ ____ rent _____
8. min ____ t ____ _____
9. a ____ cu ____ e _____
10. es ____ ecial ____ y _____
11. nic ____ ____ l _____
12. th ____ ____ r _____
13. b ____ ____ ght _____
14. d ____ ne _____
15. e ____ ____ ept _____
16. prob ____ ____ ly _____
17. bu ____ ____ _____
18. the ____ ____ _____
19. the ____ ' ____ e _____
20. af ____ e ____ t _____

34 Grade 6 • Unit 1 • Week 3

Name _____

Vocabulary • **Related Words**

Expand your vocabulary by adding or removing **inflectional endings, prefixes, or suffixes** to a base word to create different forms of a word.

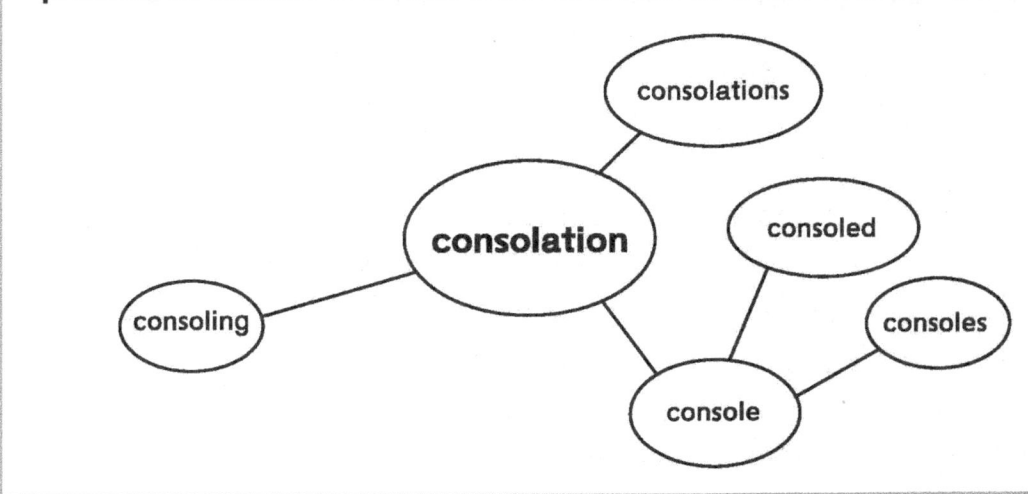

- **consolation**
  - consolations
  - consoled
  - consoles
  - console
  - consoling

Write as many words related to *indispensable* as you can. Write them on each icon image on the tablet.

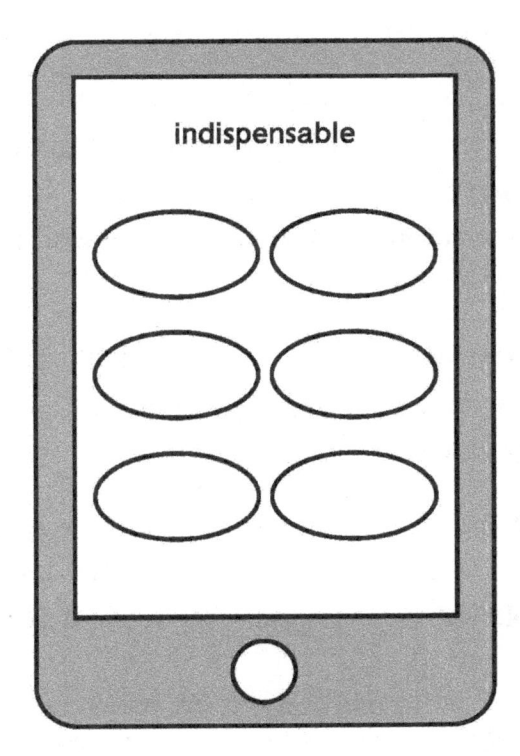

indispensable

Grade 6 • Unit 1 • Week 3

Vocabulary • High-Frequency Words

Name _____

> Remember that **high-frequency words** are the most common words in the English language. Because you read and write them often, you will probably be able to recognize many of these words instantly. Take a look at the following examples.

apple	neighbor	between	market	sheep
across	afternoon	furniture	kitchen	cool
branch	hungry	beautiful	fruits	dollar
sandwich	country	sweater	pictures	hour

Complete the paragraph using the high-frequency words in the box.

On Saturday _____, we decided to go for a drive in the _____. It was a _____ autumn day; every _____ of every tree was loaded with colorful leaves. The sun was shining, but there was a _____ breeze, so I wore my _____.

After an _____ on the road, we stopped at an antique store that our _____ recommended. This charming shop was in an old barn and sold _____ and framed _____ from the nineteenth century. Just _____ the street was a green pasture where _____ and cows quietly grazed.

Next we found a nearby farmer's _____ with stalls full of late-season _____ and vegetables. Dad got a jug of _____ cider, and Jane bought a pumpkin for only a _____.

Suddenly we were all _____, so we looked for a place where we could get a _____ and a bowl of soup. Grandpa's Cozy _____, _____ the old mill and the grain silo, seemed like the perfect place.

With a partner, write more about an afternoon in the country. Use as many high-frequency words as you can.

36 Grade 6 • Unit 1 • Week 3

Grammar • Clauses

Name _____

- A **clause** is a group of words with a subject and a verb.
- An **independent clause** forms a complete thought and can be a sentence.

    I enjoy reading.

- A **dependent clause** is not a complete thought and cannot stand as a sentence.

    When I'm at the beach

- A **subordinating conjunction** connects a dependent and independent clause. Words such as *after, although, as, because, until, when,* and *while* are subordinating conjunctions.

    I enjoy reading <u>when</u> I'm at the beach.

Write *I* beside each independent clause. Write *D* beside each dependent clause. Then rewrite each dependent clause so that it is part of a sentence. Underline the subordinating conjunction in the sentence.

1. When I go to the library. _____

_____

2. Because I like to learn about famous people in history. _____

_____

3. Most of my friends prefer fiction. _____

_____

4. Although I enjoy fiction. _____

_____

5. Until it's time to go home. _____

_____

In your writer's notebook, write about an adventure that you had. Include at least two sentences with dependent clauses. Circle the subordinating conjunctions.

Grammar • Complex Sentences

Name _____

- A **complex sentence** is an independent clause and one or more dependent clauses: *The veterinarian helped my dog when he injured his paw.*
- **Relative pronouns** (*who, whose, whom, which,* and *that*) join independent and dependent clauses.
- **Relative adverbs** (*where, when,* and *why*) join independent and dependent clauses.

For each sentence, write the dependent clause on the line. Circle the relative pronoun or adverb.

1. Today I went to a movie with my sister, who loves action films.

   _____

2. We went to a theater where she often goes with her friends.

   _____

3. She heard about this movie from a friend whose brother loved it.

   _____

4. When I go to a movie with friends, we usually choose something light and funny.

   _____

Reading/Writing Connection

Read the excerpt from "The Writing on the Wall." Underline the dependent clauses that include a relative pronoun or adverb. Then write a new sentence using a relative pronoun or adverb.

> When my mother reminded me that the classes in New York would be taught by real, working artists, I felt a glimmer of excitement. And when she told me I could stay with my aunt and her family who live in the city, it seemed sort of crazy not to go.

_____

_____

38 Grade 6 • Unit 1 • Week 4

Grammar • Mechanics: Punctuating Complex Sentences

Name _____

- Some dependent clauses are essential to the meaning of the sentence. Do not use commas to set off these clauses.

  The plane was delayed <u>because of bad weather in the area</u>.

- Some clauses are nonessential. They do not affect the basic meaning of the sentence. Use commas to set off these clauses.

  My brother, <u>who is younger than I,</u> beat me in the race.

- Dashes or parentheses can also set off nonessential clauses.

  Last night <u>(during the storm)</u> the electricity went out in the house!

Decide whether the clause is essential or nonessential to the meaning of the sentence. Write an *E* for essential and an *N* for nonessential. If needed, rewrite the sentence using the correct punctuation.

1. I want to buy a present for my dad whose birthday is next week. _____

   _____

2. I would like to buy him a wristwatch because he does not have one. _____

   _____

3. He loves the watch, that sits in the window of the jewelry store. _____

   _____

4. I will look for a similar one that is not so expensive. _____

   _____

5. My grandmother's watch which she has had for twenty years came from a

   department store. _____

   _____

   _____

In your writer's notebook, write about activities you enjoy in the fall. Check your work for correct punctuation.

Grammar • Proofreading

Name _____

> - A **complex sentence** contains an independent clause and one or more dependent clauses.
> - A **subordinating conjunction** or a **relative pronoun** connects a dependent and independent clause.
> - Do not use commas to set off clauses that are essential to the meaning of the sentence.
> - Use commas, dashes, or parentheses to set off nonessential clauses.

Rewrite the sentences. Correct the capitalization and punctuation mistakes, adding punctuation as needed. Draw a line under the complex sentences.

1. although I like sports and snow I have never learned to ski

   _____

2. my scout troop is going skiing this December

   _____

3. All the scouts will take skiing lessons, before we hit the big slopes

   _____

4. we will spend the night at Sugar Loaf Camp which is near the ski hill.

   _____

5. This is, the camp where I learned, how to swim when I was eight

   _____

6. in summer, we sleep in tents, because the nights are warm

   _____

7. this winter the nights will be very cold

   _____

8. I am glad that we will sleep in a cabin!

   _____

English: Grammar • **Apply**

Name _____

What was your favorite reading selection or other text you read this week? Write a paragraph describing what you learned from it or why you enjoyed it. When you're done, exchange your writing with a partner. Proofread your partner's writing. Remember to apply the grammar you have learned this week.

_____
_____
_____
_____
_____
_____
_____
_____
_____
_____
_____
_____
_____
_____

Spelling • *r*-Controlled Vowels

Name _____

Fold back the paper along the dotted line. Use the blanks to write each word as it is read aloud. When you finish the test, unfold the paper. Use the list at the right to correct any spelling mistakes.

1. _____
2. _____
3. _____
4. _____
5. _____
6. _____
7. _____
8. _____
9. _____
10. _____
11. _____
12. _____
13. _____
14. _____
15. _____
16. _____
17. _____
18. _____
19. _____
20. _____

Review Words
21. _____
22. _____
23. _____

Challenge Words
24. _____
25. _____

1. search
2. starve
3. rumor
4. reward
5. sparkle
6. bargain
7. parched
8. pursue
9. servant
10. torch
11. earnest
12. mourn
13. fierce
14. pierce
15. urge
16. wharf
17. court
18. weird
19. favorite
20. burnt
21. library
22. minute
23. caught
24. sphere
25. aeronautics

42 Grade 6 • Unit 1 • Week 4

Phonics/Spelling • Word Sort

Name _____

A vowel followed by the letter *r* is called an *r*-controlled vowel.

Read the following words out loud: **sm<u>ar</u>t, h<u>ear</u>ty, sh<u>are</u>d, w<u>ear</u>s, fo<u>r</u>lo<u>r</u>n, m<u>ore</u>, c<u>our</u>se**. Notice how the /är/ and /ôr/ sounds can have different spellings.

When the vowels *e, i,* and *u* are followed by *r,* the sound is usually /ûr/. Read the following words out loud: **f<u>er</u>n, visit<u>or</u>, squ<u>ir</u>m, p<u>ur</u>ple**. Notice how the same sound can be spelled with different vowels.

SPELLING TIP

The /ûr/ sound at the end of the word is usually spelled *-er,* but it may also be spelled *-or* as in *visitor, -ar* as in *dollar,* or *-ur* as in *femur.*

Read the words in the box. Write the spelling words that contain the *r*-controlled vowel pattern.

search	sparkle	servant	fierce	court
starve	bargain	torch	pierce	weird
rumor	parched	earnest	urge	favorite
reward	pursue	mourn	wharf	burnt

ar
1. _____
2. _____
3. _____
4. _____
5. _____
6. _____

er
7. _____

or
8. _____
9. _____
10. _____

ur
11. _____
12. _____
13. _____

ear
14. _____
15. _____

our
16. _____
17. _____

ier
18. _____
19. _____

eir
20. _____

Grade 6 • Unit 1 • Week 4   43

Spelling • Word Meaning

Name _____

search	sparkle	servant	fierce	court
starve	bargain	torch	pierce	weird
rumor	parched	earnest	urge	favorite
reward	pursue	mourn	wharf	burnt

A. Write the spelling word that is similar in meaning to the first two words.

1. preferred, well-liked, _____
2. hunt, seek, _____
3. nudge, prod, _____
4. go after, chase, _____
5. ferocious, vicious, _____
6. thirsty, dry, _____
7. cut-rate, deal, _____
8. serious, firm, _____
9. penetrate, puncture, _____
10. hunger, crave, _____

B. Write the spelling word that best completes each sentence.

11. The class heard a _____ about the football team.
12. The athlete lit the Olympic _____ to begin the games.
13. Workers unloaded boxes from the ship and onto the _____.
14. The team was already warming up on the basketball _____.
15. Marco didn't understand Lee's _____ joke.
16. The _____ prepared the palace for the royal family.
17. The pie crust was _____ because I left it in the oven too long.
18. The family will _____ the loss of its pet cat.
19. The sunlight made the ring _____ in the store window.
20. She didn't want a _____ for finding the lost puppy.

44   Grade 6 • Unit 1 • Week 4

Spelling • Proofreading

Name _____

Six misspelled words are in the paragraphs below. Underline each misspelled word. Then write the words correctly on the lines.

Many national parks erge backpackers to exercise caution when hiking in faverite areas that may be a bit remote. For example, it's important to sign in before setting out. Then park rangers will know where hikers are in case they need to serch for a missing person.

It is also important to pack enough bottled water so that you don't become parcht. Park rangers recommend taking extra food so that you don't strve. Wearing sunscreen, even on overcast days, will prevent your skin from being bernt by the sun's rays.

1. _____ 3. _____ 5. _____

2. _____ 4. _____ 6. _____

Writing Connection — Write about how you would prepare for a trip to an outdoor recreation area. Describe how you would be cautious when walking or hiking there. Use four or more words from the spelling list.

_____
_____
_____
_____
_____
_____
_____
_____
_____
_____
_____

Phonics/Spelling • **Review**

Name _____

> **Remember**
>
> Words with *r*-controlled vowel sounds can be spelled in different ways. The /ôr/ sound can be spelled *or* as in *for*, *our* as in *tour*, and *ar* as in *reward*. The /ûr/ sound can be spelled *er* as in *fern*, *ear* as in *earth*, *ur* as in *fur*, and *or* as in *honor*. The /îr/ can be spelled *eir* as in *weird* and *ier* as in *tier*.

search	sparkle	servant	fierce	court
starve	bargain	torch	pierce	weird
rumor	parched	earnest	urge	favorite
reward	pursue	mourn	wharf	burnt

A. Circle the spelling word in each row that rhymes with the word in bold type. Write the spelling word on the line.

1. **perch**   each   search   parch   _____
2. **morph**   core   forth   wharf   _____
3. **drew**   feud   pursue   spewed   _____
4. **torn**   form   stern   mourn   _____
5. **jargon**   bargain   logging   gone   _____
6. **consumer**   runner   rumor   more   _____
7. **carve**   art   starve   car   _____
8. **chord**   bared   reward   short   _____
9. **beard**   heard   weird   card   _____
10. **sort**   court   search   forth   _____

B. Write the missing letters to complete the spelling word.

11. sp __ __ kle

12. e __ __ nest

13. p __ __ __ ce

14. b __ __ nt

15. p __ __ ched

16. t __ __ ch

17. fav __ __ ite

18. __ __ ge

19. f __ __ __ ce

20. s __ __ vant

46 Grade 6 • Unit 1 • Week 4

Vocabulary Strategy • Context Clues

Name _____

Identify the boldfaced word in each passage. Note its position in the sentence and the words that come before and after. On the lines below, write the word's part of speech. Then use the clues in the surrounding text to write a definition for the word.

1. Ty lives in the **adjacent** house. Since he's right next door, I can always find him immediately when I need help with my homework.

   _____

2. "Where has that cat gotten to?" Mom said with a sigh. Max, our friendly German shepherd, was always easy to find, but Mr. Whiskers was such an **elusive** animal.

   _____

3. The first step in making steel is to **smelt** iron ore. In this process, heat is applied to melt the ore and separate the metal from it.

   _____

4. After the earthquake, a great **chasm** formed in the earth. The crack was so wide and deep that a house could have fallen into it.

   _____

5. "You should **omit** this sentence from your paragraph," said Ms. Jaffe. "It's better to just get right to the point." My teacher was always telling me to leave words, sentences, and even whole paragraphs out of my essays. *Less is more* seemed to be her motto.

   _____

6. Hannah frowned at the scene outside her window. The pouring rain was showing no signs of letting up, and she should have started her walk to school over ten minutes ago. *Why did I have to lose* my umbrella? she thought to herself. Then she pulled her raincoat tightly around her and **reluctantly** stepped out into the storm.

   _____

Vocabulary Strategy • Context Clues

Name _____

Read the following sentences from "Smart Start." Underline the context clues that help you figure out the meaning of the word in bold. Then write the word's meaning on the line.

1. Math had always been torture for Alex. For extra humiliation, his little sister had **accelerated** and was taking the same math subject as he, despite being almost two years younger.

   _____

2. Soon the bird base was complete, and he was partway into making the crane. So **absorbed** was he, that he didn't hear the footsteps of the person approaching his table.

   _____

3. Alex recognized that Sophia was making an effort to put him at ease, so he **granted** her a quick smile. "What made you start to like it?" he asked politely.

   _____

Use what you know about context clues to explain the following word in a sentence: *pastime*. **Be sure to include context clues that explain the word's meaning.**

_____

_____

Grammar • Run-on Sentences

Name _____

> - A **run-on sentence** results when two main or independent clauses are joined with no punctuation or coordinating conjunction.
> - A run-on sentence may be two main clauses separated by only a comma, two main clauses with no punctuation between them, or two main clauses with no comma before the coordinating conjunction.
>
>   *The bird flew to the bird feeder it ate all the seeds.* (incorrect)
>
>   *The bird flew to the bird feeder, and it ate all the seeds.*

Read each sentence. If the sentence is correct, write *C* on the line. If it is a run-on sentence, write *R*.

1. The blue jay is one of the many birds native to North America it is a member of the crow family. _____

2. Blue jays can be aggressive and they often chase other smaller birds. _____

3. Blue jays are known for warning other birds when a predator is near. _____

4. Blue jays are slow fliers hawks and owls can usually catch them easily. _____

5. Blue jays are protective of their nests, they can be aggressive toward humans who come too close. _____

6. Blue jays have a reputation for raiding nests and stealing eggs, but this behavior may not be very common. _____

7. Young blue jays like to find and carry around brightly colored objects. _____

8. The blue jay is an omnivore it eats animals, grains, nuts, seeds, and fruit. _____

In your writer's notebook, write about an exciting moment you had with your family or friends. Be sure to use compound sentences in your writing. Reread your work when you are done. Check for run-on sentences.

Grade 6 • Unit 1 • Week 5   49

Grammar • Comma Splices

Name _____

- The use of a comma in a run-on sentence that has two main clauses is called a **comma splice**.
  Dominique went to school, she rode her bike there. (incorrect)
- To correct a comma splice, replace the comma with a period and create two sentences. *Dominique went to school. She rode her bike there.*

Read each sentence. Put a C on the line after each correct sentence. Rewrite sentences that have a comma splice. Correct the comma splice by creating two sentences.

1. The Mustangs are a high school football team in our town, they are one of the top teams in the conference.

   _____

   _____

2. My cousin, Preston, plays for the Mustangs, he is a linebacker.

   _____

3. The Mustangs play in a stadium on Highland Drive, beside the school.

   _____

4. Football is popular in our town, almost everyone attends the Friday night games.

   _____

   _____

Reading/Writing Connection Read the excerpt from "Making Money: A Story for Change." Combine the sentences on the lines below. Edit your work to avoid comma splices and run-on sentences.

> They grew crops and raised animals for food. So the first form of currency was probably livestock.

_____

_____

50 Grade 6 • Unit 1 • Week 5

Grammar • Mechanics: Correcting Run-on Sentences

Name _____

- Correct a run-on sentence by dividing it into two sentences.
- Correct a run-on sentence by changing it into a compound sentence connected by a comma and a coordinating conjunction.
- Correct a run-on sentence by inserting a semicolon or a conjunction.

Rewrite each run-on sentence correctly.

1. Scientists study wildlife in order to protect it the study of the cheetah is an example.

   _____

   _____

2. The cheetah is found mainly in Africa it is also found in parts of the Middle East.

   _____

   _____

3. The cheetah has been called a natural running machine it is able to reach speeds of 60 to 70 miles per hour.

   _____

   _____

4. Its feet have large pads with sharp edges these special pads help the cheetah grip the ground.

   _____

   _____

5. The cheetah is an endangered species it is even extinct in India and Northern Africa.

   _____

   _____

Grammar • Proofreading

Name _____

> - A **run-on sentence** results when two main or independent clauses are joined with no punctuation or coordinating conjunction. The use of a comma in a run-on sentence that has two main clauses is called a **comma splice**. *My cat sleeps all day, he likes to lay in the sun.* (incorrect)
> - To correct a comma splice, replace the comma with a period and create two sentences. *My cat sleeps all day. He likes to lay in the sun.*
> - Correct a run-on sentence by dividing it into two sentences or changing it into a compound sentence connected by a comma and a coordinating conjunction.
> - Correct a comma splice with a semicolon or a conjunction with the comma.

Proofread each sentence. Rewrite each sentence correctly, correcting run-on sentences and comma splices.

1. Manuel calls his grandfather Luis Abuelito, he always tells Manuel stories about his childhood in Mexico.

   _____

   _____

2. Abuelito and Manuel share stories about their friends but their favorite thing to talk about is soccer.

   _____

   _____

3. He is an artist so he teaches Manuel how to paint landscapes and portraits.

   _____

   _____

4. Abuelito paints landscapes of Mexico, his favorites are golden sunsets.

   _____

English: Grammar • **Apply**

Name _____

What was your favorite reading selection or other text you read this week? Write a paragraph describing what you learned from it or why you enjoyed it. When you're done, exchange your writing with a partner. Proofread your partner's writing. Remember to apply the grammar you have learned this week.

Spelling • Compound Words

Name _____

Fold back the paper along the dotted line. Use the blanks to write each word as it is read aloud. When you finish the test, unfold the paper. Use the list at the right to correct any spelling mistakes.

1. _____
2. _____
3. _____
4. _____
5. _____
6. _____
7. _____
8. _____
9. _____
10. _____
11. _____
12. _____
13. _____
14. _____
15. _____
16. _____
17. _____
18. _____
19. _____
20. _____

Review Words
21. _____
22. _____
23. _____

Challenge Words
24. _____
25. _____

1. brother-in-law
2. science fiction
3. after-school
4. wading pool
5. old-fashioned
6. question mark
7. teenager
8. nearsighted
9. self-respect
10. northwest
11. full-time
12. windshield
13. watermelon
14. twenty-five
15. heartbeat
16. fingernail
17. seaweed
18. eyelid
19. seashell
20. all-star
21. fierce
22. urge
23. bargain
24. barbed wire
25. fire escape

Name _____

Phonics/Spelling • Word Sort

Compound words are made up of two or more words. They can be closed, open, or hyphenated.
- *Mailbox* is an example of a closed compound word.
- *Living room* is an example of an open compound word.
- *Merry-go-round* is an example of a hyphenated compound word.

Decoding Words

The word *boardwalk* is made up of two smaller words: *board* and *walk*. Read the two words together.

Read the words in the box. Write the spelling words that follow the pattern.

brother-in-law	old-fashioned	self-respect	watermelon	seaweed
science fiction	question mark	northwest	twenty-five	eyelid
after-school	teenager	full-time	heartbeat	seashell
wading pool	nearsighted	windshield	fingernail	all-star

open

1. _____
2. _____
3. _____

hyphenated

4. _____
5. _____
6. _____
7. _____

8. _____
9. _____
10. _____

closed

11. _____
12. _____
13. _____
14. _____

15. _____
16. _____
17. _____
18. _____
19. _____
20. _____

Look through this week's readings for more words to sort. Read the words aloud. Then create a word sort for a partner in your writer's notebook.

Grade 6 • Unit 1 • Week 5   55

Spelling • Word Meaning

Name _____

brother-in-law	old-fashioned	self-respect	watermelon	seaweed
science fiction	question mark	northwest	twenty-five	eyelid
after-school	teenager	full-time	heartbeat	seashell
wading pool	nearsighted	windshield	fingernail	all-star

A. Write the spelling word that matches each definition.

1. the hard surface at the end of a finger _____
2. regard for oneself as a human being _____
3. glass used to protect occupants of a vehicle _____
4. involving one's full attention _____
5. unable to see distant objects clearly _____
6. a shallow area of water for children to play in _____
7. the hard exterior of a marine organism _____
8. a fold of skin that protects the eye _____
9. plant growing in the sea, especially marine algae _____
10. the compass point midway between north and west _____

B. Write the spelling word that best completes each sentence.

11. The _____ game usually takes place in February.
12. I could feel my _____ increase as I ran up the hill.
13. This author enjoys writing _____.
14. My mother's brother is my father's _____.
15. I loved my grandparents' _____ recipes from long ago.
16. It's a tradition to serve _____ at the 4th of July barbecue.
17. A _____ usually has a lot of homework during the week.
18. She will be _____ years old in June.
19. That sentence doesn't need a _____ at the end of it.
20. Marco has several _____ activities, including karate.

56 Grade 6 • Unit 1 • Week 5

Spelling • Proofreading

Name _____

There are four misspelled words in the first paragraph and three in the second. Underline each misspelled word. Then write the words correctly on the lines.

   On display at many aquariums is a wide assortment of marine life. Hidden among the seeweed, you might spy a sea-shell or a camouflaged sea creature. Many aquariums hold after school programs for children. A teanager would also enjoy the wide variety of educational and interactive offerings.

1. _____   3. _____

2. _____   4. _____

   By the time many basketball players are twenty five years old, they have been playing professionally for five or six years. A player who performs at the highest level usually becomes an allstar. Because of the intense workouts and rigorous travel schedule, playing professional basketball is more than a fultime job.

5. _____   7. _____

6. _____

Writing Connection Write about marine life or about a personal experience with a sport. Use at least four words from the spelling list.

_____
_____
_____
_____
_____
_____
_____

Phonics/Spelling • **Review**

Name _____

> **Remember**
>
> A compound word is made up of two or more words. They can be closed, open, or hyphenated. You can more easily spell and figure out the meaning of a compound word by breaking it into its smaller component words.

brother-in-law	old-fashioned	self-respect	watermelon	seaweed
science fiction	question mark	northwest	twenty-five	eyelid
after-school	teenager	full-time	heartbeat	seashell
wading pool	nearsighted	windshield	fingernail	all-star

Fill in the missing syllable or word to complete the compound word. Then write the spelling word on the line.

1. _____ mark _____
2. wind_____ _____
3. finger_____ _____
4. _____-fashioned _____
5. full-_____ _____
6. _____-school _____
7. self-_____ _____
8. science _____ _____
9. brother-_____-law _____
10. _____melon _____
11. teen_____ _____
12. _____sighted _____
13. all-_____ _____
14. wading _____ _____
15. twenty-_____ _____
16. _____shell _____
17. heart_____ _____
18. eye_____ _____
19. north_____ _____
20. sea_____ _____

58 Grade 6 • Unit 1 • Week 5

Vocabulary • Related Words

Name _____

Expand your vocabulary by adding or removing inflectional endings, prefixes, or suffixes to a base word to create different forms of a word.

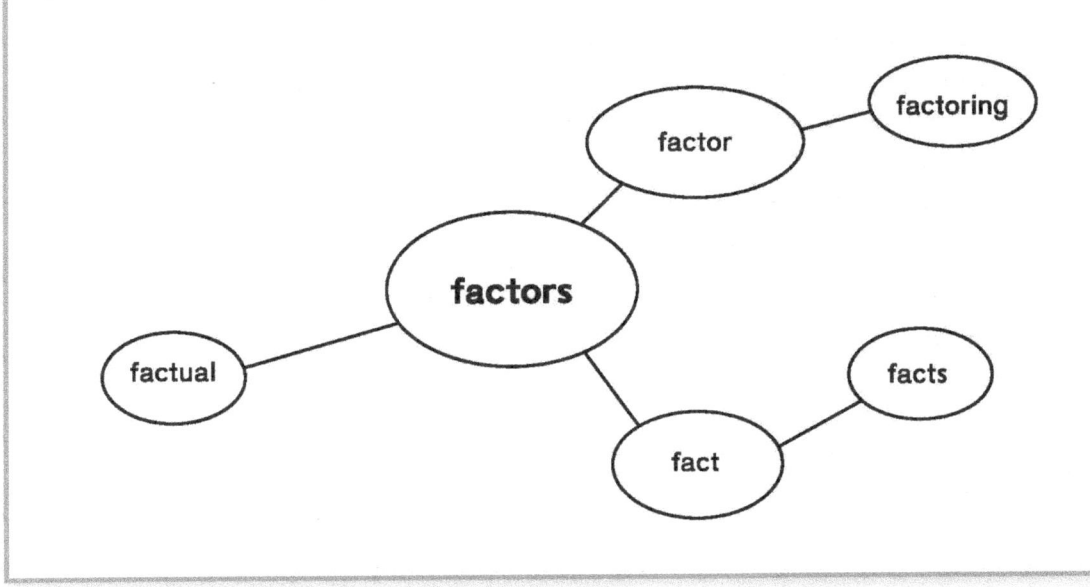

- factors
  - factor
    - factoring
  - factual
  - fact
    - facts

Write as many related words to "manufactured" on the wallet as you can. Use your notes from "The Big Picture of Economics" or a dictionary to help you. Add more lines if you can think of more words.

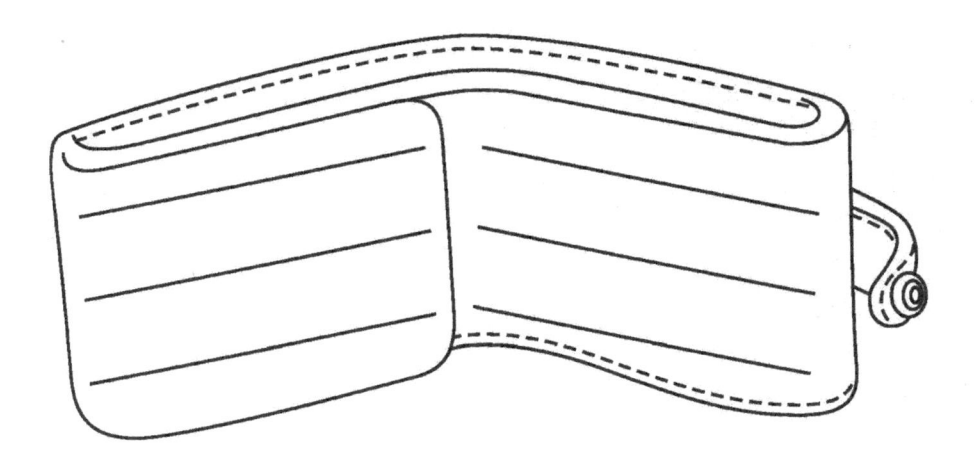

Vocabulary • Root Words

Name _____

Read the following sentences from "The Ups and Downs of Inflation." Write a definition of the word in bold, using context clues and the meaning of the root word.

1. From earning to spending and everything in between, **inflation** affects what happens to your money. Simply put, inflation is when prices rise. You are able to purchase fewer items with each dollar you have.

   root word: inflate

   _____

2. With fewer skateboards to sell, each one will be more **valuable** to buyers.

   root word: value

   _____

3. This **shortage** of supply can lead to what is called "cost-push" inflation.

   root word: short

   _____

4. Another way prices can be pushed higher is if the **government** decides to print lots more money.

   root word: govern

   _____

5. With inflation, the desire for goods and services is greater than the economy's **ability** to meet the demand.

   root word: able

   _____

60 Grade 6 • Unit 1 • Week 5

Grammar • Common and Proper Nouns

Name _____

- A **noun** names a person, place, thing, or idea.
- A **common noun** names any person, place, thing, or idea, and it is not capitalized: *scientist, restaurant, hammer, opinion.*
- A **proper noun** names a specific person, place, thing, or idea. It is capitalized: *Clara Barton, The Library of Congress, Friday, Fourth of July.*

Read each sentence. Underline each common noun once. Underline each proper noun twice.

1. My friend Kyle collects stamps from around the world.

2. Kyle brought his collection to school to show the class.

3. His favorites are from Portugal, New Zealand, and China.

4. Our librarian Mrs. Paquette said the library has books and magazines that tell about the hobby.

5. Many websites also feature information on stamps, and how to start a collection.

6. Some people collect stamps by category, such as animals, famous people, or landmarks.

7. Kyle has an old stamp from the United States with a picture of Albert Einstein.

8. Lions, leopards, and giraffes are some of the animals on his stamps from Africa.

9. A stamp from England shows the ruins at Stonehenge.

10. The stamps with butterflies from Malaysia are the most colorful.

In your writer's notebook, write a paragraph about an organization that helps people. Include three proper nouns. Check your work for correct capitalization and punctuation.

Grade 6 • Unit 2 • Week 1   61

Grammar • Concrete and Abstract Nouns

Name _____

- A **concrete noun** names something you can see, feel, hear, smell, or taste: *rain, lightning, cookies, coffee.*
- An **abstract noun** names something you cannot see, feel, hear, smell, or taste: *freedom, energy, holiday, anger, bravery.*

Read each sentence. Underline the concrete nouns. Put brackets [ ] around the abstract nouns.

1. My grandmother has vivid memories of her childhood.

2. She tells us about the city where she lived as a young girl.

3. Using my imagination, I can picture her apartment.

4. Every morning, her family had fresh bread from the bakery across the street.

5. They sat around a big table and discussed their plans for the day.

6. Sometimes they talked about politics or sports.

7. After dinner, the children played on the sidewalk, while their parents visited.

8. She enjoyed the friendliness of their neighborhood.

Reading/Writing Connection

Read this excerpt from "Who Created Democracy?" Circle the abstract nouns. Then choose two abstract nouns to use in your own sentence.

> As some powerful state governments tried to promote their ideas and force their wills on the nation, many people realized that a compromise between state governments and a new federal government would be necessary.

_____

_____

Grammar • Mechanics: **Punctuating Business Letters**

Name _____

> - In the opening of a business letter, capitalize the salutation, the person's name, and his or her abbreviated title: *Dear Mrs. Joseph:*
> - Use a colon after the salutation of a business letter. Use a comma after the closing: *Sincerely, Randi*

A. Match each group of words in the left column with the rule in the right column that will correct its mistake.

1. Dear Mrs. ramirez: Capitalize the person's abbreviated title.

2. Best regards: Use a comma after the closing.

3. Dear Mr. Olson   Capitalize the person's name.

4. dear Ms. Chu: Use a colon after the salutation.

5. Dear dr. Danko: Capitalize the salutation.

B. Rewrite the salutation and closing from Exercise A below.

6. Dear Mrs. ramirez: _____

7. Best regards: _____

8. Dear Mr. Olson _____

Connect to Community Talk to a parent or another trusted adult about some of your favorite brands and products. Together, compose a business letter describing why you enjoy the products. Then research the company together to find whom to send the letter. Edit and proofread your letter or correct capitalization.

_____
_____
_____
_____

Grade 6 • Unit 2 • Week 1   **63**

Grammar • Proofreading

Name _____

- A **common noun** names any person, place, thing, or idea and is not capitalized unless it begins a sentence.
- A **proper noun** names a specific person, place, thing, or idea and is always capitalized.
- In the opening of a business letter, capitalize the salutation, the person's name, and his or her abbreviated title.
- Use a colon after the salutation of a business letter. Use a comma after the closing.

Proofread the business letter for errors in capitalization and punctuation. Underline the letters that you think should be capitalized. Put brackets [ ] around the capital letters that you think should not be capitalized. Correct the punctuation.

707 scarlet avenue
denton, texas 76201
october 11 2014

city printers Company
456 Center street
dallas texas 75217

dear Sir or Madam

My school needs an affordable printing company to produce our basketball Programs. Could you please tell me what you would charge to print a 24-page program? The Text and Photographs will be in black and white. We will need the programs by december 2.

Thank you for your assistance.

Sincerely

nate williams

64 Grade 6 • Unit 2 • Week 1

English: Grammar • **Apply**

Name _____

What was your favorite reading selection or other text you read this week? Write a paragraph describing what you learned from it or why you enjoyed it. When you're done, exchange your writing with a partner. Proofread your partner's writing. Remember to apply the grammar you have learned this week.

_____
_____
_____
_____
_____
_____
_____
_____
_____
_____
_____
_____
_____
_____

Spelling • Irregular Plurals

Name _____

Fold back the paper along the dotted line. Use the blanks to write each word as it is read aloud. When you finish the test, unfold the paper. Use the list at the right to correct any spelling mistakes.

1. _____ 1. echoes
2. _____ 2. photos
3. _____ 3. data
4. _____ 4. scarves
5. _____ 5. volcanoes
6. _____ 6. shelves
7. _____ 7. media
8. _____ 8. bacteria
9. _____ 9. wolves
10. _____ 10. dominoes
11. _____ 11. solos
12. _____ 12. thieves
13. _____ 13. wives
14. _____ 14. cuffs
15. _____ 15. staffs
16. _____ 16. buffaloes
17. _____ 17. sheriffs
18. _____ 18. tornadoes
19. _____ 19. sopranos
20. _____ 20. loaves

Review Words
21. _____ 21. old-fashioned
22. _____ 22. windshield
23. _____ 23. question mark

Challenge Words
24. _____ 24. halves
25. _____ 25. wharves

Phonics/Spelling • Word Sort

Name _____

Most nouns are made plural by adding -s to the end of the word. Other nouns have irregular spellings in their plural form.

- To form the plural of nouns ending in a consonant followed by *o*, add *-s* or *-es*, as in *tacos* and *heroes*.
- In words that end in *-f* or *-fe*, change it to *-v* plus *-es* to form the plural, as in *halves*. For words ending in *-ff*, add *-s*, as in *cliffs*.
- Some nouns have no spelling change when they are in the plural form: *data, fish*.

SPELLING TIP

There are some words that do not add a letter to the end to make the plural form. These words either change the vowel (*man* to *men*), change the word, or keep their singular form (*deer, fish*). Memorizing these spellings will help you to remember them.

Read the words in the box. Write the spelling words that match the plural spelling patterns.

echoes	volcanoes	wolves	wives	sheriffs
photos	shelves	dominoes	cuffs	tornadoes
data	media	solos	staffs	sopranos
scarves	bacteria	thieves	buffaloes	loaves

-s

1. _____
2. _____
3. _____

-oes

4. _____
5. _____

6. _____
7. _____
8. _____

-ves

9. _____
10. _____
11. _____

12. _____
13. _____
14. _____

-ffs

15. _____
16. _____
17. _____

plurals that don't end in -s

18. _____   19. _____   20. _____

Grade 6 • Unit 2 • Week 1   **67**

Spelling • Word Meaning

Name _____

echoes	volcanoes	wolves	wives	sheriffs
photos	shelves	dominoes	cuffs	tornadoes
data	media	solos	staffs	sopranos
scarves	bacteria	thieves	buffaloes	loaves

A. Read the word histories. Fill in each blank with a spelling word.

1. _____: an Old English word *scylfe* meaning "ledge" or "crag"

2. _____: a Latin word *solus*, which means "alone"

3. _____: a Latin word *supra*, which means "above"

B. Write the spelling word that matches each definition below.

4. small living things that often cause disease _____

5. criminals who take other people's property _____

6. repeating of sounds _____

7. shaggy-haired animals living on the North American plains _____

8. destructive funnel-shaped clouds _____

9. rectangular-shaped blocks used for playing games _____

10. wild canines that hunt in packs _____

11. mass communication, such as newspapers, TV, and the Internet _____

12. sturdy walking sticks _____

13. married women _____

14. law enforcement officers _____

15. openings in the Earth's crust that let out ash and lava _____

16. folded-up material around the bottom of pants _____

17. baked bread _____

18. garments worn around the head or neck _____

19. pictures made by a camera _____

20. collected facts or information _____

Spelling • Proofreading

Name _____

Six misspelled words are in the paragraphs below. Underline each misspelled word. Then write the words correctly on the lines.

If you're planning a trip to Yellowstone National Park, be sure to take your camera. You'll want to take lots of photoes of the wildlife there. Before you drive through the park, pick up a wildlife book that provides important datas on the animals you will see from a distance. When you park in designated areas, do not leave valuables in your car. Thiefs have been known to break into parked vehicles.

You might also take a pair of binoculars. Keep them handy as you drive. You might spot some buffalos interacting with a wolf. Or when you're in your motel late at night, you might hear the echos of wolfs howling.

1. _____ 3. _____ 5. _____

2. _____ 4. _____ 6. _____

Writing Connection Write about a trip you've taken or would like to take to a national park or wildlife area. Use at least four words from the spelling list.

_____
_____
_____
_____
_____
_____
_____
_____
_____
_____

Grade 6 • Unit 2 • Week 1   69

Phonics/Spelling • Review

Name _____

Remember

While most nouns become plural by adding -s or -es to the end of the word, irregular nouns form plurals in other ways.

- In words that end in -f or -fe, such as *shelf* and *knife*, change the -f to -v plus -es to form the plural: *shelves, knives*.
- Some irregular nouns are made plural by adding different endings (*ox, oxen*), changing vowels (*goose, geese*), or changing the word (*person, people*).
- Still other irregular plurals remain in their singular form: *fish, deer, species*.

echoes	volcanoes	wolves	wives	sheriffs
photos	shelves	dominoes	cuffs	tornadoes
data	media	solos	staffs	sopranos
scarves	bacteria	thieves	buffaloes	loaves

Fill in the missing letters of each word to form a spelling word. Then write the spelling word on the line.

1. thie __ __ s _____
2. cuf __ __ _____
3. sopran __ __ _____
4. wol __ __ s _____
5. sherif __ __ _____
6. sta __ f __ _____
7. tornad __ e __ _____
8. phot __ __ _____
9. buffal __ __ s _____
10. volcan __ __ s _____
11. da __ __ _____
12. loa __ e __ _____
13. shel __ e __ _____
14. sol __ __ _____
15. wi __ __ s _____
16. domin __ e __ _____
17. med __ __ _____
18. scar __ __ s _____
19. bacter __ __ _____
20. ech __ e __ _____

Grade 6 • Unit 2 • Week 1

Vocabulary • Content Words

Name _____

Content words are words that are specific to a field of study. For example, words like *government, colonists,* and *patriots* are social studies content words.

Authors use content words to explain a concept or idea. Sometimes you can figure out what a content word means by using context clues. You can also use a dictionary to help you find the meaning of unfamiliar content words.

Go on a word hunt with a partner through "The Democracy Debate." Find as many content words related to the history of democracy as you can. Write them in the chart below.

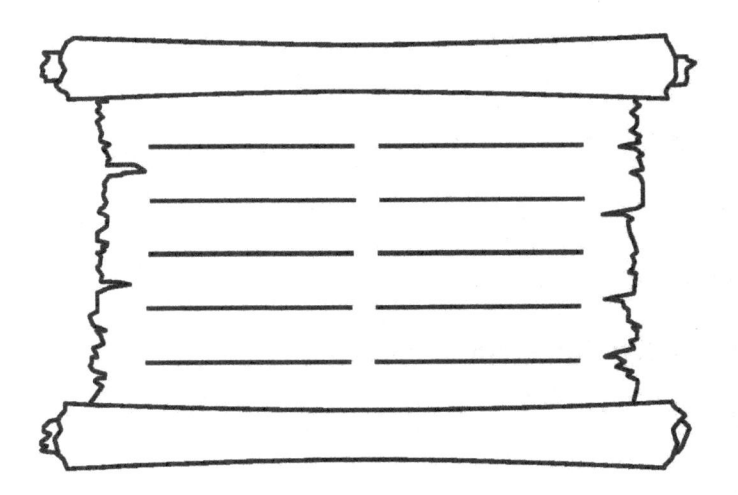

CONNECT TO CONTENT

"The Democracy Debate" gives facts about the history of democracy. It introduces the reader to ancient philosophers and their views on a democratic government. The author uses content words that help you understand this social studies topic.

Circle two words that you were able to figure out the meaning of using context clues. Write the words and what they mean on the lines.

_____
_____
_____
_____

Grade 6 • Unit 2 • Week 1   71

Vocabulary • Spiral Review

Name _____

Write the vocabulary word from the box that answers each clue below. You may use a dictionary to confirm word meanings.

salaries	consolation	manufactured	formula
pulverize	cascaded	basically	inventory
factors	sarcastic	fluctuate	available

1. This word might describe someone's sense of humor. _____
2. This describes what you can do with a sledgehammer. _____
3. This verb can refer to the rise and fall of temperature. _____
4. This word is a synonym for *essentially*. _____
5. This describes how a waterfall moved down a cliff. _____
6. This word describes what workers earn from their employers. _____
7. This word describes an award you get that isn't first place. _____
8. This word is a synonym for *elements*. _____
9. This is a word for all the items for sale at a store. _____
10. This word can describe a friend who is free to go to movies. _____
11. This word might describe an equation. _____
12. This describes the final product of an automobile plant or a paper mill. _____

_____

COLLABORATE With a partner, write more clues for the vocabulary words. Trade your clues with another pair and work together to figure out the answers.

Grammar • Singular and Plural Nouns

Name _____

- A **singular noun** names one person, place, thing, or idea.
- A **plural noun** names more than one person, place, thing, or idea. Most plural nouns are formed by adding -s or -es to a singular noun.
    beaches, bicycles, pears, boxes
- If a word ends in *y* and the letter in front of the *y* is a vowel, then add -s.
    toy, toys; monkey, monkeys; play, plays
- If the letter in front of the *y* is a consonant, then drop the *y* and add -ies.
    flurry, flurries; city, cities

Read each sentence. Underline each singular noun. Put brackets [ ] around each plural noun.

1. Our library has three new computers.

2. Students can use a computer to do projects.

3. They can research a historical person or write reports.

4. Each teacher has an account, and each student has a special password.

5. All the books and magazines in the library are cataloged on the computer.

Reading/Writing Connection — **Read the excerpt from "The Democracy Debate." Two singular nouns are underlined. Describe how to form the plural form of each noun on the lines below.**

About 350 B.C., Aristotle wrote in his book *Politics* that a government that tries to restrict power to a few educated men would not work. It would benefit only the rich. A democracy run by common people would not work either, because such people might not make wise decisions.

_____

_____

Grade 6 • Unit 2 • Week 2   73

Grammar • **Special Changes to Make Plurals**

Name _____

- If a noun ends in -f, sometimes add -s, but sometimes change the f to a v and add -es to form the plural: reef, reefs; half, halves.
- If a noun ends in -lf, change the f to a v and add -es to form the plural: wolf, wolves; calf, calves.
- For most nouns ending in -fe, change the f to a v and add -s to form the plural: safe, safes; life, lives.

A. Underline the misspelled plural nouns in each sentence. Write the words correctly on the line. Some plural nouns are spelled correctly.

1. The children wore coats and scarfs when they raked the leafs. _____

2. Chefs need knifes when they prepare most dishs. _____

3. Andrew Lang wrote storys about elfs and fairies. _____

4. Passing the bluffes, the river rafters heard the howls of wolfs. _____

B. Write the plural form of each singular noun.

5. life _____

6. shelf _____

7. hoof _____

8. roof _____

9. thief _____

10. giraffe _____

In your writer's notebook, write about a place you have visited. Draw one line under each singular noun and two lines under each plural noun.

Grammar • Mechanics: Using Commas in a Series, Punctuating Letter Parts

Name _____

> - Use commas to separate three or more words, phrases, or clauses in a sentence.
> - Use commas after all elements you are separating, except the last one of the series: *I need to buy yeast, flour, and salt for my bread recipe.*
> - When writing a business letter, follow the salutation with a colon. Follow the closing with a comma.

Rewrite each incorrect item, correcting the punctuation. If the item is correct, write correct.

1. Dear Sir or Madam,

   _____

2. I am interested in a career in broadcasting on television in radio or, in another news medium.

   _____
   _____

3. I would like to be a news anchor, sportscaster reporter or producer.

   _____
   _____

4. Please send me information about what these careers are like, what I should study in school, and which activities could help me prepare.

   _____
   _____

5. Sincerely;

   _____

Grammar • Proofreading

Name _____

- Most plural nouns are formed by adding -s or -es to a singular noun.
- If a word ends in a vowel and y, add -s. If the word ends in a consonant and y, drop the y and add -ies.
- If a noun ends in -f, sometimes add -s, but sometimes change the f to a v and add -es. If a noun ends in -lf, change the f to a v and add -es. For most nouns ending in -fe, change the f to a v and add -s.
- Use commas to separate three or more words, phrases, or clauses in a sentence. Use a comma after each element except the last one of the series.
- In a business letter, follow the salutation with a colon. Follow the closing with a comma.

Proofread for errors. Rewrite the sentences using the correct plural forms and correct punctuation.

COMMON ERRORS

Certain nouns, such as *information, milk, snow,* and *furniture*, always take the singular form. Example: *There is too much furniture in this room.*

1. Dear Principal Jacobs,

   _____

2. A winter storm left a fresh blanket of snow on lawns streets and driveways, in our neighborhood.

   _____
   _____

3. The bushs trees and leafs glisten with ice and snow.

   _____

4. Icicles hang from the roofes cables and branchs.

   _____

> In your writer's notebook, write a paragraph describing the neighborhood around your school. Use commas to list details of the neighborhood. Then read through your work and correct any comma errors.

76 Grade 6 • Unit 2 • Week 2

English: Grammar • **Apply**

Name _____

What was your favorite reading selection or other text you read this week? Write a paragraph describing what you learned from it or why you enjoyed it. When you're done, exchange your writing with a partner. Proofread your partner's writing. Remember to apply the grammar you have learned this week.

_____
_____
_____
_____
_____
_____
_____
_____
_____
_____
_____
_____
_____
_____

Spelling • Inflectional Endings

Name _____

Fold back the paper along the dotted line. Use the blanks to write each word as it is read aloud. When you finish the test, unfold the paper. Use the list at the right to correct any spelling mistakes.

1. _____ 1. sloped
2. _____ 2. stifling
3. _____ 3. marveled
4. _____ 4. sipped
5. _____ 5. encouraged
6. _____ 6. permitting
7. _____ 7. orbiting
8. _____ 8. credited
9. _____ 9. labored
10. _____ 10. uttered
11. _____ 11. referred
12. _____ 12. hovered
13. _____ 13. totaled
14. _____ 14. accused
15. _____ 15. patrolling
16. _____ 16. reviving
17. _____ 17. surrounding
18. _____ 18. unraveling
19. _____ 19. confiding
20. _____ 20. regretting

Review Words
21. _____ 21. echoes
22. _____ 22. shelves
23. _____ 23. media

Challenge Words
24. _____ 24. interpreted
25. _____ 25. swiveling

78 Grade 6 • Unit 2 • Week 2

Phonics/Spelling • Word Sort

Name _____

The inflectional endings *-ed* and *-ing* change the verb tense. *-ed*: past; *-ing*: present

- When a word ends with a consonant and *e*, drop the *e* and add *-ed* or *-ing*: hik**ed**, hik**ing** (hike).
- When a word ends with a vowel and a consonant, double the final consonant and add *-ed* or *-ing*: gri**nned**, gri**nning** (grin). There are some exceptions: **edited, editing**.

SPELLING TIP

When a word ends in *y*, change the *y* to *i* before adding *-ed*: **spied** (spy), **cried** (cry), **tried** (try).

Write the spelling words that match the inflectional ending patterns.

sloped	encouraged	labored	totaled	surrounding
stifling	permitting	uttered	accused	unraveling
marveled	orbiting	referred	patrolling	confiding
sipped	credited	hovered	reviving	regretting

double final consonant and -ed

1. _____
2. _____

-ed without doubled consonant

3. _____
4. _____
5. _____
6. _____
7. _____

8. _____

drop e before adding -ed

9. _____
10. _____
11. _____

double final consonant and -ing

12. _____
13. _____
14. _____

-ing without doubled consonant

15. _____
16. _____
17. _____

drop e before adding -ing

18. _____
19. _____
20. _____

Grade 6 • Unit 2 • Week 2

Name _____

Spelling • Word Meaning

sloped	encouraged	labored	totaled	surrounding
stifling	permitting	uttered	accused	unraveling
marveled	orbiting	referred	patrolling	confiding
sipped	credited	hovered	reviving	regretting

A. Read the word histories. Fill in each blank with a spelling word.

1. _____: Latin—*permittere*, "to let through"

2. _____: Latin—*orbis*, "a wheel or ring"

3. _____: Latin—*mirari*, "to wonder"

4. _____: Latin—*revivere*, "to live again"

B. Write the spelling word that matches each definition below.

5. feeling sad about a loss _____

6. hung in the air, or suspended above _____

7. revealing in private; telling secretly _____

8. unable to breathe easily _____

9. drank a little at a time _____

10. at an angle _____

11. gave hope or confidence _____

12. becoming undone _____

13. publicly stated or acknowledged _____

14. going through an area to make sure it's safe _____

15. expressed through speech _____

16. added up _____

17. worked hard _____

18. sent to for information or help _____

19. charged with wrongdoing _____

20. encircling _____

Spelling • Proofreading

Name _____

There are three misspelled words in each paragraph. Underline each misspelled word. Then write the words correctly on the lines.

Have you ever marvelled at how beautiful the sky is at night? Have you ever seen any unusually bright, glimmering objects orbitting in the night sky? Many people have contacted the National UFO Reporting Center when they've seen strange objects that hoverd overhead. Many of these unexplainable events have been instances of mistaken identity.

1. _____ 2. _____ 3. _____

People are pleased by the fact that crime has dropped considerably in Los Angeles over the past few years. Some people have creditted the police chief for his efforts to reduce crime. More police cars are patroling city streets as well as surroundding neighborhoods in the city.

4. _____ 5. _____ 6. _____

Writing Connection Write about something you observed in science class. Use four or more words from the spelling list.

_____
_____
_____
_____
_____
_____
_____
_____
_____
_____

Phonics/Spelling • **Review**

Name _____

Remember

The inflectional endings -ed and -ing are added to verbs to create new verb forms and tenses. Most base words do not change when adding -ed or -ing, such as when add becomes added or adding.

- For base words that end with a consonant and e, drop the final e and add -ed or -ing: taste, tasted, tasting.
- For many words that end in a vowel and a consonant, double the final consonant before adding -ed or -ing: flip, flipped, flipping.

sloped	encouraged	labored	totaled	surrounding
stifling	permitting	uttered	accused	unraveling
marveled	orbiting	referred	patrolling	confiding
sipped	credited	hovered	reviving	regretting

Fill in the missing letters of each word to form a spelling word. Then write the spelling word on the line.

1. regre __ __ __ ng _____
2. tota __ __ d _____
3. hove __ __ d _____
4. orbi __ __ ng _____
5. confid __ __ __ _____
6. slop __ __ _____
7. encoura __ __ __ _____
8. si __ __ ed _____
9. unravel __ __ __ _____
10. permi __ __ ing _____
11. labo __ __ __ _____
12. revi __ __ __ __ _____
13. utte __ __ __ _____
14. surround __ __ __ _____
15. accu __ __ __ _____
16. refer __ __ __ _____
17. marvel __ __ _____
18. credi __ __ __ _____
19. patrol __ __ __ _____
20. stifl __ __ __ _____

82 Grade 6 • Unit 2 • Week 2

Vocabulary Strategy • Word Origins

Name _____

When you look up a word in the dictionary, you will usually find the word's **etymology**, or its **origin**, and the history of its use and development. This etymology often reveals that the word comes from an ancient Greek, Latin, or Old English word or root. For example, the entry for the word *aquarium* shows that it comes from the Latin word *aqua* meaning "water."

> **a·quar·i·um** (ə kwâr' ē əm) *noun* 1. a tank, bowl, or similar container in which fish, other water animals, and water plants are kept 2. a building used to display collections of fish, other water animals, and water plants. [Latin fr. *aqua* water.]

Study each dictionary entry. Then answer the questions that follow.

> **ag·ri·cul·ture** (a' gri kəl' chər) *noun.* the science, art, or business of cultivating the soil, producing crops, and raising livestock; farming. [Middle English, fr. Middle French, fr. Latin *agricultura*, fr. *ager* field + *cultura* cultivation.]
>
> **com·fort** (kum(p)' fərt) *verb* 1. to ease the grief or sorrow of; console: *We tried to comfort the crying baby.* 2. to give hope to; cheer: *Knowing your friends will be there should comfort you.* [Middle English, fr. Old French *conforter*, fr. Late Latin *confortare* to strengthen greatly, fr. Latin *com-* + *fortis* strong.]

1. Which languages does the word *comfort* come from?

   _____

2. What does the Late Latin word *confortare* mean? _____

3. What does the Latin root *fortis* mean? _____

4. Which Latin word does *agriculture* come from? _____

5. What does the Latin root *ager* mean? _____

6. What does the Latin root *cultura* mean? _____

Grade 6 • Unit 2 • Week 2   83

Vocabulary Strategy • Greek and Latin Prefixes

Name _____

Read each sentence below from "What is a Democracy?" and the meaning of each prefix. Write the meaning of the word in bold on the first line. Then use that word in a sentence of your own.

1. "The **United** States of America is a democracy."
   The Latin prefix *uni-* means "as one."

   Meaning: _____
   Sentence: _____

2. "Without **telephones** or other ways to keep people in touch, the town meetings were also social gatherings for the public."
   The Greek prefix *tele-* means "distant, far apart."

   Meaning: _____
   Sentence: _____

3. "Voters met to solve problems for the good of all, making it possible for people to participate directly in **legislation**."
   The Latin prefix *leg-* means "law."

   Meaning: _____
   Sentence: _____

4. "As the need for government **extended** to cities, states, and the nation as a whole, the town meeting became impractical."
   In *extended*, the Latin prefix *ex-* means "out."

   Meaning: _____
   Sentence: _____

84 Grade 6 • Unit 2 • Week 2

Grammar • More Plural and Collective Nouns

Name _____

- To form the **plural** of some nouns ending in *f* or *fe*, change *f* to *v* and add *-es* or *-s*: *shelf, shelves* or *wife, wives*.
- To form the plural of a noun that ends in a vowel followed by *o*, add *-s*: *video, videos* or *rodeo, rodeos*.
- To form the plural of a noun that ends in a consonant followed by *o*, add *-s* or *-es*: *avocado, avocados* or *volcano, volcanoes*.
- A **collective** noun names a group. It can be singular or plural: *class, team*.

A. Write the plural form of each singular noun on the line.

1. tomato _____ 3. life _____

2. patio _____ 4. photo _____

B. Circle the collective noun in each row.

5. players, team, coach

6. group, members, leaders

7. band, musicians, instruments

8. brothers, sisters, family

Reading/Writing Connection Read this excerpt from "Yaskul's Mighty Trade." On the lines below, describe how to create the plural forms of the two underlined singular nouns.

Father points to a small alcove, a <u>shelf</u> we have carved in the <u>wall</u>. "The thieves missed our wool rugs and sacks of salt. But all our lazuli stones are gone!"

_____

_____

Grade 6 • Unit 2 • Week 3 85

Grammar • Irregular Plural Forms

Name _____

> - Some nouns have **irregular plural forms**. These plurals do not end in *-s*.
>   *tooth, teeth; child, children*
> - Some nouns, like *fish*, stay the same whether singular or plural.
>   *buffalo, moose*

Circle the correct plural form of each singular noun.

1. sheep — sheep, sheeps
2. foot — feet, foot
3. goose — geese, gooses
4. deer — deer, deers
5. tooth — toothes, teeth
6. louse — louse, lice
7. ox — oxen, oxes
8. elk — elks, elk
9. woman — womans, women
10. moose — moose, meese

Write a short fictional passage in your writer's notebook about an animal of your choice. Use two irregular plural nouns in your writing. You can choose an irregular plural noun from the questions above, or think of your own.

86 Grade 6 • Unit 2 • Week 3

Grammar • Mechanics: Use Correct Plural Forms

Name _____

- Change the *f* to *v* and add *-es* or *-s* to form the plural of some nouns ending in *f* or *fe*.
- Add *-s* to form the plural of nouns ending in a vowel followed by *o*.
- Add *-s* or *-es* to nouns ending in a consonant followed by *o*.
- Some nouns have an irregular plural form. Other nouns stay the same whether singular or plural.

Read each sentence. If the sentence contains an incorrect plural form, underline the incorrect noun and write its correct plural form on the line. If the sentence is correct, write *correct* on the line.

1. The dogs guided the flock of sheeps through the open gate. _____

2. The market sells fresh tomatoes, potatos, corn, and radishes. _____

3. It is important to brush your dog's tooths. _____

4. My dad took photos of moose, bison, deers, and elk on our hike. _____

5. The childrens waited patiently for their turns on the swings. _____

6. Please keep the knifes in their protective sleeves. _____

Writing Connection Write a paragraph using the plural form of the following nouns: echo, piano, musician and person. Be sure to proofread your writing and share it with a partner.

_____
_____
_____
_____
_____

Grammar • Proofreading

Name _____

- To form the plural of some nouns ending in *f* or *fe*, change *f* to *v* and add *-es* or *-s*.
- To form the plural of a noun that ends in a vowel followed by *o*, add *-s*. To form the plural of a noun that ends in a consonant followed by *o*, add *-s* or *-es*.
- A collective noun names a group. It can be singular or plural.
- Some nouns have irregular plural forms. These plurals do not end in *-s*.
- Some nouns stay the same whether singular or plural: *trout, deer, moose*.

Proofread for errors. Rewrite the sentences using correct plural forms. Correct mistakes in capitalization or punctuation.

1. before television was invented, families gathered around their radioes and listened to broadcast entertainment.

   _____

   _____

2. some programs brought classical music into the lifes of listeners across the United States.

   _____

   _____

3. mens, womans, and children also enjoyed comedys

   _____

4. comic book heros came to life with actors to voice them

   _____

5. with Television, network studioes could produce programs that showed bears, elks, fish, and other wildlife in their natural habitats

   _____

   _____

88   Grade 6 • Unit 2 • Week 3

English: Grammar • **Apply**

Name _____

What was your favorite reading selection or other text you read this week? Write a paragraph describing what you learned from it or why you enjoyed it. When you're done, exchange your writing with a partner. Proofread your partner's writing. Remember to apply the grammar you have learned this week.

Grade 6 • Unit 2 • Week 3

Spelling • Closed Syllables

Name _____

Fold back the paper along the dotted line. Use the blanks to write each word as it is read aloud. When you finish the test, unfold the paper. Use the list at the right to correct any spelling mistakes.

1. _____
2. _____
3. _____
4. _____
5. _____
6. _____
7. _____
8. _____
9. _____
10. _____
11. _____
12. _____
13. _____
14. _____
15. _____
16. _____
17. _____
18. _____
19. _____
20. _____

Review Words
21. _____
22. _____
23. _____

Challenge Words
24. _____
25. _____

1. factor
2. banner
3. victim
4. mental
5. formal
6. pantry
7. ballot
8. prosper
9. pumpkin
10. muffler
11. ragged
12. kingdom
13. barren
14. necklace
15. wallet
16. ponder
17. funnel
18. dwelling
19. snapshot
20. fabric
21. sloped
22. totaled
23. surrounding
24. verdict
25. garment

Phonics/Spelling • Word Sort

Name _____

A **closed syllable** is a syllable that ends in a consonant and has a short vowel sound. When dividing a word that starts with a closed syllable, look for the consonants after the first short vowel sound.

- Words divided between a double consonant: *sum/mer, rot/ten*
- Words divided between different consonants: *bun/ker, cac/tus*

DECODING WORDS

When two consonants come between two vowels in a word, divide the syllable between the consonants: *dinner, din/ner.*

Read the words in the box. Write the spelling words that contain the matching closed syllable patterns. Then draw a slash (/) between the syllables.

factor	formal	pumpkin	barren	funnel
banner	pantry	muffler	necklace	dwelling
victim	ballot	ragged	wallet	snapshot
mental	prosper	kingdom	ponder	fabric

closed syllables with double consonants, as in *classic: clas/sic*	closed syllables with different consonants, as in *whisper: whis/per*

Look through this week's selections for more words with closed syllables to sort. Record them in your writer's notebook. Draw a slash between the syllables.

Grade 6 • Unit 2 • Week 3

Spelling • Word Meaning

Name _____

factor	formal	pumpkin	barren	funnel
banner	pantry	muffler	necklace	dwelling
victim	ballot	ragged	wallet	snapshot
mental	prosper	kingdom	ponder	fabric

A. Write the spelling word that best completes each analogy.

1. *Casual* is to *school* as _____ is to *wedding*.

2. *Anthill* is to *ant* as _____ is to *king*.

3. *Ring* is to *finger* as _____ is to *neck*.

4. *Rubber* is to *sneakers* as _____ is to *clothing*.

B. Write the spelling word that matches each definition below.

5. storeroom for food items _____

6. well-worn or torn _____

7. pocket-sized case for holding money _____

8. large, round, yellowish-orange fruit of the squash family _____

9. to think deeply _____

10. paper used to make a voting choice _____

11. person badly treated or taken advantage of _____

12. cone-shaped device used when pouring _____

13. a scarf worn around the neck for warmth _____

14. piece of cloth used to decorate or advertise _____

15. photograph _____

16. process involving the mind _____

17. to be successful _____

18. structure or house to live in _____

19. unable to sustain life _____

20. something that contributes to a result _____

92 Grade 6 • Unit 2 • Week 3

Spelling • Proofreading

Name _____

There are six misspelled words in the paragraphs below. Underline each misspelled word. Then write the words correctly on the lines.

Cinderella lived in a large country home with her stepmother and two stepsisters. While her family ate scones topped with raspberries and whipped cream, Cinderella toiled in the pantree, stocking the shelves with food. One night, there was a formle dance in the kingdam, but Cinderella was not allowed to go.

Even if she had been allowed to go to the dance, Cinderella couldn't because she had only one dress to wear. It was very old and raged. Clearly, she was a vicktim of her wicked stepmother's cruelty. While her stepmother put on a nekless of sapphires and rubies to wear to the dance, Cinderella was on her hands and knees scrubbing the floor.

1. _____ 2. _____ 3. _____

4. _____ 5. _____ 6. _____

Writing Connection — Write about something you've seen or observed at school. Use four or more words from the spelling list.

_____
_____
_____
_____
_____
_____
_____
_____
_____
_____

Phonic/Spelling • **Review**

Name _____

> **Remember**
>
> A **closed syllable** is a syllable that ends in one or more consonants and usually has a short vowel sound. The word *dentist* has two closed syllables: *den* and *tist*.
>
> • Words divided between a double consonant: *mit/ten, gut/ter, ten/nis*.
>
> • Words divided between different consonants: *gum/drop, mag/net*.

factor	formal	pumpkin	barren	funnel
banner	pantry	muffler	necklace	dwelling
victim	ballot	ragged	wallet	snapshot
mental	prosper	kingdom	ponder	fabric

Fill in the missing letters of each word to form a spelling word. Then write the spelling word on the line.

1. mu ___ ___ ler _____
2. ba ___ ___ en _____
3. nec ___ ___ ace _____
4. ba ___ ___ er _____
5. ra ___ ___ ed _____
6. kin ___ ___ om _____
7. me ___ ___ al _____
8. fa ___ ___ or _____
9. wa ___ ___ et _____
10. fo ___ ___ al _____
11. fa ___ ___ ic _____
12. ba ___ ___ ot _____
13. pro ___ ___ er _____
14. vi ___ ___ im _____
15. pum ___ ___ in _____
16. pa ___ ___ ry _____
17. fu ___ ___ el _____
18. sna ___ ___ hot _____
19. dwe ___ ___ ing _____
20. po ___ ___ er _____

94 Grade 6 • Unit 2 • Week 3

Vocabulary • Related Words

Name _____

Expand your vocabulary by adding or removing inflectional endings, prefixes, or suffixes to a base word to create different forms of a word.

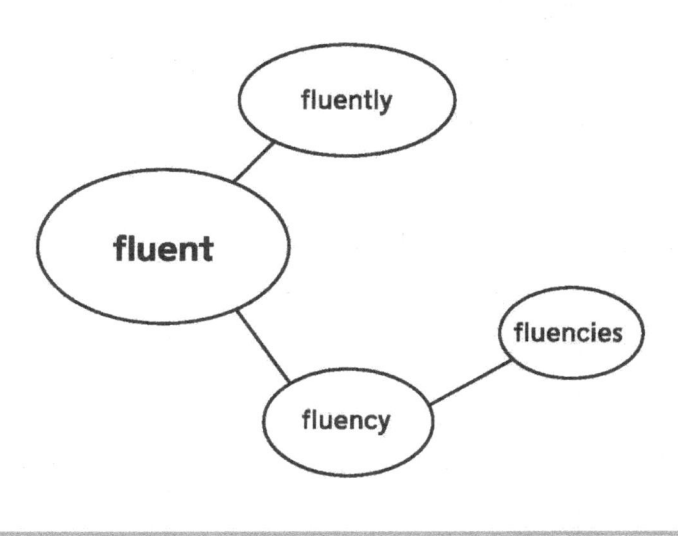

- fluent
- fluently
- fluency
- fluencies

Read the word below. Add or remove prefixes, suffixes, and inflectional endings to form related words and write them in the blanks. Use a print or online dictionary to help you.

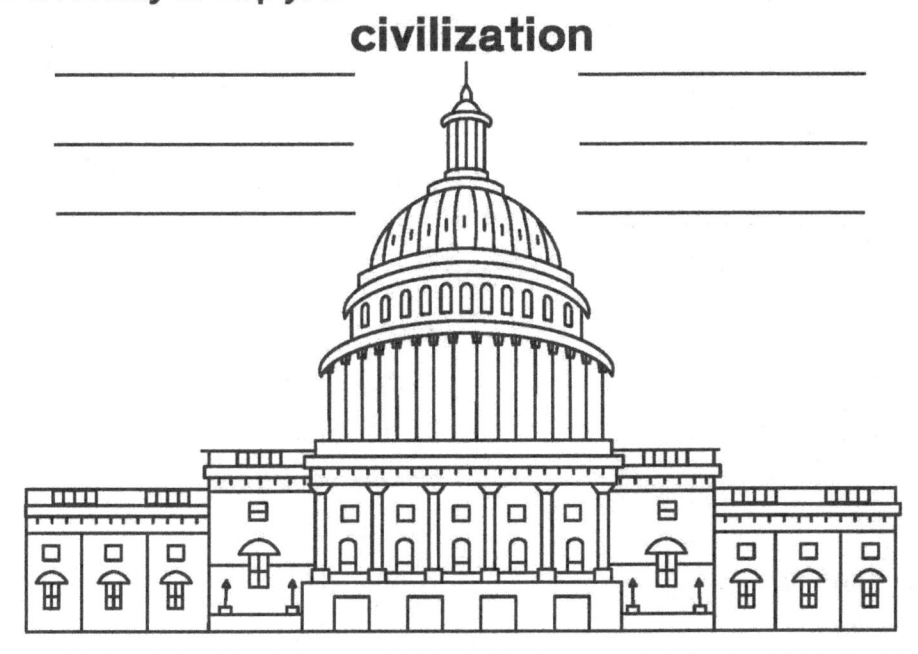

civilization

Vocabulary • Spiral Review

Name _____

Use the words in the box and the clues below to help you solve the crossword puzzle.

heinous	speculation	restrict	scalding
promote	glimmer	dynamic	principal
preceded	foundation	aspiring	withstood

Across
3. shimmer
5. act of determining why
9. basis
10. very hot
11. limit or confine
12. came before

Down
1. shockingly bad
2. most important
4. seeking a goal
6. help to grow
7. energetic
8. endured

96 Grade 6 • Unit 2 • Week 3

Grammar • Possessive Nouns

Name _____

- A **possessive noun** names who or what owns something.
- A possessive noun is **singular** when it names one owner.
- A possessive noun can be **common** or **proper**.
- Add an apostrophe and *-s* to make a singular noun possessive, even when the noun ends in *s*: *the squirrel's tail, Douglas's bicycle, the bus's door.*

Rewrite the noun in parentheses ( ) as a possessive noun.

1. The (zookeeper) job requires him to work on Saturdays. _____

2. The most popular attraction is the big (cat) area. _____

3. The (leopard) spots help to camouflage her in the wild. _____

4. The length of the (giraffe) neck allows him to reach his food. _____

5. The (hippopotamus) habitat has a pond. _____

6. We went to (Hallie) favorite place, the duck pond. _____

7. The (swan) wingspan was amazing to see. _____

8. The (pond) surface was covered with lily pads. _____

9. (James) laughter echoed through the reptile house. _____

10. The (walrus) tusks were about three feet long! _____

In your writer's notebook, write a short passage about a special event that you attended. Include five singular possessive nouns. Check to make sure you used apostrophes correctly.

Name _____

Grammar • **Plural Possessive Nouns**

- A possessive noun is **plural** when it names more than one owner.
- If a plural noun is regular and ends in -s, add an apostrophe to make it possessive: *schools', snakes'.*
- If a plural noun is irregular and does not end in -s, add an apostrophe and -s to make it possessive: *fish's, women's.*

Write the plural possessive for each plural noun.

1. pandas _____
2. pythons _____
3. donkeys _____
4. geese _____
5. boxes _____
6. elk _____
7. mice _____
8. goats _____
9. sharks _____
10. oxen _____
11. walruses _____
12. deer _____

Reading/Writing Connection Read the paragraph from "The Genius of Roman Aqueducts." Circle the irregular plural noun. On the lines below, describe how to make the possessive form of the irregular plural noun you circled.

> Most children in Rome knew how water was transported to their city. But did you ever wonder where the water you drink comes from? Or how it got to your faucet?

_____
_____

98 Grade 6 • Unit 2 • Week 4

Grammar • Mechanics: **Forming Plural and Possessive Nouns**

Name _____

- Be careful not to confuse plural nouns with possessive nouns.
- Plural nouns do not use apostrophes. They are often formed by adding -s or -es to a singular noun.
- Possessive nouns are formed by adding an apostrophe or an apostrophe and -s.

A. Label the following nouns as S for singular, SP for singular possessive, P for plural, or PP for plural possessive.

1. building's _____
2. cars _____
3. area's _____
4. base _____
5. women's _____
6. socks _____
7. James's _____
8. dress _____
9. students _____
10. hamsters' _____
11. Brandon's _____
12. hat's _____
13. teeth _____
14. children's _____
15. cactus _____

B. Write the possessive form of each word in parentheses.

16. Unfortunately, the (water) surface was rough and choppy. _____
17. The (boat) captain warned the passengers to wear life jackets. _____
18. The (passengers) life jackets were bright orange. _____

Think of a special gift that you gave someone. Write a paragraph describing the gift, using possessive nouns. Describe the gift in detail.

Grade 6 • Unit 2 • Week 4

Name _____

Grammar • Proofreading

- A **possessive noun** names who or what owns something. A possessive noun can be **common** or **proper**.
- A singular possessive noun names one owner. A plural possessive noun names more than one owner.
- If a plural noun is regular and ends in -s, add an apostrophe to make it a possessive noun.
- If a plural noun is irregular and does not end in -s, add an apostrophe and -s to make it possessive.

Proofread each sentence. Rewrite it using the correct possessive or plural form of the nouns. Correct mistakes in capitalization and punctuation.

COMMON ERRORS

Sometimes an apostrophe is included by mistake. If a plural noun does not have or own something, then it is not possessive and should not have an apostrophe.

1. the department stores elevator carries peoples to every floor

   _____
   _____

2. the elevators buttons show that this store has four floor for customers shopping

   _____
   _____

3. womens clothing areas are on the second and third floor's.

   _____
   _____

4. you will find the mens suits on the first floor near the stores entrance?

   _____
   _____

English: Grammar • **Apply**

Name _____

What was your favorite reading selection or other text you read this week? Write a paragraph describing what you learned from it or why you enjoyed it. When you're done, exchange your writing with a partner. Proofread your partner's writing. Remember to apply the grammar you have learned this week.

Spelling • **Open Syllables**

Name _____

Fold back the paper along the dotted line. Use the blanks to write each word as it is read aloud. When you finish the test, unfold the paper. Use the list at the right to correct any spelling mistakes.

1. _____
2. _____
3. _____
4. _____
5. _____
6. _____
7. _____
8. _____
9. _____
10. _____
11. _____
12. _____
13. _____
14. _____
15. _____
16. _____
17. _____
18. _____
19. _____
20. _____

Review Words

21. _____
22. _____
23. _____

Challenge Words

24. _____
25. _____

1. brutal
2. secure
3. panic
4. cabin
5. fever
6. voter
7. vanish
8. nylon
9. detect
10. resist
11. labor
12. focus
13. rival
14. recite
15. topic
16. amid
17. unit
18. rotate
19. vital
20. lament
21. victim
22. wallet
23. snapshot
24. mural
25. civic

102 Grade 6 • Unit 2 • Week 4

Phonics/Spelling • Word Sort

Name _____

Syllables can divide after the first vowel (V/CV). These syllables, which end in vowels, are called **open syllables**. In **open syllables**, the vowel sound is usually long: *spo/ken, re/cent*.

Syllables can divide after the consonant that follows the first vowel (VC/V). These syllables, which end in consonants, are called **closed syllables**. In closed syllables, the vowel sound is usually short: *shiv/er, com/et, ban/ish*.

DECODING WORDS

The word *robot* has two syllables. The first syllable, *ro*, ends with the long *o* sound. It is an open syllable. The second syllable, *bot*, ends with a consonant and has a short *o* sound. It is a closed syllable. Blend the two syllables together: /rō/ /bot/.

Read the words in the box. Write the spelling words that match the syllable patterns. Then draw a slash (/) between the syllables.

brutal	fever	detect	rival	unit
secure	voter	resist	recite	rotate
panic	vanish	labor	topic	vital
cabin	nylon	focus	amid	lament

long *a*, as in *baby*, *ba/by*

1. _____

long *e*, as in *retell*, *re/tell*

2. _____
3. _____
4. _____
5. _____

long *i* sound, as in *pilot*, *pi/lot*

6. _____
7. _____

8. _____

long *o*, as in *cobra*, *co/bra*

9. _____
10. _____
11. _____

variant vowel /u/

12. _____

long *u*, as in *cubic*, *cu/bic*

13. _____

short vowel open syllables

14. _____
15. _____
16. _____

short vowel closed syllables

17. _____
18. _____
19. _____
20. _____

Grade 6 • Unit 2 • Week 4   103

Spelling • Word Meaning

Name _____

brutal	fever	detect	rival	unit
secure	voter	resist	recite	rotate
panic	vanish	labor	topic	vital
cabin	nylon	focus	amid	lament

A. Write the spelling word that belongs with each group of words.

1. repeat, retell, _____
2. idea, subject, _____
3. notice, discover, _____
4. grieve, regret, _____
5. competitor, challenger, _____

B. Write the spelling word that matches each definition below.

6. disappear _____
7. safe _____
8. a kind of man-made fabric _____
9. absolutely necessary _____
10. citizen who casts a ballot _____
11. small house made of logs _____
12. to stand up to or actively oppose _____
13. work _____
14. to make an image clear; to give attention to _____
15. fear _____
16. cruel _____
17. standard amount used for measuring _____
18. surrounded by _____
19. to turn on an axis or center _____
20. rise in body temperature _____

104   Grade 6 • Unit 2 • Week 4

Spelling • Proofreading

Name _____

There are three misspelled words in each paragraph below. Underline each misspelled word. Then write the words correctly on the lines.

Last year, before my brother went off to college, my family took a trip to Maine. We stayed in a cabbin ammid the trees and tried to focis on just spending time together.

1. _____ 2. _____ 3. _____

My family and I spent a few days at a cottage on Lake Michigan. When we returned from a hike one day, we could dettect that someone or something had been there. How could that happen? All the doors and windows were seccure. We started to pannic until my mother discovered that a raccoon had gotten in through the pet door!

4. _____ 5. _____ 6. _____

Writing Connection

Write about a trip you and your family have taken. Use at least four words from the spelling list.

_____
_____
_____
_____
_____
_____
_____
_____

Grade 6 • Unit 2 • Week 4

Phonics/Spelling • **Review**

Name _____

> **Remember**
> - **Open syllables** divide after the first vowel (V/CV). In open syllables, the vowel sound is usually long: *pa/per, spi/der.*
> - **Closed syllables** divide after the consonant that follows the first vowel (VC/V). In closed syllables, the vowel sound is usually short: *lem/on, riv/er.*

brutal	fever	detect	rival	unit
secure	voter	resist	recite	rotate
panic	vanish	labor	topic	vital
cabin	nylon	focus	amid	lament

Fill in the missing letters of each word to form a spelling word. Then write the spelling word on the line.

1. f ___ ___ er _____
2. ___ ___ it _____
3. n ___ ___ on _____
4. r ___ ___ ate _____
5. v ___ ___ er _____
6. r ___ ___ al _____
7. c ___ ___ in _____
8. va ___ ___ sh _____
9. d ___ ___ ect _____
10. f ___ ___ us _____
11. br ___ ___ al _____
12. ___ ___ id _____
13. r ___ ___ ite _____
14. pa ___ ___ c _____
15. v ___ ___ al _____
16. l ___ ___ or _____
17. t ___ ___ ic _____
18. r ___ ___ ist _____
19. l ___ ___ ent _____
20. s ___ ___ ure _____

Vocabulary Strategy • Thesaurus

Name _____

> A print or digital **thesaurus** is a resource that lists a word's synonyms and antonyms. When writing, use a thesaurus to find the most appropriate words to convey your ideas and feelings. You can also consult a thesaurus to define words and to better understand shades of meaning of synonyms.

Use the digital thesaurus entry below to help you revise the paragraph. Write the specific synonym or antonym that best replaces the generic word in parentheses.

cold (kōld)
Part of Speech: adjective
Definition: at a low or relatively low temperature
Synonyms: arctic, below freezing, biting, bitter, bleak, bone-chilling, brisk, chilly, cool, inclement, nippy, numbing, polar, raw, shivery, snowy, stinging, wintry
Antonyms: baking, balmy, blazing, blistering, boiling, broiling, burning, close, feverish, fiery, flaming, heated, humid, muggy, oven-like, roasting, scalding, scorching, searing, sizzling, smoking, steaming, stuffy, sultry, summery, sweltering, tropical, warm

The first (cold) _____ days of autumn always remind me of the winter my family and I spent in Norway. When we first arrived in Oslo in November, it was not terribly (cold) _____, but only a (cold) _____ 45 degrees. That all changed quickly when we headed north! The dark December days were the (coldest) _____ I had ever experienced. The second we went outside, our faces were blasted by the (cold) _____ breeze. We could see our breath in the (cold) _____ air. Luckily, our little house was usually cozy and (hot) _____. We spent many hours by the fireplace, thawing our hands over a (hot) _____ fire.

Grade 6 • Unit 2 • Week 4 107

Vocabulary Strategy • Connotations and Denotations

Name _____

A. Read each of the following excerpts from the passage, "Kush, A Land of Archers." Then explain how the tone of the sentence would change if the word in bold were replaced by the word in parentheses.

1. Archers of all ages came to demonstrate their skill, and the best athletes earned **recognition** (glory).

   _____

   _____

2. At first Mother looked **surprised** (amazed).

   _____

   _____

3. "Oh, little Markos, give yourself time to grow!" my older brother **wheedled** (pleaded), ruffling my hair with his oversized hands.

   _____

   _____

4. Ignoring him, I walked with **purpose** (boldness) to the archery field.

   _____

   _____

B. Write a few sentences explaining whether the word in bold has a positive or negative connotation and why.

5. "My arrow had **plunged** into the most distant target of all."

   _____

   _____

   _____

108 Grade 6 • Unit 2 • Week 4

Grammar • Appositives

Name _____

> - An **appositive** is a noun or pronoun placed next to a noun or pronoun to identify it: *This is my friend, <u>Vijay</u>. James Madison's wife, <u>Dolley</u>, was an influential first lady.*
> - An **appositive phrase** includes the appositive and the words that modify the appositive: *My twin brother, <u>the president of the sixth grade class</u>, planned a fund-raiser.*

Read each sentence. If the sentence contains an appositive, write *A* on the line and underline the appositive word or phrase. If the sentence does not contain an appositive, write *N*.

1. Herpetology, the study of snakes and other reptiles, is my favorite subject. _____

2. Some sources claim that an Australian snake, the inland taipan, is the most venomous land snake. _____

3. The snake I like best, the king cobra, is another dangerous snake. _____

4. The mamba, a venomous snake of Africa, is a relative of the cobra. _____

5. Cottonmouths, or water moccasins, live in the southeastern United States. _____

6. Cottonmouths are often confused with copperheads. _____

7. The copperhead, a type of pit viper, is less venomous than the cottonmouth. _____

8. New World coral snakes, North American snakes, have very potent venom. _____

In your writer's notebook, describe a reptile, bird, insect, or other creature you think is interesting. Use at least three appositives or appositive phrases in your writing.

Grade 6 • Unit 2 • Week 5 109

Grammar • Essential and Nonessential Appositives

Name _____

- An **essential** or **restrictive appositive** defines a noun so the sentence is easier to understand: *My friend Jacob performs in plays.*
- A **nonessential** or **nonrestrictive appositive** is not necessary to understand the sentence: *My dog, a black lab, likes to visit the dog park.*

Underline the appositive in each sentence. Write *E* if the appositive is essential. Write *N* if the appositive is nonessential.

1. The spelling bee, a yearly event at our school, is exciting to watch. ____

2. Our local television station, KJBR-TV, broadcasts the spelling bee each year. ____

3. About fifty students, all sixth graders, compete in the spelling bee each year. ____

4. Mrs. Bates, our school principal, is one of the judges. ____

5. My friend Katie won the top prize this year. ____

6. Katie was the only student who could spell the word *spaghetti*. ____

7. David Bedner, a boy in my class, won second place. ____

8. Last year's winner, Victor Martinez, presented the awards. ____

Reading/Writing Connection

Read the lines from "Ozymandias." Circle the appositive phrase. Then write two sentences of your own including appositives or appositive phrases.

And on the pedestal these words appear:
'My name is Ozymandias, king of kings:
Look on my works, ye Mighty, and despair!'

_____
_____

110 Grade 6 • Unit 2 • Week 5

Grammar • Mechanics: Using Commas, Dashes, and Parentheses

Name _____

> - Use commas to set off nonessential appositives.
>   *My brother, who loves to bake, made a lemon meringue pie.*
> - Use dashes to show a strong break in thought within a sentence.
>   *The pie—gooey and delicious—was quickly devoured by our family.*
> - Use parentheses to set off nonessential facts within a sentence.
>   *My other brother (the youngest sibling) prefers to eat instead of cook.*

Read each set of sentences. Circle the letter of the sentence that is punctuated correctly.

1. a. Two of my classmates—Savannah—and Will ride home with me after school.
   b. Two of my classmates, Savannah (and Will) ride home with me after school.
   c. Two of my classmates, Savannah and Will, ride home with me after school.

2. a. His sister gave all the money she raised ($25.00) to the charity.
   b. His sister gave all the money, she raised $25.00, to the charity.
   c. His sister gave all the money she raised—$25.00 to the charity.

3. a. Everyone in the family even, the pets, prefers cold weather.
   b. Everyone in the family (even the pets prefers) cold weather.
   c. Everyone in the family—even the pets—prefers cold weather.

4. a. The dog a black and white (terrier) will come home with us next week.
   b. The dog, a black and white terrier, will come home with us next week.
   c. The dog—a black and white—terrier will come home with us next week.

5. a. Mr. Kowalski, our scout leader, led the hike up the mountain.
   b. Mr. Kowalski our scout leader—led the hike up the mountain.
   c. Mr. Kowalski (our scout leader led the hike up the mountain.

In your writer's notebook, write about something interesting you did with classmates. Include three appositives in your writing. Remember, appositives are a great way to add details to your writing.

Grammar • Proofreading

Name _____

> - An **appositive** is a noun or pronoun placed next to a noun or pronoun to identify it.
> - An **appositive phrase** includes the appositive and the words that modify the appositive.
> - An **essential** or **restrictive appositive** defines a noun so the sentence is easier to understand.
> - A **nonessential** or **nonrestrictive appositive** is not necessary to understand the sentence. Use commas to set off nonessential appositives.

Proofread each sentence. Then rewrite the sentence correctly. Use commas to set off the nonessential appositives. Correct mistakes in capitalization or punctuation.

1. ruben a boy in my class is a great swimmer.

   _____

2. He swims for the city team the Jacksonville Jets.

   _____

3. Ruben one of two boys in his Family has three sisters

   _____

4. Ruben's sister Bella swims for the Jets too.

   _____

5. bella a fourth-grader is one of the top swimmers on the team

   _____

112 Grade 6 • Unit 2 • Week 5

English: Grammar • **Apply**

Name _____

What was your favorite reading selection or other text you read this week? Write a paragraph describing what you learned from it or why you enjoyed it. When you're done, exchange your writing with a partner. Proofread your partner's writing. Remember to apply the grammar you have learned this week.

_____
_____
_____
_____
_____
_____
_____
_____
_____
_____
_____
_____
_____
_____

Spelling • Consonant + *le* Syllables

Name _____

Fold back the paper along the dotted line. Use the blanks to write each word as it is read aloud. When you finish the test, unfold the paper. Use the list at the right to correct any spelling mistakes.

1. _____ 1. simple
2. _____ 2. royal
3. _____ 3. national
4. _____ 4. valuable
5. _____ 5. survival
6. _____ 6. muscle
7. _____ 7. whistle
8. _____ 8. squabble
9. _____ 9. durable
10. _____ 10. incurable
11. _____ 11. scramble
12. _____ 12. scruple
13. _____ 13. quadruple
14. _____ 14. noodle
15. _____ 15. squiggle
16. _____ 16. throttle
17. _____ 17. securable
18. _____ 18. beagle
19. _____ 19. dimple
20. _____ 20. bicycle

Review Words
21. _____ 21. panic
22. _____ 22. labor
23. _____ 23. unit

Challenge Words
24. _____ 24. literal
25. _____ 25. timetable

Phonics/Spelling • **Word Sort**

Name _____

When a word ends with the letters *le*, the final syllable usually includes the preceding consonant. This is called a **consonant + le syllable**. It is the final stable syllable that always ends with the sound /əl/. Examples include *beetle* (bee/tle) and *stable* (sta/ble).

Words that end in a consonant + *el* or *al* often divide in the same way: *medal* (me/dal), *label* (la/bel).

DECODING WORDS

The word *example* has three syllables. It ends with the final stable syllable *ple*, pronounced /pəl/. Blend the sounds in each syllable together: /ig/ /zam/ /pəl/.

Write the spelling words that contain the matching pattern. Then draw a slash (/) between the syllables.

simple	survival	durable	quadruple	securable
royal	muscle	incurable	noodle	beagle
national	whistle	scramble	squiggle	dimple
valuable	squabble	scruple	throttle	bicycle

-ple

1. _____
2. _____
3. _____
4. _____

–ble

5. _____
6. _____
7. _____

8. _____
9. _____
10. _____

-tle

11. _____
12. _____

-cle

13. _____
14. _____

-dle

15. _____

-gle

16. _____
17. _____

-al

18. _____
19. _____
20. _____

Look through this week's selections for more words with consonant + *le* syllables to sort. Record them in your writer's notebook.

Grade 6 • Unit 2 • Week 5   115

Spelling • Word Meaning

Name _____

simple	survival	durable	quadruple	securable
royal	muscle	incurable	noodle	beagle
national	whistle	scramble	squiggle	dimple
valuable	squabble	scruple	throttle	bicycle

A. Write the spelling word that goes with each word history.

1. *simplus:* Latin; "single" _____
2. *skvabbel:* Scandinavian; "quarrel" _____
3. *throte:* Middle English; "throat" _____
4. *hwistle:* Old English; "tubular musical instrument" _____
5. *nudel:* German; "narrow strip of dried dough" _____

B. Write the spelling word that best completes each sentence.

6. The British _____ palace is in London.
7. The family adopted a _____ from the animal shelter.
8. The gate is _____ if you close it tightly.
9. Gold jewelry is considered _____.
10. The _____ on his paper sort of looked like the letter *s*.
11. The value of this painting will probably _____ over time!
12. An _____ disease is one from which people cannot recover.
13. Our _____ anthem is "The Star-Spangled Banner."
14. Her main _____ was about not texting while driving.
15. Our conservation efforts help in the _____ of endangered species.
16. The _____ race was televised worldwide on Saturday.
17. His leg _____ was tight before he exercised.
18. The baby has the cutest _____ when she smiles.
19. The raincoat is made of _____ cloth that will last for years.
20. I will have to _____ to be ready by 5 o'clock.

Spelling • Proofreading

Name _____

There are six misspelled words in the paragraphs below. Underline each misspelled word. Then write the words correctly on the lines.

    Long ago, each animal in the village had only one kind of food to eat. It was enough for their survivle, but the animals grew tired of eating the same thing. "I can't eat another noodel," Spider declared. "I don't mind if we have to scrambel for food. I just want something different to eat." Fox agreed. Rabbit was tired of eating carrots, so the three friends went to see Owl.

    Owl had a simpel plan. "If all four of us combine our food into a stew, we'll have quadrupal the food." The animals did as Owl suggested and had a feast fit for a royale family.

1. _____ 2. _____ 3. _____

4. _____ 5. _____ 6. _____

Writing Connection — Write about something you and your friends would like to do. Use at least four words from the spelling list.

_____
_____
_____
_____
_____
_____
_____
_____
_____
_____

Phonics/Spelling • **Review**

Name _____

> **Remember**
>
> When a word ends with the letters *le*, the final syllable usually includes the preceding consonant. For example, *giggle* divides as *gig/gle*. A **consonant + *le* syllable** is a type of **final stable syllable** that ends with the sound /əl/.
>
> Words that end in a consonant + *el* or *al* often divide in the same way: *channel (chan/nel)*, *legal (le/gal)*. Read the word *steeple* aloud: /stē/ /pəl/. In the first syllable, the digraph *ee* makes the long *e* sound. The second syllable is a final stable syllable.

Fill in the missing letters of each word to form a spelling word. Then write the spelling word on the line.

1. survi __ __ __   _____
2. squab __ __ __   _____
3. bicy __ __ __   _____
4. mus __ __ __   _____
5. valua __ __ __   _____
6. dim __ __ __   _____
7. whis __ __ __   _____
8. natio __ __ __   _____
9. dura __ __ __   _____
10. bea __ __ __   _____
11. throt __ __ __   _____
12. secura __ __ __   _____
13. squig __ __ __   _____
14. ro __ __ __   _____
15. incura __ __ __   _____
16. scru __ __ __   _____
17. noo __ __ __   _____
18. scram __ __ __   _____
19. quadru __ __ __   _____
20. sim __ __ __   _____

Vocabulary • Related Words

Name _____

Expand your vocabulary by adding or removing inflectional endings, prefixes, or suffixes to a base word to create different forms of a word.

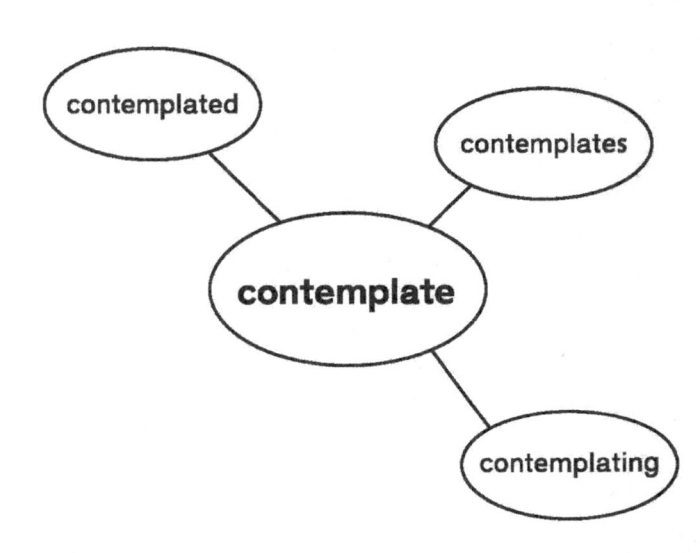

- contemplated
- contemplates
- **contemplate**
- contemplating

Read the word below. Add inflectional endings, prefixes, or suffixes to form related words. Write them on the lines of sheet music below. Use a print or electronic dictionary to help you.

lyric

Vocabulary Strategy • **Personification**

Name _____

Read each passage from the poem, "At Grandmother's House." Then answer the questions about personification.

1. I see foxes and mule deer and rabbits
   Dancing as though the desert were their stage.

    What is personified? _____

    What is its human action? _____

2. Nature proudly displays
   Her work for us to savor.

    What is personified? _____

    What is its human action? _____

3. When the sun bows low, I see
   A rainbow like a party favor.

    What is personified? _____

    What is its human action? _____

4. She points to stars and planets
   While the flames perform their ballet.

    What is personified? _____

    What is its human action? _____

5. A quilt she made just for me
   That holds me in its arms all night.

    What is personified? _____

    What is its human action? _____

Grammar • Action Verbs

Name _____

- An **action verb** expresses a **physical** or **mental** action. An action verb must agree with its subject: *Sylvia practices the piano everyday.*
- A **direct object** receives the action of the verb in a sentence and tells whom or what is affected by the verb's action.
  Sylvia practices the piano everyday.

Underline the action verb in each sentence. Put brackets [ ] around the direct object.

1. The students displayed their talents in the variety show.
2. The school principal introduced each act.
3. Wilson played the drums.
4. Adam performed a solo.
5. Matthew wrote an original song for the show.
6. Isabelle told jokes in a comedy act.
7. Mrs. Hernandez and Mr. Underwood judged the contest.
8. Matthew won the top prize.

Reading/Writing Connection

Read the excerpt from "Facing the Storm." Circle the direct object that corresponds to each underlined action verb.

"Just think about the birds," Isabel said as they carried each cage up to the reptile house. The hawks screeched and beat their wings when they felt the wind.

Grade 6 • Unit 3 • Week 1   121

Grammar • Direct Objects and Indirect Objects

Name _____

> - A **direct object** receives the action of the verb in a sentence and tells whom or what is affected by the verb's action: *Savion gave his dog a treat*.
> - An **indirect object** appears before the direct object and tells to whom or for whom the action is done: *Savion gave his dog a treat*.

Draw one line under the action verb. Draw two lines under the indirect object. Put brackets [ ] around each direct object.

1. Grace handed her mother the notebook.

2. Jackie tossed me the basketball.

3. Ben played the class a recording.

4. The teacher taught the group the song.

5. Mr. Yamada bought his daughter a winter coat.

6. Zane's grandmother knitted him a red scarf.

7. The waiter gave each person a menu.

8. The chef prepared the customers a special meal.

9. The host showed his guests a good time.

10. The guests thanked him for the invitation.

Write a short passage describing a school performance. Edit and proofread your work. Make sure that all subjects and verbs agree.

Grammar • Mechanics: Quotation Marks and Dialogue

Name _____

> - Use quotation marks before and after someone's exact words.
> - Begin a quotation with a capital letter.
> - Place commas and periods inside quotation marks: *"I made note cards to help me study for my science test," said Theo.*
> - If a quotation comes at the end of a sentence, use a period, question mark, or exclamation point to end it: *He said, "Don't be late to the movie theater!"*
> - If the sentence continues after a quotation is given, use a comma, question mark, or exclamation point to close the quotation.
>   *"There will be an assembly tomorrow afternoon," said Mr. Sinha.*

Rewrite each sentence using the correct capitalization and punctuation.

1. Can you suggest a good book asked Martin

   _____

2. what types of books interest you asked the librarian

   _____

3. Martin replied i like mysteries and science fiction

   _____

4. let me show you some of our newest mysteries the librarian suggested

   _____

5. Martin exclaimed these look great

   _____

Writing Connection Write the dialogue of a conversation you had today. Then read and act out your dialogue with a partner. Edit your work for correct punctuation.

_____

_____

_____

Grammar • Proofreading

Name _____

> - An **action verb** is a word that expresses action. It tells what the subject does or did.
> - A **direct object** tells whom or what is affected by the verb's action. An **indirect object** appears before the direct object and tells to whom or for whom the action is done.
> - Use quotation marks before and after someone's exact words.
> - Begin a quotation with a capital letter.
> - Commas and periods always appear inside quotation marks.
> - If a quotation comes at the end of a sentence, use a period, question mark, or exclamation point to end it. If the sentence continues after a quotation is given, use a comma, question mark, or exclamation point to close the quotation.

Proofread the sentences. Then rewrite them correctly using correct capitalization or punctuation. Correct mistakes made with verbs that do not agree with their subjects.

1. madeleine said "my family give good care our pets"

   _____

2. "Should I brush the cat's thick coat every day" she asked?

   _____

3. "my father walk the dog every morning. Madeleine added."

   _____

4. madeleine said. "my brother give them food and water"

   _____

5. "we love our pets," exclaimed Madeleine.

   _____

124 Grade 6 • Unit 3 • Week 1

English: Grammar • Apply

Name _____

What was your favorite reading selection or other text you read this week? Write a paragraph describing what you learned from it or why you enjoyed it. When you're done, exchange your writing with a partner. Proofread your partner's writing. Remember to apply the grammar you have learned this week.

Spelling • **Vowel Team Syllables**

Name _____

Fold back the paper along the dotted line. Use the blanks to write each word as it is read aloud. When you finish the test, unfold the paper. Use the list at the right to correct any spelling mistakes.

1. _____ 1. guaranteed
2. _____ 2. creatures
3. _____ 3. poisonous
4. _____ 4. appointment
5. _____ 5. exploit
6. _____ 6. earthbound
7. _____ 7. streamline
8. _____ 8. wealthy
9. _____ 9. healthy
10. _____ 10. shoulder
11. _____ 11. straighten
12. _____ 12. moisten
13. _____ 13. pedigree
14. _____ 14. volunteer
15. _____ 15. impeach
16. _____ 16. spoilage
17. _____ 17. treasures
18. _____ 18. toughest
19. _____ 19. ceiling
20. _____ 20. equality

Review Words
21. _____ 21. valuable
22. _____ 22. survival
23. _____ 23. bicycle

Challenge Words
24. _____ 24. maintained
25. _____ 25. weightlessness

Phonics/Spelling • Word Sort

Name _____

> When a vowel sound is spelled with more than one letter, the syllable is called a **vowel team syllable**. Two, three, or four letters can work together to form a single vowel sound: ar*ou*nd, m*oo*n, t*igh*ten, app*oi*nt, entert*ai*n.
>
> In *tighten*, three letters form one sound, /ī/. Two letters that form one sound, such as *ou* in *around*, are called **digraphs**.

DECODING WORDS

Fountain has two vowel team spellings —*ou* and *ai*. Vowel team spellings, like the digraphs *ou* and *ai*, must stay in the same syllable. Blend the syllables together: *foun-tain*: /foun/ /tən/.

Read the words in the box. Write the spelling words that contain the matching vowel team. If a word has more than one vowel team, choose one way to sort it.

guaranteed	exploit	healthy	pedigree	treasures
creatures	earthbound	shoulder	volunteer	toughest
poisonous	streamline	straighten	impeach	ceiling
appointment	wealthy	moisten	spoilage	equality

ee
1. _____
2. _____

ea
3. _____
4. _____
5. _____
6. _____
7. _____
8. _____

ua
9. _____
10. _____

oi
11. _____
12. _____
13. _____
14. _____
15. _____

ou
16. _____
17. _____
18. _____

ai
19. _____

ei
20. _____

Grade 6 • Unit 3 • Week 1

Spelling • Word Meaning

Name _____

guaranteed	exploit	healthy	pedigree	treasures
creatures	earthbound	shoulder	volunteer	toughest
poisonous	streamline	straighten	impeach	ceiling
appointment	wealthy	moisten	spoilage	equality

A. Write the spelling word that is a synonym for each word below.

1. use _____
2. rich _____
3. unbend _____
4. accuse _____
5. riches _____
6. most difficult _____
7. dampen _____
8. robust _____
9. toxic _____
10. pure-bred _____

B. Write the spelling word that best completes each sentence.

11. There are many sea _____ living in the ocean, including sea otters, sharks, and whales.

12. They installed an overhead fan in the living room _____.

13. She is the best _____ at the animal shelter.

14. Jake rested the tray of dishes on his left _____ and carried it into the kitchen.

15. Many products advertised on TV are _____ to last at least a year.

16. I have a doctor's _____ on Friday afternoon.

17. The spacecraft will be _____ in a few days.

18. The toy company needs to _____ its production facility.

19. _____ was an important issue during the Civil Rights Movement.

20. _____ can happen when food is not refrigerated.

Spelling · Proofreading

Name _____

There are six misspelled words in the paragraphs below. Underline each misspelled word. Then write the words correctly on the lines.

Once there was a young man who was in love with the daughter of a welthy farmer. The farmer didn't think anyone was good enough for his daughter. The young man said, "I may not have a fancy pedigrea, but I am a hard worker. I am helthy, and I love your daughter."

To prove himself, the young man became a voluntear on the farm and performed difficult jobs. He worked in the fields until he could hardly strayghten himself up. The farmer finally said, "Men who are willing to *say* they love someone are common. Men who are willing to *show* they love someone are like tresures. Welcome to the family."

1. _____   2. _____   3. _____

4. _____   5. _____   6. _____

Writing Connection Write a story about a time when you or someone you know showed honesty. Use at least four words from the spelling list.

_____
_____
_____
_____
_____
_____
_____
_____

Phonics/Spelling • Review

Name _____

Remember

In a **vowel team syllable**, two or more letters work together to make one vowel sound. For example, in the word *bright*, the letters *igh* work together to make the long *i* sound. In the word *trailer*, the letters *ai* make the long *a* sound. When two letters stand for a single sound, it is also called a **digraph**. Read the word *trailer* aloud, keeping the digraph *ai* in the same syllable: /trā/ /lər/.

guaranteed	exploit	healthy	pedigree	treasures
creatures	earthbound	shoulder	volunteer	toughest
poisonous	streamline	straighten	impeach	ceiling
appointment	wealthy	moisten	spoilage	equality

Fill in the missing letters of each word to form a spelling word. Write the spelling word on the line. Then circle the vowel team or teams in each word.

1. p ___ ___ sonous _____
2. volunt ___ ___ ___ _____
3. sp___ ___ lage _____
4. imp ___ ___ ch _____
5. guarant ___ ___ d _____
6. cr ___ ___ tures _____
7. m ___ ___ sten _____
8. tr ___ ___ sures _____
9. app ___ ___ ntment _____
10. eq ___ ___ lity _____
11. str ___ ___ mline _____
12. c ___ ___ ling _____
13. w ___ ___ lthy _____
14. earthb ___ ___ nd _____
15. sh ___ ___ lder _____
16. pedigr ___ ___ _____
17. t ___ ___ ghest _____
18. expl ___ ___ t _____
19. str ___ ___ ghten _____
20. h ___ ___ lthy _____

130 Grade 6 • Unit 3 • Week 1

Vocabulary • Related Words

Name _____

Expand your vocabulary by adding or removing inflectional endings, prefixes, or suffixes to a base word to create different forms of a word.

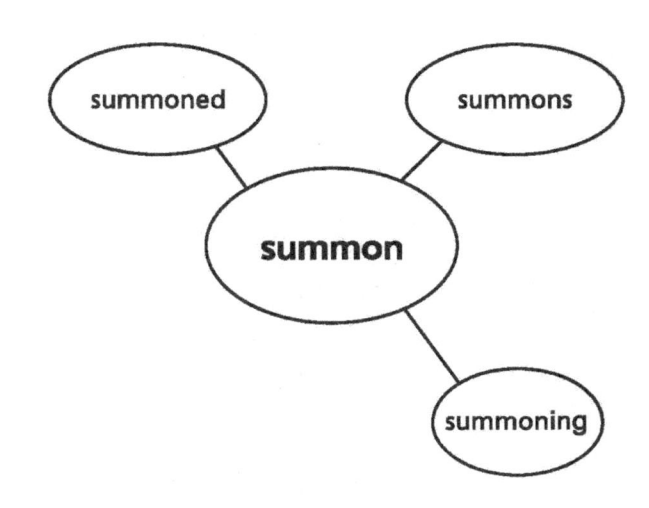

- summoned
- summons
- summon
- summoning

Read the word below. Add or remove inflectional endings, prefixes, or suffixes to form related words and write them on the puzzle pieces. Use a print or online dictionary to help you.

persistent

Grade 6 • Unit 3 Week 1   131

Vocabulary • **Spiral Review**

Name _____

Score some goals! Match the vocabulary words on the left with the definitions on the right. Use a dictionary if you need to.

1. fluent   puts energy into doing something

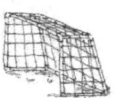

2. majestic   forceful or full of energy

3. perception   a sudden change that causes distress

4. commerce   think seriously about

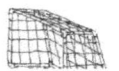

5. commemorate   using sharp or ironic words

6. exerts   lonely and miserable

7. forlorn   related to family or life at home

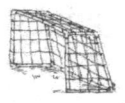

8. contemplate   honor or remember something

9. upheaval   grand and impressive

10. dynamic   buying and selling of products

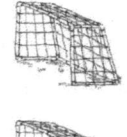

11. domestic   able to speak or write well

12. sarcastic   the way someone looks at an issue

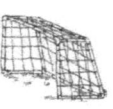

132   Grade 6 • Unit 3 • Week 1

Grammar • Verb Tenses

Name _____

> - The **present tense** of a verb tells what a subject is doing now.
>
>   Louis <u>plays</u> video games with his brother.
>
> - The **past tense** tells what has already happened. It is usually formed by adding -d or -ed to the base form of the verb.
>
>   We <u>played</u> a game in science class.
>
> - The **future tense** tells what is going to happen. It is usually formed by adding the helping verb will to the base form of the verb.
>
>   Samantha <u>will play</u> soccer in the fall.

A. Write the past tense of each verb.

1. climb _____

2. pretend _____

3. examine _____

4. pick _____

5. charge _____

B. Write the future tense of each verb.

6. excuse _____

7. travel _____

8. watch _____

Write about a goal that you accomplished last year. Then write about a goal you want to accomplish this year. Edit and proofread your work. Make sure all verb tenses are correct.

Grade 6 • Unit 3 • Week 2   133

Grammar • Subject-Verb Agreement

Name _____

> - Verbs must agree with their subjects in number: A **singular subject** requires a **singular verb**, and a **plural subject** requires a **plural verb**.
> - Present tense verbs with a single subject add -s to the base.
>   *Julia walks her dog each morning.*
> - Present tense verbs with a plural subject do not add -s.
>   *Cole and Remy walk to school every day.*

Rewrite each sentence using the correct present tense form of the verb in parentheses.

1. A hiker (walk, walks) along trails that are not very steep.

   _____

2. Rock climbers (choose, chooses) steeper slopes.

   _____

3. Smooth rocks (require, requires) special climbing techniques.

   _____

4. A rock climber (need, needs) special equipment to ascend a mountain.

   _____

5. Steel spikes (help, helps) the climber reach the top.

   _____

Reading/Writing Connection Read the excerpt from "Facing the Storm." Circle the verbs in each sentence. Then, write three of your own sentences using correct subject-verb agreement.

> "I've sent the other volunteers home, but I need you girls to help Mr. Garza get the storm shutters down in here and in the aviary."

_____

_____

134 Grade 6 • Unit 3 • Week 2

Grammar • Mechanics: **Subject-Verb Agreement**

Name _____

- A verb may have more than one subject. More than one subject for the same verb is called a compound subject. Treat a compound subject like a plural subject and do not add -s to the verb.
- A collective noun is considered singular if it names the group as a whole. It is considered plural if it refers to the group's members as individuals.

Rewrite the sentences. Use the correct verb in parentheses so that the subjects and verbs agree.

1. The football team (practice, practices) every day after school.

   _____

2. The players and coaches (meet, meets) on the field.

   _____

3. Reese (carry, carries) equipment from the gym.

   _____

4. Shoulder pads and helmets (protect, protects) the players.

   _____

5. The team (drink, drinks) water during and after practice.

   _____

Writing Connection

Write a paragraph about a sport or game that you like to play. Describe the activity in detail using action verbs. Make sure to use the correct subject-verb agreement.

_____

_____

_____

Grade 6 • Unit 3 • Week 2 135

Grammar • Proofreading

Name _____

> - The **present tense** of a verb tells what a subject is doing now. The **past tense** tells what has already happened. Add -*d* or -*ed* to most verbs to show past tense. The **future tense** tells what is going to happen. Add the helping verb *will* to show future tense.
> - A present tense verb must agree with its subject. Present tense verbs with a single subject add -*s* to the base. Present tense verbs with a plural subject do not add -*s*.
> - Treat a compound subject like a plural subject and do not add -*s* to the verb.
> - A collective noun is considered singular if it names the group as a whole. It is considered plural if it refers to the group's members acting individually.

Proofread the sentences for mistakes. Put brackets [ ] around incorrect verb tenses. Rewrite the sentences correctly.

1. elephants lives in herds

   _____

2. female elephants and calves travels together.

   _____

3. Typically, a strong female elephant lead the herd

   _____

4. the herd move from place to place looking for food

   _____

5. elephants eats leaves, grass, fruit, and other foods from plants

   _____

136   Grade 6 • Unit 3 • Week 2

English: Grammar • **Apply**

Name _____

What was your favorite reading selection or other text you read this week? Write a paragraph describing what you learned from it or why you enjoyed it. When you're done, exchange your writing with a partner. Proofread your partner's writing. Remember to apply the grammar you have learned this week.

Spelling • r-Controlled Vowel Syllables

Name _____

Fold back the paper along the dotted line. Use the blanks to write each word as it is read aloud. When you finish the test, unfold the paper. Use the list at the right to correct any spelling mistakes.

1. _____   1. actor
2. _____   2. stroller
3. _____   3. scatter
4. _____   4. daughter
5. _____   5. platter
6. _____   6. customer
7. _____   7. ancestor
8. _____   8. flavor
9. _____   9. mirror
10. _____   10. vinegar
11. _____   11. bachelor
12. _____   12. behavior
13. _____   13. calendar
14. _____   14. waiter
15. _____   15. singular
16. _____   16. maneuver
17. _____   17. observer
18. _____   18. wander
19. _____   19. traitor
20. _____   20. janitor

Review Words
21. _____   21. wealthy
22. _____   22. exploit
23. _____   23. ceiling

Challenge Words
24. _____   24. clamor
25. _____   25. rescuer

Grade 6 • Unit 3 • Week 2

Phonics/Spelling • **Word Sort**

Name _____

When a vowel is followed by the letter *r*, the two combine to form a special vowel sound. Both the vowel and the *r* must remain in the same syllable. Here are some examples of *r*-controlled vowel syllables:

ter as in *crater*   *cor* as in *coral*

mar as in *marvel*   *thir* as in *thirteen*

Read each word aloud. Listen to the effect the *r* has on each vowel sound.

DECODING WORDS

The word *margin* has two syllables. In the first syllable, the vowel *a* is followed by an *r*. That means that the letters *ar* work together to form an *r*-controlled vowel team, and the *ar* stays in the same syllable. Blend the sounds: /mär/ /jin/.

Read the words in the box. Write the spelling words that contain the matching *r*-controlled patterns.

actor	platter	mirror	calendar	observer
stroller	customer	vinegar	waiter	wander
scatter	ancestor	bachelor	singular	traitor
daughter	flavor	behavior	maneuver	janitor

-ar	-or	-er

Look through this week's selections for more words with *r*-controlled vowel syllables to sort. Create a word sort for a partner in your writer's notebook.

Grade 6 • Unit 3 • Week 2 139

Spelling • Word Meaning

Name _____

actor	platter	mirror	calendar	observer
stroller	customer	vinegar	waiter	wander
scatter	ancestor	bachelor	singular	traitor
daughter	flavor	behavior	maneuver	janitor

A. Write the spelling word that best completes each sentence.

1. He used the _____ to take his baby to the park.
2. The _____ ran the American flag up the flag pole.
3. With his binoculars, Marco is a keen _____ of wildlife.
4. Let's sort the nouns according to whether they are _____ or plural.
5. The teacher complimented her class on their pleasant _____.
6. The _____ of the frozen yogurt is sweet and delicious.
7. I made an olive oil and _____ salad dressing.
8. The _____ served salad before the main course.
9. My dad prepared a _____ of appetizers for the party.
10. The _____ was convincing in his role as a doctor.

B. Write the spelling word that matches each definition.

11. someone who betrays his or her country _____
12. to distribute or spread in all directions _____
13. a relative who lived long ago _____
14. glass that reflects images _____
15. man who is not married _____
16. chart showing months, weeks, and days of the year _____
17. female human offspring _____
18. someone who pays for goods or services _____
19. to move around without a destination in mind _____
20. to move or handle with skill _____

Spelling • Proofreading

Name _____

There are five misspelled words in the first paragraph below and four misspelled words in the second paragraph. Underline each misspelled word. Then write the words correctly on the lines.

The customur brought his daughtor into the grocery store. While the child sat in her strollor, the father looked at different items to buy. First, he put a small bottle of vinegur in his basket, thinking he would use it to make salad dressing. As the man moved around the store, the little girl was on her best behavur.

1. _____ 2. _____ 3. _____

4. _____ 5. _____

The acter was very convincing in his role as a waitor. For example, he carried an incredibly heavy plattor of dishes through the restaurant and into the kitchen. He was able to maneuvore around many tables that were spaced closely together. He was so convincing that I forgot that the man was acting!

6. _____ 7. _____ 8. _____ 9. _____

Writing Connection — Write about a scene you've observed at a grocery store or restaurant. Use four or more words from the spelling list.

_____
_____
_____
_____
_____
_____
_____
_____
_____

Phonics/Spelling • **Review**

Name _____

Remember

When a vowel is followed by the letter *r*, the two combine to form a special **r-controlled vowel** sound. Both the vowel and the *r* must remain in the same syllable. As you read the following words aloud, listen carefully to the vowel sound in each underlined syllable: vis**itor**, /vi/ /zi/ /tər/; haz**ard**, /haz/ /ərd/; all**ergy**, /a/ /lər/ /jē/; dis**turb**, /dis/ /tərb/

actor	platter	mirror	calendar	observer
stroller	customer	vinegar	waiter	wander
scatter	ancestor	bachelor	singular	traitor
daughter	flavor	behavior	maneuver	janitor

Write the r-controlled vowel syllable that ends each word. Then write the spelling word on the line.

1. wan ___ ___ ___ _____
2. custo ___ ___ ___ _____
3. ances ___ ___ ___ _____
4. ac ___ ___ ___ _____
5. obser ___ ___ ___ _____
6. behav ___ ___ ___ _____
7. plat ___ ___ ___ _____
8. jani ___ ___ ___ _____
9. calen ___ ___ ___ _____
10. strol ___ ___ ___ _____
11. trai ___ ___ ___ _____
12. maneu ___ ___ ___ _____
13. bache ___ ___ ___ _____
14. vine ___ ___ ___ _____
15. mir ___ ___ ___ _____
16. fla ___ ___ ___ _____
17. daugh ___ ___ ___ _____
18. wai ___ ___ ___ _____
19. scat ___ ___ ___ _____
20. singu ___ ___ ___ _____

142   Grade 6 • Unit 3 • Week 2

Vocabulary Strategy • Word Relationships

Name _____

> When you come across an unfamiliar word, look for other words in the surrounding text that have certain relationships to that word. These words might give you a clue to the word's meaning. Look at the following example:
>
> **The ancient castle was crumbling, but many of the elements were still intact. We saw the towers and a space that might have been the dungeon. The stone keep rose three stories above the grounds.**
>
> This paragraph describes **parts** of a **whole**—a castle. This clue tells you that a *keep*, in this context, is a part of a castle. Other word relationships that can help you find a word's meaning are **cause/effect** and **item/category**.

Read each passage. Use the given word relationship clue to write a definition for the boldfaced word.

1. **cause/effect**

   The rocks in the tundra had clearly suffered the effects of **weathering**. After constant freezing and thawing, they had cracked and broken into smaller pieces.

   _____

2. **part/whole**

   A volcano generally consists of several main parts. The dome is the steep mound created by the build-up of magma. The **vent** is the circular hole or large crack through which magma and gases escape from inside the earth.

   _____

3. **item/category**

   Woodwinds include flutes and instruments with reeds, or thin strips of material that vibrate to produce sounds. Some woodwinds actually have two reeds bound together. These include the oboe and the **bassoon**.

   _____

Grade 6 • Unit 3 • Week 2   143

Vocabulary Strategy • Paragraph Clues

Name _____

Read each passage from "Poppy and the Junior Tigers." Underline the context clues that help you figure out the meaning of each word in bold. Then write the word's meaning on the line.

1. Not only were the Junior Tigers not interested in dribbling drills, but they also **balked** at running drills and shooting drills. Although Poppy had tried to explain just how important the drills were to performing well, the Junior Tigers just didn't appear to care.
   _____

2. Poppy called out, "Kia, you're begging for someone to steal the ball. Pass lower! Rosa, stop **fiddling** with your hair and focus!"
   _____

3. "Really?" asked Mike, looking **crestfallen**, his usual grin gone. "But I like basketball."
   _____

4. "Carl, don't run with the ball, but don't trip over it, either." Mike, a tall, skinny kid who enjoyed hogging the ball, smirked and said, "Yeah, Carl, love your **coordination**."
   _____

5. To Poppy's surprise, the Junior Tigers actually lined up without the usual shoving and pushing. They took turns shooting at the basket in an almost orderly **fashion**.
   _____

Grammar • **Main and Helping Verbs**

Name _____

- A **main verb** shows the main action or state of being in a sentence.

    Beau and his mom cook dinner on Thursday nights.

- A **helping verb** helps the main verb show tense. Helping verbs include forms of *be, do,* and *have,* as well as *will, can, may, should,* and *must.*

    They will make steamed dumplings for dinner tomorrow.

- A **verb phrase** consists of a main verb and one or more helping verbs.

    Beau has enjoyed learning how to cook.

Write the verb phrases in the following sentences.

1. The northern states have suffered a drought. _____

2. The weather has been hot and dry for weeks. _____

3. The farmers have hoped for rain. _____

4. A good rain should save the dry crops. _____

5. The harvest season is approaching. _____

6. The weather may turn cooler next month. _____

Connect to Community

Talk to a parent or another trusted adult about your local newspapers. Read articles together from a print or digital newspaper. Then pretend you are a journalist for your school newspaper. Write an article about a special event that happened at your school. Proofread your work for correct verb tenses.

_____
_____
_____
_____

Grammar • Perfect Tenses and Progressive Forms

Name _____

- **Perfect tenses** use a form of *have* followed by a past participle, which is usually the *-ed* form of the verb.

- **Present perfect** tells about an action that occurred at an indefinite time in the past: *I have finished my science experiment.* **Past perfect** tells about an action that occurred before another event in the past: *After Tia had finished her dinner, she played outside.* **Future perfect** adds the helping verb *will* and tells about an action that will start and finish in the future: *I will have walked two miles.*

- **Progressive forms** use a form of *be* followed by a present participle, which is the *-ing* form of the verb.

- **Present progressive** tells about an action that is happening now: *I am working on my essay.* **Past progressive** tells about an action that took place while another action was occurring: *I was telling them about the field trip.* **Future progressive** adds the helping verb *will* and tells about an action that will occur while another happens: *I will be going to dance class after school.*

Write the tense of each verb phrase.

1. will be studying _____
2. am cooking _____
3. have talked _____
4. will have arrived _____
5. was talking _____
6. had remained _____

Reading/Writing Connection

Read the sentence from "Jewels of the Sea." Circle the past perfect in the sentence below. Then write two sentences of your own using the past perfect tense.

> "Even though the women had lived all their lives by the sea, they did not know how to swim!"

_____

_____

146 Grade 6 • Unit 3 • Week 3

Grammar • Mechanics: Avoiding Verb Tense Shifts

Name _____

- Avoid shifting from one verb tense to another in the same sentence when the actions occur at the same time.
- When actions occur at different times, however, a shift makes sense.
  Yesterday, Jaclyn <u>made</u> a bird house, and she <u>will</u> <u>hang</u> it tomorrow.

A. Read each pair of sentences. Put an X beside the incorrect sentence in which the verb tenses shift.

1. Today, my family went to the store and shops for school supplies. _____
   Today, my family went to the store and shopped for school supplies. _____

2. We looked for the things we needed the most. _____
   We look for the things we needed the most. _____

3. I needed notebooks for English class and chose some red ones. _____
   I needed notebooks for English class and choose some red ones. _____

B. Rewrite each sentence below using the correct tense of the verb in parentheses ( ).

4. Yesterday the weather was warm and sunny, but right now it (has looked) cold and rainy outside.

   _____

   _____

5. The temperature is dropping, and tomorrow we (had) ice everywhere.

   _____

6. On winter afternoons, I pull on my skates and (had played) ice hockey with my friends.

   _____

In your writer's notebook, write about how the weather forecast influences your activities. Check your work to make sure your verb tenses are written correctly.

Grammar • Proofreading

Name _____

> - A **main verb** shows the main action or state of being. A **helping verb** helps the main verb show tense. Helping verbs include forms of *be, do,* and *have,* as well as *will, can, may, should,* and *must*. A **verb phrase** consists of a main verb and one or more helping verbs.
> - Main and helping verbs form different **verb tenses**. Avoid shifting verb tenses in a sentence unless the actions occur at different times.

Proofread each sentence for mistakes. Rewrite the sentence correctly. Then underline any verb phrases.

1. Juan is plan a surprise party for his brother

   _____

2. his brother turned ten tomorrow.

   _____

3. Juan has pick some fun games and activities?

   _____

4. last week he invites the guests.

   _____

5. Today, Juan has prepare food for the party,

   _____

6. The guests gathering early for the party

   _____

7. Everyone hides and will shout, "Surprise!

   _____

8. Juan's brother liked parties, and he loved this one.

   _____

148 Grade 6 • Unit 3 • Week 3

English: Grammar • **Apply**

Name _____

What was your favorite reading selection or other text you read this week? Write a paragraph describing what you learned from it or why you enjoyed it. When you're done, exchange your writing with a partner. Proofread your partner's writing. Remember to apply the grammar you have learned this week.

Spelling • Frequently Misspelled Words

Name _____

Fold back the paper along the dotted line. Use the blanks to write each word as it is read aloud. When you finish the test, unfold the paper. Use the list at the right to correct any spelling mistakes.

1. _____
2. _____
3. _____
4. _____
5. _____
6. _____
7. _____
8. _____
9. _____
10. _____
11. _____
12. _____
13. _____
14. _____
15. _____
16. _____
17. _____
18. _____
19. _____
20. _____

Review Words 21. _____
22. _____
23. _____

Challenge Words 24. _____
25. _____

1. address
2. against
3. always
4. answer
5. because
6. believe
7. brought
8. children
9. cousin
10. doesn't
11. dollar
12. enough
13. guess
14. instead
15. people
16. receive
17. straight
18. until
19. usually
20. woman
21. flavor
22. calendar
23. behavior
24. foreign
25. official

150 Grade 6 • Unit 3 • Week 3

Phonics/Spelling • Word Sort

Name _____

Many words are frequently misspelled because they contain consonants or vowels that do not follow regular spelling patterns. To help you read and write **frequently misspelled words**, look for familiar spelling patterns, make sure each syllable has a vowel or vowel team, or use memory devices to help you remember how to spell the word.

To spell the word *island*, remember that an *island* **is land** surrounded by water.

SPELLING TIP

Memory tricks and mnemonic devices like, "*i* before *e*, except after *c*, or when sounding like *a*, as in *neighbor* and *weigh*" can help you remember how to spell words like: *receive, believe, achieve* and *piece*.

Read the words in the box. Write the spelling words that contain the matching vowel sound in the first syllable.

address	because	cousin	guess	straight
against	believe	doesn't	instead	until
always	brought	dollar	people	usually
answer	children	enough	receive	woman

short vowel sound

1. _____
2. _____
3. _____
4. _____
5. _____
6. _____
7. _____

8. _____
9. _____
10. _____
11. _____

long vowel sound

12. _____
13. _____
14. _____

15. _____
16. _____

other vowel sounds

17. _____
18. _____
19. _____
20. _____

Look through this week's selections for more frequently misspelled words to sort. Then create a sort for a partner in your writer's notebook.

Spelling • Word Meaning

Name _____

address	because	cousin	guess	straight
against	believe	doesn't	instead	until
always	brought	dollar	people	usually
answer	children	enough	receive	woman

A. Write the spelling word that each clue describes.

1. unsure of an answer _____
2. someone related to me _____
3. the plural of *person* _____
4. the opposite of *give* _____
5. American money _____
6. the plural of *child* _____
7. *25 Pine Street* _____
8. the opposite of *never* _____
9. the singular of *women* _____
10. to have faith or to trust _____

B. Write the spelling word that best completes each sentence.

11. I voted _____ the candidate with no experience.
12. She wasn't sure how to _____ the question.
13. Jorge went swimming _____ it was a hot, sunny day.
14. Mara _____ her duffel bag to soccer practice.
15. He _____ have enough money for the bus fare.
16. Jake thought two turkey burgers were more than _____ to eat!
17. I will buy sneakers _____ of a new baseball cap.
18. The workers painted a _____ line down the middle of the road.
19. We'll have to wait _____ it snows before we can go skiing.
20. I _____ have cereal and orange juice for breakfast.

Spelling • Proofreading

Name _____

A. There are four misspelled words in each paragraph below. Underline each misspelled word. Then write the words correctly on the lines.

It is important to teach young childrin to memorize their name, addres, and phone number. This information is critical to know in case they get lost. Practice having your child say each piece of information. If he or she does'nt know an anser, give a helpful clue or reminder.

1. _____ 2. _____ 3. _____ 4. _____

Many peepul in our country beleive it is their responsibility to vote. When you vote, you will vote for or agenst a representative. It is important to vote becuz that is how we can improve our country and make it a better place in which to live.

5. _____ 6. _____ 7. _____ 8. _____

Writing Connection Write about something that you think is important. Use at least four words from the spelling list.

_____
_____
_____
_____
_____
_____
_____
_____
_____
_____

Spelling • Review

Name _____

Remember

Frequently misspelled words often contain consonants or vowels that do not follow regular spelling patterns. Looking for familiar spelling patterns, making sure each syllable has a vowel or vowel team, or using memory devices can help you remember how to spell these words.

address	because	cousin	guess	straight
against	believe	doesn't	instead	until
always	brought	dollar	people	usually
answer	children	enough	receive	woman

A. Fill in the missing letters of each word. Then write the spelling word on the line.

1. inst __ __ d _____
2. ag __ __ nst _____
3. p __ __ ple _____
4. a __ __ ays _____
5. wom __ __ _____

6. unt __ __ _____
7. chi __ __ __ en _____
8. do __ __ __ 't _____
9. c __ __ sin _____
10. us __ __ lly _____

B. Circle the spelling word that rhymes with the bold word. Write the word.

11. **mess** best address desk
_____

12. **weight** straight delay white
_____

13. **confess** jest missed guess
_____

14. **caught** brought cough laugh
_____

15. **weave** relieves believe relive
_____

16. **clause** raise sought because
_____

17. **collar** bowler molar dollar
_____

18. **rough** rogue enough brought
_____

19. **deceive** grief sieve receive
_____

20. **prancer** dance answer antler
_____

154   Grade 6 • Unit 3 • Week 3

Vocabulary • Related Words

Name _____

Expand your vocabulary by adding or removing inflectional endings, prefixes, or suffixes to a base word to create different forms of a word.

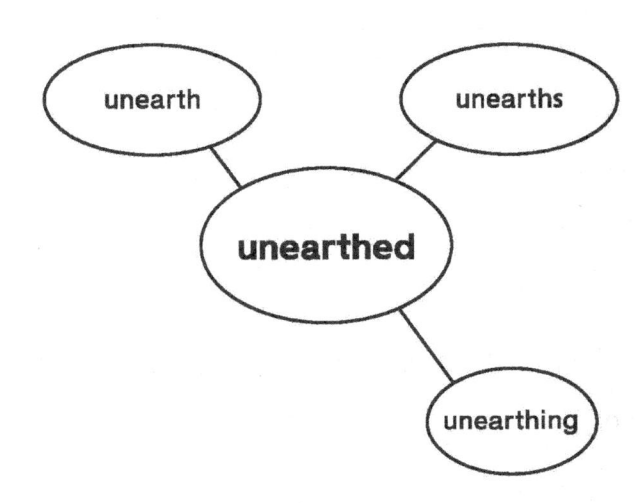

- unearth
- unearths
- **unearthed**
- unearthing

Read the word below. Add or remove inflectional endings, prefixes or suffixes to form related words and write them in the blank cogs. Use a print or online dictionary to help you.

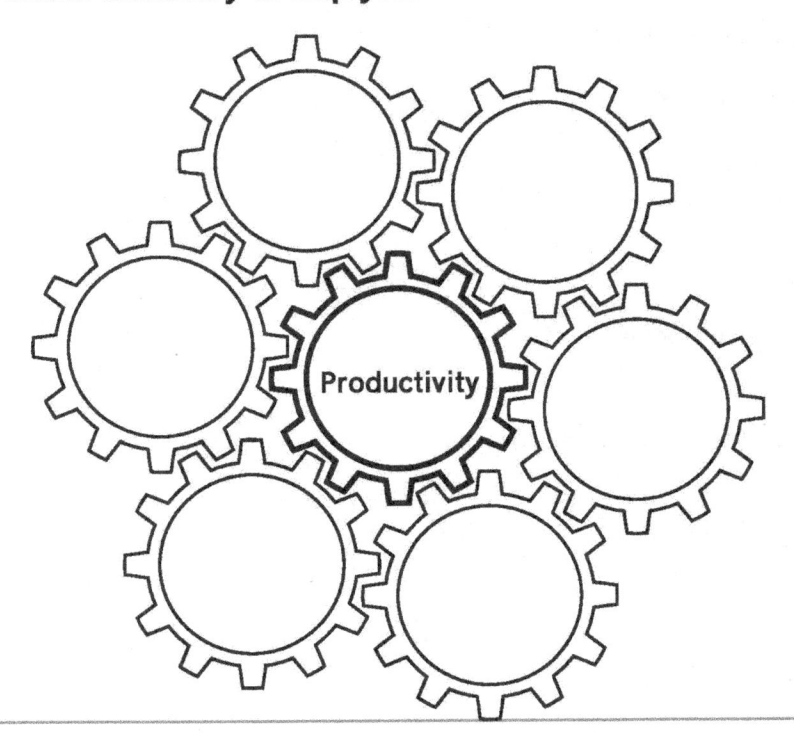

Productivity

Grade 6 • Unit 3 • Week 3 155

Vocabulary • Spiral Review

Name _____

Read the clues. Complete the puzzle with the vocabulary words. Then write the letters in the boxes to solve the riddle. Use a dictionary if you need help.

phobic	feebly	stifling	roused
skewed	dilemma	alcove	summon
utmost	persistent	vastness	recoiled

1. a difficult problem or choice to be made _ _ _ ☐ _ _
2. having a fear of something _ _ ☐ _ _ _
3. call upon something for a certain action _ ☐ _ _ _ _
4. continuing in spite of opposition _ _ _ _ _ _ _ ☐ _
5. the quality of being very large _ _ _ ☐ _ _ _
6. weakly _ ☐ _ _ _ _
7. small space set back in a wall _ _ _ ☐ _
8. fell back suddenly in fear _ _ _ _ _ ☐ _
9. woken up from sleep ☐ _ _ _ _ _
10. took an indirect route _ ☐ _ _ _ _
11. suffocating or very close ☐ _ _ _ _ _ _ _
12. of the greatest degree or amount _ ☐ _ _ _ _

What is the tallest mountain in the world?

☐ ☐ ☐ ☐ ☐   ☐ ☐ ☐ ☐ ☐ ☐ ☐

156 Grade 6 • Unit 3 • Week 3

Grammar • Linking Verbs

Name _____

- A **linking verb** links the subject of a sentence with an adjective or a noun.
- Forms of *be,* when they stand alone, are always linking verbs.
    She *is* a chemical engineer.
- The verbs *seem, appear, look, sound, taste,* and *feel* can also be linking verbs. *The students appear excited for their spring concert.*

For each sentence, write the linking verb.

1. Today is the first day of camp. _____

2. The lake looks calm at sunrise. _____

3. The birds sound peaceful in the trees. _____

4. Campers feel good after a restful sleep. _____

5. Breakfast is oatmeal and bacon. _____

6. The campers appear hungry. _____

7. The food smells great! _____

8. Hot oatmeal tastes delicious. _____

9. The weather feels warm. _____

10. Ducks and squirrels are our neighbors here! _____

In your writer's notebook, write a thank you letter to a teacher at your school. In your letter explain how they helped you or how they made school special for you. Edit and proofread your work.

Grammar • Predicate Nouns and Adjectives

Name _____

- A sentence is made up of a subject and a predicate.
- A **predicate noun** is a noun that follows a linking verb and renames or identifies the subject: *The basketball game is <u>tomorrow</u>.*
- A **predicate adjective** is an adjective that follows a linking verb and describes the subject: *The granola bars are <u>chewy</u>.*

A. Read each sentence and underline the linking verb. Then write the predicate noun on the blank line.

1. Today is Saturday. _____
2. Saturday is our day for errands. _____
3. These items are the groceries for today. _____
4. The first thing is apples. _____

B. Read each sentence and underline the linking verb. Then write the predicate adjective on the blank line.

5. These apples look good. _____
6. The green ones taste sour. _____
7. That type is crunchy. _____

Reading/Writing Connection

Read the sentence from "Jewels from the Sea." Circle the linking verb and underline the predicate adjective. Then write a new sentence with a linking verb and predicate adjective.

"They made very little money, and some would say the women were impoverished."

_____
_____
_____

158 Grade 6 • Unit 3 • Week 4

Grammar • Mechanics: **Titles**

Name _____

- Italicize or underline titles of long works, such as novels, plays, films, newspapers, magazines, artworks, and albums.
- Use quotation marks around titles of short works, such as short stories, essays, magazine articles, songs, and poems.
- Capitalize all the important works in titles, along with the first and last words.
- Capitalize linking verbs in titles.

Write each title correctly on the line. Use an underline for long works and quotation marks for short works. The words in parentheses ( ) tell you whether the work is long or short.

1. the call of the wild (book)

   _____

2. my favorite vacation (essay)

   _____

3. the baltimore sun (newspaper)

   _____

4. washington crossing the delaware (painting)

   _____

5. stopping by woods on a snowy evening (poem)

   _____

6. this land is your land (song)

   _____

In your writer's notebook, record an interview with a classmate. Ask them about their favorite books, movies, and songs. Edit your work to check for correct capitalization.

Grammar • Proofreading

Name _____

> - A **linking verb** links the subject of a sentence with an adjective or a noun. Common linking verbs include *seem, appear, look, sound, taste, feel* and forms of *be*.
> - A **predicate noun** is a noun that follows a linking verb and renames or identifies the subject. A **predicate adjective** is an adjective that follows a linking verb and describes the subject.
> - Italicize or underline titles of long works, such as novels, plays, films, newspapers, magazines, artworks, and albums. Use quotation marks around titles of short works, such as short stories, essays, magazine articles, songs, and poems.
> - Capitalize all the important words in titles, along with the first and last words of the title. Capitalize all linking verbs in a title.

Rewrite the sentences correctly. Watch for mistakes with linking verbs, capitalization, and punctuation.

1. My favorite <u>book</u> is peter pan.

   _____

2. that magazine, science monthly, sounds interesting.

   _____

3. the title of my Article is the game seemed lost

   _____

4. At the game, we sang take me out to the ballgame.

   _____

5. dog barking at the moon are a Painting by Joan Miro.

   _____

6. <u>the village blacksmith</u> is my favorite poem?

   _____

160 Grade 6 • Unit 3 • Week 4

English: Grammar • Apply

Name _____

What was your favorite reading selection or other text you read this week? Write a paragraph describing what you learned from it or why you enjoyed it. When you're done, exchange your writing with a partner. Proofread your partner's writing. Remember to apply the grammar you have learned this week.

Spelling • Words with Prefixes

Name _____

Fold back the paper along the dotted line. Use the blanks to write each word as it is read aloud. When you finish the test, unfold the paper. Use the list at the right to correct any spelling mistakes.

1. _____ 1. superhuman
2. _____ 2. independent
3. _____ 3. incomplete
4. _____ 4. supermarket
5. _____ 5. outstanding
6. _____ 6. uncommon
7. _____ 7. untangle
8. _____ 8. incredible
9. _____ 9. outpost
10. _____ 10. enlist
11. _____ 11. superstar
12. _____ 12. outlaw
13. _____ 13. proclaim
14. _____ 14. unsightly
15. _____ 15. unknown
16. _____ 16. prolong
17. _____ 17. enrich
18. _____ 18. enlarge
19. _____ 19. outfield
20. _____ 20. outcry

Review Words
21. _____ 21. address
22. _____ 22. cousin
23. _____ 23. people

Challenge Words
24. _____ 24. indistinct
25. _____ 25. unequal

Name _____

Phonics/Spelling • Word Sort

A prefix is a group of letters added to the beginning of a word that changes the word's meaning. For example:

- **un-** ("not" or "opposite of"): <u>un</u>well
- **pro-** ("for" or "forward"): <u>pro</u>crastinate
- **in-** ("not" or "opposite of"): <u>in</u>action
- **out-** ("in a manner that surpasses"): <u>out</u>bid
- **en-** ("put into" or "cause to be"): <u>en</u>close
- **super-** ("over"): <u>super</u>size

DECODING WORDS

Look at the beginning part of the word *unknown*. The prefix *un-* means "not." Use the prefix to figure out the word's meaning. The word *unknown* means "not known."

Write the spelling words that contain the matching prefix. Then draw a slash (/) between the prefix and the base word in each spelling word.

superhuman	outstanding	outpost	proclaim	enrich
independent	uncommon	enlist	unsightly	enlarge
incomplete	untangle	superstar	unknown	outfield
supermarket	incredible	outlaw	prolong	outcry

un-
1. _____
2. _____
3. _____
4. _____

in-
5. _____
6. _____
7. _____

en-
8. _____
9. _____
10. _____

pro-
11. _____
12. _____

out-
13. _____
14. _____
15. _____
16. _____
17. _____

super-
18. _____
19. _____
20. _____

Look through this week's selections for more words with prefixes to sort. Create a word sort for a partner in your writer's notebook.

Spelling • Word Meaning

Name _____

superhuman	outstanding	outpost	proclaim	enrich
independent	uncommon	enlist	unsightly	enlarge
incomplete	untangle	superstar	unknown	outfield
supermarket	incredible	outlaw	prolong	outcry

A. Write the spelling word that has a meaning similar to each word below.

1. unusual _____
2. extend _____
3. engage _____
4. criminal _____
5. announce _____
6. unbelievable _____
7. self-reliant _____
8. unfamiliar _____
9. unfinished _____
10. unattractive _____

B. Write the spelling word that best completes each sentence.

11. Can we _____ this family photo?
12. After swimming, I had to _____ my hair.
13. The audience cheered when the _____ appeared on stage.
14. A group of soldiers waited at the _____ for the army to arrive.
15. He must have _____ strength to lift those heavy boxes.
16. Vitamins and minerals are often added to foods to _____ them.
17. What _____ work you did on your report!
18. There was a public _____ over the library's closing.
19. The Taylors went to the _____ for their weekly shopping.
20. Lily caught the fly ball in the _____.

Spelling • Proofreading

Name _____

There are six misspelled words in the paragraphs below. Underline each misspelled word. Then write the words correctly on the lines.

I'll never forget last night's baseball game. My favorite team's souperstar was up at bat. He is known for hitting grand-slam home runs. I'm sure the players in the outfeeld were really nervous because the bases were loaded. The pitcher unleashed the ball. With suprhuman strength, the batter hit the ball out of the ballpark.

The team scored four runs! It was an inncredible play by an owtstanding player. The fans cheered wildly, and the players ran onto the field to preclaim themselves the winners.

1. _____ 2. _____ 3. _____

4. _____ 5. _____ 6. _____

Writing Connection — **Write about a sports event you've attended or watched on TV. Use at least four words from the spelling list.**

_____
_____
_____
_____
_____
_____
_____
_____
_____

Phonics/Spelling • **Review**

Name _____

> **Remember**
>
> A prefix is a group of letters added to the beginning of a word that changes the word's meaning. These are some common prefixes:
> - *un-* "not" or "opposite of"
> - *pro-* ("for" or "forward"): <u>pro</u>active
> - *in-* "not" or "opposite of"
> - *out-* ("in a manner that exceeds or surpasses"): <u>out</u>bid
> - *en-* ("put into or onto" or "cause to be"): <u>en</u>close
> - *super-* ("over"): <u>super</u>size

superhuman	outstanding	outpost	proclaim	enrich
independent	uncommon	enlist	unsightly	enlarge
incomplete	untangle	superstar	unknown	outfield
supermarket	incredible	outlaw	prolong	outcry

Write each word's prefix. Then write the spelling word on the line.

1. _____ field _____
2. _____ list _____
3. _____ star _____
4. _____ law _____
5. _____ sightly _____
6. _____ cry _____
7. _____ post _____
8. _____ tangle _____
9. _____ claim _____
10. _____ complete _____
11. _____ credible _____
12. _____ long _____
13. _____ large _____
14. _____ rich _____
15. _____ market _____
16. _____ standing _____
17. _____ dependent _____
18. _____ common _____
19. _____ known _____
20. _____ human _____

Vocabulary Strategy • Greek and Latin Roots

Name _____

Many words we use in English contain roots from the ancient languages of Greek and Latin. It is helpful to know the meanings of the most common **Greek and Latin roots.** When you recognize these roots in an unfamiliar word, you can use their meanings to help you define that word. Take a look at these roots and their meanings:

Greek root *log,* as in *apology,* means "word."

Greek root *scop,* as in *periscope,* means "see."

Greek root *therm,* as in *thermostat,* means "heat."

Latin root *aud,* as in *audible,* means "hear."

Latin root *loc,* as in *location,* means "place."

Latin root *ped,* as in *biped,* means "foot."

Choose a Greek root and a Latin root from the box above. Write each root below a house. Then fill the house with words containing that root. Use a dictionary to help you. Then write a definition for two of the words.

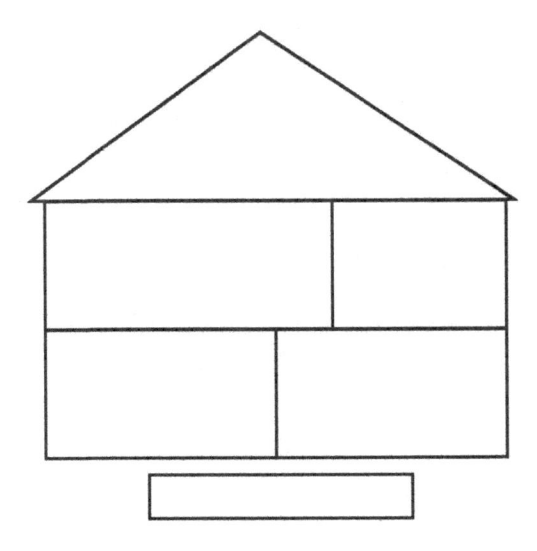

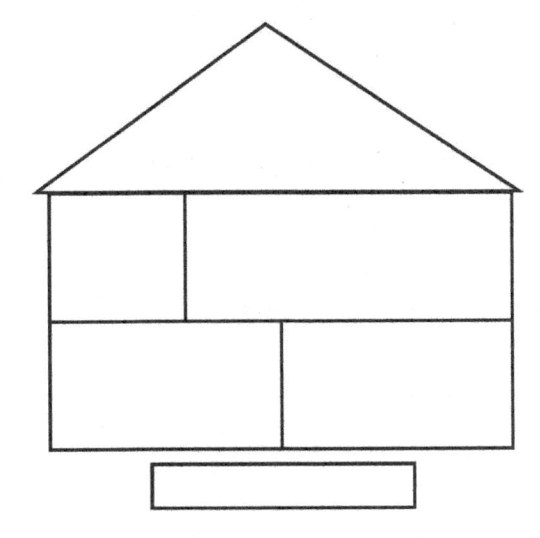

Grade 6 • Unit 3 • Week 4   167

Vocabulary Strategy • **Prefixes and Suffixes**

Name _____

A. Choose the prefix *un-* or *trans-* to change the meaning of each word below. Then use each word in a sentence.

1. clean _____

2. helpful _____

3. form _____

4. port _____

5. available _____

B. Read the words below. On the line provided write how the part of speech or how the word changes when a suffix is added.

6. sanitary ⟶ sanitation

7. transport ⟶ transportation

8. plan ⟶ planner

9. outside ⟶ outsiders

168 Grade 6 • Unit 3 • Week 4

Grammar • Irregular Verbs

Name _____

- Form the past tense and past participle of a **regular verb** by adding -ed.

  I <u>watched</u> a movie with my friend Adam.

- The past tense and past participle of an **irregular verb** are formed differently. In some irregular verbs, a vowel changes. In others, the spelling changes: I <u>ran</u> over to my friends at recess. Sandy should have <u>known</u> to bring an umbrella on the field trip.

Present	Past	Past Participle
begin	began	have begun
ring	rang	have rung
tell	told	have told
go	went	have gone
blow	blew	have blown
sink	sank	have sunk
break	broke	have broken
know	knew	have known
see	saw	have seen
stand	stood	have stood

Read each sentence. On the line, write the correct form of each verb in parentheses ( ).

1. The sound of applause (break) the silence of the theater. _____

2. The audience (stand) to show their appreciation. _____

3. Sylvia (know) her performance was a success. _____

4. Sylvia's dad (throw) a rose onto the stage. _____

5. Her mom (blow) Sylvia a kiss from the audience. _____

6. "We have never (see) such a great show!" said Cody. _____

In your writer's notebook, write about a special day from this past month. Edit your work to be sure you used the past tense correctly.

Grammar • **Special Spellings**

Name _____

- Some irregular verbs have special spellings when used with the helping verbs *have, has,* or *had.*

   The lake <u>had frozen</u> over during the winter.

Present	Past	Past Participle (with *have, had,* or *has*)
think	thought	thought
sing	sang	sung
freeze	froze	frozen
wear	wore	worn
teach	taught	taught
choose	chose	chosen
leave	left	left

Each sentence contains an incorrect form of an irregular verb. Write the correct form on the line.

1. We had thinked today would be a good day to go skating. _____

2. Indeed, the ice freezed solidly overnight. _____

3. However, we have chose to go sledding instead. _____

4. We have weared our warmest clothes. _____

5. Dylan has leaved his hat and gloves at home. _____

6. Sledding without my hat teached me a lesson about cold weather. _____

Reading/Writing Connection Read the sentence from "Is Your City Green?" Underline the irregular verb. Then write two sentences using verbs from the chart at the top of the page.

"Since passengers who have chosen to ride trains are not driving their cars, less fuel is burned."

_____

_____

Grammar • Mechanics: **Contractions with Helping and Irregular Verbs**

Name _____

- A contraction is a single word made by combining two words and leaving out one or more letters. An apostrophe replaces the missing letters.
- A contraction can be formed with a pronoun and a helping verb. (we have = we've; he would = he'd)
- A contraction can be formed with a pronoun and the present tense form of the irregular verb be. (I am = I'm; we are = we're)

A. Write the contractions for the following pronouns and helping verbs.

1. she had _____
2. they have _____
3. we are _____

B. Read each sentence. Rewrite the sentence, changing the pronoun and verb in parentheses ( ) to a contraction.

4. (I am) beginning to think the train is never going to arrive.

   _____

5. (We have) been waiting on the platform for more than an hour.

   _____

6. Aunt Roberta says (she will) ask why the train is delayed.

   _____

Writing Connection Write a paragraph about a decision that you made in the past. Think about what you would have done differently. Use three contractions in your writing.

_____

_____

_____

Grade 6 • Unit 3 • Week 5   171

Name _____

Grammar • Proofreading

> - The past tense and past participle of a **regular verb** are formed by adding the letters *-ed*.
> - The past tense and past participle of some **irregular verbs** are formed by changes in spelling.
> - A contraction is a single word formed by combining two words and leaving out some letters. An apostrophe replaces the missing letters.
> - A contraction can be formed with a pronoun and a helping verb. (*we have* = *we've*; *I am* = *I'm*)

Proofread each sentence. Rewrite the sentence correctly using the correct form of the irregular verb. Add commas and apostrophes where needed.

1. Mr. Darus, the band director, wanted to speak to Dylan, but Dylan had already went home.

   _____
   _____

2. He leaved school early for an appointment with his dentist Dr. Akagi.

   _____

3. Im not sure whether Dylan knowed about the appointment.

   _____

4. His mother had telled the principal this morning.

   _____

5. Dylan had thinked hed be able to stay after school for band practice.

   _____

English: Grammar • **Apply**

Name _____

What was your favorite reading selection or other text you read this week? Write a paragraph describing what you learned from it or why you enjoyed it. When you're done, exchange your writing with a partner. Proofread your partner's writing. Remember to apply the grammar you have learned this week.

Spelling • Suffixes *-ion* **and** *-tion*

Name _____

Fold back the paper along the dotted line. Use the blanks to write each word as it is read aloud. When you finish the test, unfold the paper. Use the list at the right to correct any spelling mistakes.

1. _____
2. _____
3. _____
4. _____
5. _____
6. _____
7. _____
8. _____
9. _____
10. _____
11. _____
12. _____
13. _____
14. _____
15. _____
16. _____
17. _____
18. _____
19. _____
20. _____

Review Words
21. _____
22. _____
23. _____

Challenge Words
24. _____
25. _____

1. inspire
2. inspiration
3. consult
4. consultation
5. separate
6. separation
7. illustrate
8. illustration
9. instruct
10. instruction
11. observe
12. observation
13. react
14. reaction
15. connect
16. connection
17. hesitate
18. hesitation
19. represent
20. representation
21. incomplete
22. outfield
23. supermarket
24. evaporate
25. evaporation

Phonics/Spelling • Word Sort

Name _____

The common suffixes *-ion*, *-tion*, and *-ation* are added to certain words to change them from verbs to nouns.

create	divide	discuss
creation	division	discussion

Read each pair of words. Notice how the consonant sound at the end of each verb changes when the suffix is added. The /t/ in *create* changes to /sh/ in *creation*; the /d/ in *divide* changes to /zh/ in *division*; the /s/ in *discuss* changes to /sh/ in *discussion*.

DECODING WORDS

- When the base word ends in *e*, as in *decorate* and *celebrate*, the *e* is dropped before the suffix *-ion* is added: *decoration, celebration*.

- The final syllable *-tion* is always pronounced /shən/. Read the word *action* aloud: /ac/ /shən/.

Write each pair of spelling words according to their pattern.

inspire	separate	instruct	react	hesitate
inspiration	separation	instruction	reaction	hesitation
consult	illustrate	observe	connect	represent
consultation	illustration	observation	connection	representation

add *-ion*

1. _____ _____

2. _____ _____

3. _____ _____

add *-ation*

4. _____ _____

5. _____ _____

drop *e* and add *-ation*

6. _____ _____

7. _____ _____

drop *e* and add *-ion*

8. _____ _____

9. _____ _____

10. _____ _____

Look through this week's selections for more words with the suffixes *-ion* and *-tion*. Record each word and a related word in your writer's notebook. Note any consonant sound changes.

Spelling • Word Meaning

Name _____

inspire	separate	instruct	react	hesitate
inspiration	separation	instruction	reaction	hesitation
consult	illustrate	observe	connect	represent
consultation	illustration	observation	connection	representation

A. Write the spelling word that best completes each analogy.

1. *United* is to *together* as _____ is to *apart*.
2. *Teach* is to *teacher* as _____ is to *instructor*.
3. *Composition* is to *composer* as _____ is to *illustrator*.
4. *Patrol* is to *police officer* as _____ is to *astronomer*.
5. *Steadfast* is to *firm* as _____ is to *waver*.

B. Write the spelling word that best completes each sentence.

6. There was no _____ when he made his decision.
7. Keisha had an allergic _____ when she ate the peanuts.
8. Our cell phone _____ is excellent!
9. The bird watcher made an interesting _____ about the baby birds.
10. The accused is seeking _____ by a lawyer.
11. Can you _____ the dots to solve the puzzle?
12. What _____ did your teacher give before recess?
13. Her parents will _____ with a doctor about the best treatment.
14. The artist found his _____ from the spectacular scenery.
15. The wall creates a _____ between the two zoo animals.
16. To help us imagine a story, an artist can _____ it with drawings.
17. The patient wanted a _____ with a specialist.
18. What might _____ a composer to write a new piece of music?
19. These flags each _____ a country.
20. How did you _____ when you heard the loud thunder?

176   Grade 6 • Unit 3 • Week 5

Spelling • Proofreading

Name _____

There are three misspelled words in each paragraph below. Underline each misspelled word. Then write the words correctly on the lines.

A landscape artist will observ her surroundings before beginning to paint. Her inspireation might be seeing a flock of birds soaring overhead. Or she might make a simple observeation of how river water flows along its path.

1. _____ 2. _____ 3. _____

What kind of instrukshun do people need to become cartoonists? Do they need to take art classes? A cartoonist's illustrasion can look really simple to create. But to know how to illustrait using cartoons actually takes skill and creativity.

4. _____ 5. _____ 6. _____

Writing Connection Write about something you have been inspired to do. Use at least four words from the spelling list.

_____
_____
_____
_____
_____
_____
_____
_____
_____
_____

Phonics Spelling • Review

Name _____

Remember

A suffix is a letter or group of letters added to a base word or root. Adding the suffixes *-ion, -tion* and *-ation* to certain words changes them from verbs to nouns. These suffixes also change the consonant sound in a word. For example, the /t/ in *react* changes to /sh/ when adding the suffix *-ion* to form *reaction*.

Read the following words. Notice how the suffix affects each final consonant sound.

distract	**perfect**	**eliminate**
distraction	**perfection**	**elimination**

inspire	separate	instruct	react	hesitate
inspiration	separation	instruction	reaction	hesitation
consult	illustrate	observe	connect	represent
consultation	illustration	observation	connection	representation

Write the missing letters to make a spelling word. Then write the spelling word on the line.

1. hesi __ __ __ ion _____
2. re __ __ __ __ _____
3. observa __ __ __ n _____
4. separ __ __ __ _____
5. represent __ __ __ on _____
6. connec __ __ __ n _____
7. instr __ __ __ _____
8. illustra __ __ __ n _____
9. con __ __ __ t _____
10. inspir __ __ __ on _____
11. consulta __ __ __ n _____
12. illust __ __ __ e _____
13. instruc __ __ __ n _____
14. conn __ __ __ _____
15. repre __ __ __ t _____
16. separat __ __ __ _____
17. obse __ __ __ _____
18. react __ __ __ _____
19. hesit __ __ __ _____
20. insp __ __ __ _____

Vocabulary • Content Words

Name _____

> **Content words** are words that are specific to a field of study. For example, words like *technology, energy,* and *pollution* are environmental science content words.
>
> Authors use content words to explain a concept or idea. Sometimes you can figure out what a content word means by using context clues. You can also use a dictionary to help you find the meaning of unfamiliar content words.

Go on a word hunt with a partner through "Make Your City Green!" Find content words related to the environment. Write them in the chart.

Science Words		

CONNECT TO CONTENT

"Make Your City Green!" gives facts about life in an environmentally friendly city in the future. The author describes how life will change in cities with more environmentally friendly technology.

Circle two words that you were able to figure out the meaning of using context clues. Write the words and what they mean on the lines.

_____
_____
_____
_____
_____
_____
_____

Grade 6 • Unit 3 • Week 5   179

Vocabulary Strategy • Synonyms and Antonyms

Name _____

Read each passage from "Trees for a Healthier Africa." Look at the word in bold. If the underlined word is a synonym clue write *S* after the passage. If it is an antonym clue, write *A*. Write a definition of the word in bold. Then write a sentence using the word.

1. Forests in many regions of Africa have not been **conserved**. _____
   Instead of being protected, many trees have been <u>overharvested</u>.

   _____
   _____

2. Such deforestation can cause **dire** results. Less rain, more heat, _____
   and erosion are just a few of the <u>grim</u> effects of deforestation.

   _____
   _____

3. Knowing the impact of **destroying** forests may help prevent such
   ruin in the future. People have learned what went wrong and how _____
   to <u>restore</u> the forests.

   _____
   _____

4. AWF studied the **dwindling** forests in an effort to slow CO_2 buildup.
   They made plans to <u>increase</u> tree growth instead of letting the _____
   forests shrink even more.

   _____
   _____

5. **Reversing** deforestation takes time, but many people are working _____
   to <u>turn it around</u>.

   _____
   _____

Grammar • Pronouns and Antecedents

Name _____

- A **pronoun** takes the place of one or more nouns in a sentence. A **personal pronoun** refers to a person or thing.
- Singular pronouns are *I, you, he, she, it, me, him,* and *her.*
- Plural pronouns are *we, you, they, us,* and *them.*
- An **antecedent** is the word or words that a pronoun refers to.

  <u>Sasha</u> goes to a coding club after school. <u>She</u> learns how to create games.

A. Write a pronoun to take the place of the underlined word or words. Write an S if the pronoun is singular; write a P if the pronoun is plural.

1. Eliza and Haley went to the movie together. _____

2. The movie started at 2:00 p.m. _____

3. Eliza thought the movie was great. _____

4. Other people in the audience thought so too. _____

5. After the movie, Haley's brother, Joe, walked home with the girls.
   _____

B. Circle the pronoun in each sentence. Underline the antecedent.

6. Eliza and Haley said they were hungry after the movie.

7. Haley's dad asked Eliza if she would like to stay for dinner.

8. Mr. Lawrence asked the girls to help him make a pizza.

9. Haley cut the pizza and brought it to the table.

10. After dinner, Joe washed the dishes and put them away.

> Look through your writer's notebook for a paragraph that includes pronouns. Check that each pronoun agrees with its antecedent. Also check for any spelling mistakes. You may use a dictionary to help you.

Grammar • Agreement of Pronouns and Antecedents

Name _____

- Pronouns must agree with their antecedents in **number**.
  Stella moved the chair and desk because <u>they</u> were blocking the door.
- Pronouns must agree with their antecedents in **gender**.
  Juan says <u>he</u> enjoys reading the assigned books.

A. Choose the pronoun in parentheses ( ) that correctly completes each sentence. Write it on the line.

1. My sister Elizabeth says (they, she) wants to learn a foreign language. _____

2. Elizabeth asked Mr. Stokes to help (her, us) choose a language. _____

3. Mr. Stokes said to consider the difficulty of the language and whether knowing (they, it) would be useful. _____

4. Spanish and Mandarin are both good choices because many people speak (them, it). _____

B. Fill in the blank with the appropriate pronoun.

5. Elizabeth thinks Italian and Portuguese sound beautiful, so she wants to study _____

6. However, more people speak French, so _____ is probably more useful.

Reading/Writing Connection Read the sentence from "She Had to Walk Before She Could Run." Circle the pronoun and underline the antecedent. Then write two sentences about someone you admire. Include two pronouns. Edit your work for pronoun usage and agreement.

"After the doctors removed the braces, they were amazed to see that Rudolph could walk on her own."

_____

_____

Grammar • Mechanics: **Avoiding Vague References**

Name _____

- Avoid using pronouns that refer to either of two antecedents.

  Jen went to the store with her grandmother after she got home from work. (incorrect)

  After her grandmother got home from work, Jen went with her to the store. (correct)

- Avoid referring to a hidden antecedent.
- To fix a vague pronoun reference, rephrase the sentence or replace the pronoun with a noun.

A. Read each pair of sentences. Draw an X beside the sentence that avoids vague pronoun reference.

1. My sister Amber helped our mother fill the aquarium after she got home. _____

   After our mother got home, my sister Amber helped her fill the aquarium. _____

2. The aquarium is not large, but they will have plenty of room to swim. _____

   The aquarium is not large, but the fish will have plenty of room to swim. _____

3. Amber dropped the light in the tank, but the light was not broken. _____

   Amber dropped the light in the tank, but it was not broken. _____

B. Rewrite each sentence to avoid vague pronoun reference.

4. Mom and Amber decided that she would exchange the heater at the pet store.

   _____

   _____

5. My mother returned the heater to the store, and he gave her a new one.

   _____

   _____

In your writer's notebook, write about a person that inspires you. Include at least 5 pronouns. Check to make sure that each pronoun is used correctly.

Grade 6 • Unit 4 • Week 1   183

Grammar • Proofreading

Name _____

> - A **pronoun** takes the place of one or more nouns in a sentence. A **personal** pronoun refers to a person or thing. Singular pronouns are *I, you, he, she, it, me, him,* and *her.* Plural pronouns are *we, you, they, us,* and *them.*
> - An **antecedent** is the word or words that a pronoun refers to. Pronouns must agree with their antecedents in **number** and **gender**.
> - Avoid vague pronoun reference.
> - To fix a vague pronoun reference, rephrase the sentence or replace the pronoun with a noun.

Rewrite each sentence correctly. Use correct capitalization and punctuation.

1. the Teacher greeted the students and asked him to sit down

   _____

2. henry got out his pencil, opened his book and went to sharpen it.

   _____

3. Angela asked if they could help call the roll".

   _____

4. when the bell rang, it startled the students?

   _____

5. after lunch, Jonah went to talk to Mr. carlson, his math teacher, in his office

   _____

   _____

184   Grade 6 • Unit 4 • Week 1

English: Grammar • **Apply**

Name _____

What was your favorite reading selection or other text you read this week? Write a paragraph describing what you learned from it or why you enjoyed it. When you're done, exchange your writing with a partner. Proofread your partner's writing. Remember to apply the grammar you have learned this week.

Spelling • Suffix *-ion*

Name _____

Fold back the paper along the dotted line. Use the blanks to write each word as it is read aloud. When you finish the test, unfold the paper. Use the list at the right to correct any spelling mistakes.

1. _____
2. _____
3. _____
4. _____
5. _____
6. _____
7. _____
8. _____
9. _____
10. _____
11. _____
12. _____
13. _____
14. _____
15. _____
16. _____
17. _____
18. _____
19. _____
20. _____

Review Words
21. _____
22. _____
23. _____

Challenge Words
24. _____
25. _____

1. admit
2. admission
3. permit
4. permission
5. explain
6. explanation
7. exclaim
8. exclamation
9. include
10. inclusion
11. explode
12. explosion
13. divide
14. division
15. decide
16. decision
17. omit
18. omission
19. collide
20. collision
21. separation
22. instruction
23. connection
24. expand
25. expansion

Phonics/Spelling • Word Sort

Name _____

The common suffix, *-ion* is added to certain words to change them from verbs to nouns.

submit	correct	conclude
submission	correction	conclusion

When adding the suffix *-ation*, words drop the *i* in the last syllable: **proclaim proclamation**.

Read each pair of words and notice how the spelling of each base word changed. Pay attention to how the consonant sound at the end of each verb changes when the suffix is added. The /t/ in *submit* changes to /sh/ in *submission*; the /t/ in *correct* changes to /sh/ in *correction*; the /d/ in *conclude* changes to /zh/ in *conclusion*.

SPELLING TIP

When the base word ends in *e*, the *e* is dropped before the suffix *-ion* is added: *frustrate, frustration; dictate, dictation; sedate, sedation; animate, animation; navigate; navigation.*

Write base words and words ending in *-ion* with the matching spelling pattern.

admit	explain	include	divide	omit
admission	explanation	inclusion	division	omission
permit	exclaim	explode	decide	collide
permission	exclamation	explosion	decision	collision

change *t* to *ss* and add *-ion*

1. _____ _____

2. _____ _____

3. _____ _____

change *de* to *s* and add *-ion*

4. _____ _____

5. _____ _____

6. _____ _____

7. _____ _____

8. _____ _____

drop *i* and add *-ation*

9. _____ _____

10. _____ _____

Look through this week's selections for more words with the suffix *-ion*. Record each word and its base word in your writer's notebook. Note any consonant sound changes. Then read the words aloud.

Spelling • Word Meaning

Name _____

admit	explain	include	divide	omit
admission	explanation	inclusion	division	omission
permit	exclaim	explode	decide	collide
permission	exclamation	explosion	decision	collision

A. Write the spelling word that is a synonym for each word.

1. crash _____
2. allow _____
3. exclusion _____
4. consent _____
5. describe _____
6. incorporate _____
7. determine _____
8. separation _____
9. burst _____

B. Write the spelling word that best completes each sentence.

10. What did she _____ when opening her present and seeing a kitten?

11. Drivers need a _____ to park in the neighborhood.

12. Let's _____ the snack into four pieces so we can share it.

13. They will make a _____ soon about where to go on vacation.

14. I saw the cars _____ on the slippery ice.

15. In his e-mail, Sam used several _____ points to describe his trip.

16. The _____ of games in the package made my cousin smile.

17. Did you _____ the middle paragraph of your speech?

18. He gave a good _____ of how to operate the machinery.

19. Did you hear the _____ from the volcano?

20. The family paid _____ to see the special museum exhibit.

Spelling • Proofreading

Name _____

There are four misspelled words in the first paragraph and three in the second. Underline each misspelled word. Then write the words correctly on the lines.

When a freeway colision occurs, rescue workers are immediately called to the scene. Firefighters often appear first to make sure that an exploshun doesn't occur as a result of gas leaks. Law enforcement officials deside how to handle the accident. They do not permitt other motorists to get out of their cars and approach the scene.

1. _____ 2. _____ 3. _____ 4. _____

In our town, senior citizens pay a reduced fee for admishun to the movie theater. They can also get special permishun to park near the theater. An explaination of this policy is included at the entrance to the parking lot.

5. _____ 6. _____ 7. _____

Writing Connection — **Write about some of the businesses near where you live. Use at least four words from the spelling list.**

_____
_____
_____
_____
_____
_____
_____
_____
_____
_____

Phonics/Spelling • Review

Name _____

> **Remember**
>
> The suffix, *-ion* changes certain words from verbs to nouns.
> seclude (verb)   comprehend (verb)   infect (verb)
> seclusion (noun)   comprehension (noun)   infection (noun)
> The consonant sound at the end of each verb changes when the suffix *-ion* is added.

admit	explain	include	divide	omit
admission	explanation	inclusion	division	omission
permit	exclaim	explode	decide	collide
permission	exclamation	explosion	decision	collision

A. Write the base word for each word ending in *-ion*.

1. omission _____
2. explanation _____
3. permission _____
4. collision _____
5. division _____

6. admission _____
7. inclusion _____
8. decision _____
9. explosion _____
10. exclamation _____

B. Add the suffix *-ion* to each base word to form another spelling word. Write the spelling word ending in *-ion*.

11. admit _____
12. exclaim _____
13. divide _____
14. explode _____
15. permit _____

16. omit _____
17. decide _____
18. collide _____
19. include _____
20. explain _____

Vocabulary • Content Words

Name _____

> **Content words** are words that are specific to a field of study. For example, words like *physical challenge, routine* and *opponent* are athletic content words.
>
> Authors use content words to explain a concept or idea. Sometimes you can figure out what a content word means by using context clues. You can also use a dictionary to help you find the meaning of unfamiliar content words.

COLLABORATE Go on a word hunt with a partner through "She Had to Walk Before She Could Run." Find content words related to sports competitions. Write them in the chart.

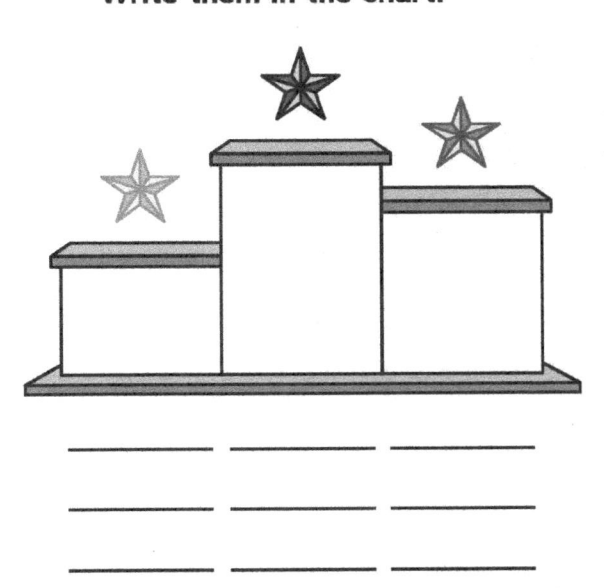

CONNECT TO CONTENT

"She Had to Walk Before She Could Run" is an inspiring true story about Wilma Rudolph's determination and strength. The author's message to the reader is that if you work hard, you can achieve your goal.

_____ _____ _____

_____ _____ _____

_____ _____ _____

Pick two words that you were able to define by using context clues. Write the words and what they mean on the lines.

_____

_____

_____

Grade 6 • Unit 4 • Week 1   191

Vocabulary • Spiral Review

Name _____

Write your best answer on the lines that follow.

1. Describe something from which you have **recoiled**.
   _____

2. If you were an **advocate** for a cause, what would that cause be? Why?
   _____

3. Describe a **dilemma** you recently faced.
   _____

4. What kind of material might make good **insulation** for a bird's nest?
   _____

5. Where would you go to find **solitude**? Why?
   _____

6. What was your **initial** thought about sixth grade?
   _____

7. What is the **optimal** time to do your homework? Why?
   _____

8. Describe a time when you have shown **ingenuity**.
   _____

9. What kind of behavior do you find **irrational**? Why?
   _____

10. Why would an **invasive** plant not be welcome in someone's yard?
    _____

11. If you had to **designate** a person to be the president of your class, who would it be? Why?
    _____

12. How do you feel when you see something that is **commonplace**?
    _____

Name _____

Grammar • **Kinds of Pronouns**

- A **subject pronoun** (*I, you, he, she, it, we, you, they*) is the subject of a sentence: *He runs every morning.*
- An **object pronoun** (*me, you, him, her, it, us, you, them*) is the object of a verb or a preposition: *Mr. Coleman will bring them.*
- A **reflexive pronoun** (*myself, yourself, himself, herself, itself, ourselves, yourselves, themselves*) is an object that is the same as the subject of the sentence: *Milan made herself lunch.*
- An **intensive pronoun** emphasizes its antecedent but does not act as an object: *Ivy herself drew the picture.*

A. Underline the pronoun in each sentence. Write *subject* if it is a subject pronoun; write *object* if it is an object pronoun.

1. Gabriella and I organized the book drive. _____

2. The class helped us decorate bins to collect the books. _____

3. They also made posters to announce the book drive. _____

4. We asked each student in our school to donate one book. _____

B. Choose the correct pronoun in parentheses ( ) to complete each sentence. Write it on the line.

5. (We, Us) awarded prizes to the students who collected the most books. _____

6. Gabriella (she, herself) collected seventeen books. _____

7. However, Luis brought (us, they) the most books. _____

8. Luis collected fifty-seven books all by (him, himself). _____

In your writer's notebook, write a passage about a time that you helped someone. Reread your work when you're done. Make sure you used pronouns correctly.

Grade 6 • Unit 4 • Week 2 193

Grammar • Uses of Subject and Object Pronouns

Name _____

- Use the **subjective case**, *I, you, he, she, we* and *they*, for pronouns that follow a linking verb, including forms of *be*. Subject pronouns are in the subjective case.

    The last to arrive was I.

- Use the **objective case**, *me, you, him, her, us, them*, for pronouns that are direct and indirect objects and objects of a preposition. Object pronouns are in the objective case.

    Andrew gave him the pen.

A. Circle the pronoun in parentheses ( ) that correctly completes each sentence. Write the case of the pronoun on the line.

1. (We, Us) had a sixth-grade field day at school, with awards for the winners.
    _____

2. The person who handed out the awards was (I, me). _____

3. (He, Him) won the top award for winning three races. _____

4. I handed (he, him) the award. _____

5. He thanked (me, I) for it. _____

6. The second place winner was (her, she). _____

7. I recognized (her, she) for jumping the farthest. _____

8. The third graders received an award because (they, them) were the helpers.
    _____

Reading/Writing Connection

Read the sentence from "She Had to Walk Before She Could Run." Circle the subjective case pronouns and underline the objective case pronouns. Then write two sentences of your own using the subjective case or objective case.

"Of her feeling of accomplishment, she said she knew it was something 'nobody could ever take away from me, ever.'"

_____

_____

194 Grade 6 • Unit 4 • Week 2

Grammar • Mechanics: **Proper Use of Pronouns**

Name _____

- Use a subject pronoun when the pronoun is the subject of a sentence or clause; use an object pronoun when the pronoun is the object of a verb or preposition.
- Use the correct form of a reflexive pronoun: *himself,* not *hisself; ourselves,* not *ourself; themselves,* not *themself* or *theirself.*
- Use a reflexive pronoun only when it refers to an antecedent.

    Keith made *himself* lunch.

Read each sentence. Rewrite the sentence using the correct subject, object, or reflexive pronoun or pronouns.

1. Kevin and Amanda helped (we, us) sort the donated items.

   _____

2. Rebecca and (me, I) put the items in boxes.

   _____

3. Kevin helped (him, he) carry the boxes to the bus.

   _____

4. When (they, them) finished, he got (hisself, himself) a drink of water.

   _____

Connect to Community — Talk to a parent or another trusted adult about a city in your state you want to learn more about. You may also use an online encyclopedia or another publication to help you research. Then write a paragraph about it. Remember to use pronouns correctly.

_____

_____

_____

_____

Grammar • Proofreading

Name _____

- A **subject pronoun** (*I, you, he, she, it, we, you, they*) is the subject of a sentence. An **object pronoun** (*me, you, him, her, it, us, you, them*) is the object of a verb or a preposition.
- A **reflexive pronoun** is an object that is the same as the subject of the sentence. An **intensive pronoun** emphasizes its antecedent but does not act as an object. Use *himself*, not *hisself*; *ourselves*, not *ourself*; *themselves*, not *themself* or *theirself*.
- Use the **subjective case** for pronouns that follow a linking verb, or form of the verb *be*. Subject pronouns are used to express subjective case.
- Use the **objective case** for direct and indirect objects as well as for objects of a preposition. Object pronouns are used to express objective case.

Proofread the sentences. Rewrite them correctly using the correct pronouns and correct capitalization and punctuation.

1. carlos made hisself a sandwich

   _____

2. ariana handed I a napkin

   _____

3. the boys theirselves painted the mural

   _____

4. her thought the colors were beautiful

   _____

5. how surprised was he when he see his uncle

   _____

6. them looked forward to spending time together

   _____

196 Grade 6 • Unit 4 • Week 2

English: Grammar • **Apply**

Name _____

What was your favorite reading selection or other text you read this week? Write a paragraph describing what you learned from it or why you enjoyed it. When you're done, exchange your writing with a partner. Proofread your partner's writing. Remember to apply the grammar you have learned this week.

Spelling • Vowel Alternation

Name _____

Fold back the paper along the dotted line. Use the blanks to write each word as it is read aloud. When you finish the test, unfold the paper. Use the list at the right to correct any spelling mistakes.

1. _____
2. _____
3. _____
4. _____
5. _____
6. _____
7. _____
8. _____
9. _____
10. _____
11. _____
12. _____
13. _____
14. _____
15. _____
16. _____
17. _____
18. _____
19. _____
20. _____

Review Words
21. _____
22. _____
23. _____

Challenge Words
24. _____
25. _____

1. compete
2. competition
3. moment
4. momentous
5. crime
6. criminal
7. refer
8. reference
9. nation
10. national
11. metal
12. metallic
13. final
14. finality
15. reside
16. resident
17. origin
18. original
19. ignite
20. ignition
21. admission
22. division
23. decision
24. acquire
25. acquisition

Phonics/Spelling • Word Sort

Name _____

Adding a suffix to the end of a word sometimes changes the vowel sound in the related word. This change in the vowel sound is called vowel alternation.

define	invite	nature
definition	invitation	natural

Read each pair of words aloud and notice the vowel-sound changes. Notice the spelling change that occurs when the suffix is added.

DECODING WORDS

Sometimes when the ending -*al* is added to a word that ends in -*e*, the -*e* is dropped before the suffix is added. For example, in *crime*, the -*e* is dropped and -*in* is added. Notice how the long *i* sound in crime changes to a short *i* in *criminal*.

Write the pairs of spelling words that contain the specified pattern.

compete	crime	nation	final	origin
competition	criminal	national	finality	original
moment	refer	metal	reside	ignite
momentous	reference	metallic	resident	ignition

no change to base word when ending is added

1. _____ _____
2. _____ _____
3. _____ _____
4. _____ _____
5. _____ _____

double consonant and add ending

6. _____ _____

drop e and add one-syllable ending

7. _____ _____
8. _____ _____

drop e and add two-syllable ending

9. _____ _____
10. _____ _____

Look through this week's selections for more words with vowel alternations. Record each word and a related word in your writer's notebook. Underline the vowel sound changes.

Spelling • Word Meaning

Name _____

compete	crime	nation	final	origin
competition	criminal	national	finality	original
moment	refer	metal	reside	ignite
momentous	reference	metallic	resident	ignition

A. Write the spelling word that belongs with each group of words.

1. light, spark, _____
2. instant, second, _____
3. bronze, silver, _____
4. thesaurus, dictionary, _____
5. Brazil, England, _____
6. homeowner, occupant, _____

B. Write the spelling word that best completes each sentence.

7. While you are in _____, stay alert and focused.

8. Our family reunion was a very _____ occasion for Grandma.

9. I liked the _____ movie better than the new remake.

10. When you study the _____ of a word, you find out what language it comes from.

11. The car won't start; the _____ needs to be repaired.

12. He will _____ to a dictionary for the correct definition.

13. Littering is a _____ in most communities.

14. In what state do you _____?

15. The chess team won the _____ competition.

16. She will _____ in the marathon on Saturday morning.

17. The food left a _____ taste in my mouth.

18. There was a _____ to their last meeting.

19. The _____ was sentenced to ten years in prison.

20. Jake's _____ day of school is Friday, June 12.

200 Grade 6 • Unit 4 • Week 2

Spelling • Proofreading

Name _____

There are four misspelled words in the first paragraph and three in the second. Underline each misspelled word. Then write the words correctly on the lines.

In 1936, Jesse Owens represented our nashun in the Olympics in Berlin, Germany. It was a momenteous occasion! Owens became the first American track and field athlete to win four gold medals in one Olympic game. The competetion was fierce, but it did not stop Owens from winning and becoming a nationol hero.

1. _____ 2. _____ 3. _____ 4. _____

When writing biographies on athletes such as a Jesse Owens, there are many referense materials at your fingertips. For example, you can referr to reliable websites on the Internet for factual information. You can also find primary source materials to add to your report, such as originall photographs, letters, and documents.

5. _____ 6. _____ 7. _____

Writing Connection Write about a competition you've attended or seen on television. Use at least four words from the spelling list.

_____
_____
_____
_____
_____
_____
_____
_____

Grade 6 • Unit 4 • Week 2 201

Name _____

Spelling • Review

Remember

Adding a suffix can change in the spelling and sound of a word. This change usually occurs after adding a suffix to the end of a base word.

cave   *narrate*   *excel*
cavity   *narrative*   *excellent*

Read each pair of words and notice how the vowel sound in each word changes when the suffix is added.

compete	crime	nation	final	origin
competition	criminal	national	finality	original
moment	refer	metal	reside	ignite
momentous	reference	metallic	resident	ignition

A. Write the missing letters to form a spelling word. Then write the word.

1. final ___ ___ ___   _____   6. crim ___ ___ ___ l   _____
2. resid ___ ___ t   _____   7. ori ___ ___ ___   _____
3. mome ___ ___   _____   8. compet ___ ___ ___ on _____
4. ref ___ ___   _____   9. origi ___ ___ ___   _____
5. na ___ ___ ___ n   _____   10. meta ___ ___ ___ c   _____

B. Circle the word that rhymes with the word in bold type. Write the word.

11. **settle** metal retail hospital _____
12. **rhyme** team crime lemon _____
13. **divide** rustle cupid reside _____
14. **rational** emotional national ration _____
15. **apprentice** momentum clearance momentous _____
16. **musician** elation ignition function _____
17. **discrete** compete abrupt create _____
18. **delight** ignite wide align _____
19. **vinyl** regal little final _____
20. **deference** dance reference clearance _____

Vocabulary Strategy • Exaggeration and Hyperbole

Name _____

> An **exaggeration** represents something as greater than it is. Writers and speakers use exaggeration to overemphasize a point. Here is an example:
>
> **This book is gigantic!**
>
> **Hyperbole** is a figure of speech consisting of extreme exaggeration that is not meant to be taken literally. Hyperbole describes a situation so over-the-top that it could not happen in real life:
>
> **It will take me a million years to read this book!**
>
> Both examples convey that the book seems extremely long to the speaker.

Read each sentence. Then explain what point the statement is trying to make.

1. I've been waiting an entire lifetime for you!

   _____

   _____

2. I might never understand this math problem!

   _____

   _____

3. There must have been 500 people at my party!

   _____

   _____

4. That pizza is larger than Mars and Jupiter combined!

   _____

   _____

5. I think I could sleep for days!

   _____

   _____

Vocabulary Strategy • Idioms

Name _____

A. Read each passage from "Jesse Owens: A Message to the World." Figure out the meaning of the idiom in bold by looking at the context and the literal meaning of the words. Write the meaning of the idiom on the line.

1. Owens tied world records for the 100-yard dash. He set new world records for the 220-yard dash, the 220-yard low hurdles, and the running broad jump. Owens's success was not just a **flash in the pan**. He was only warming up for the Olympics.

   _____

2. The man who had **carried the weight of the world** on his shoulders and triumphed at the 1936 Olympics eventually got the honors he deserved.

   _____

3. The Foundation provides finances, support, and services to young people to help them **go the extra mile** and become all they are meant to be.

   _____

B. Use each idiom below in a sentence of your own.

4. flash in the pan: _____

   _____

5. carried the weight of the world on his/her shoulders: _____

   _____

6. go the extra mile: _____

   _____

Grammar • Possessive Pronouns

Name _____

- There are three cases, or forms, of pronouns.
- **Nominative** case is used for subject pronouns and predicate pronouns.
  He walked to school. The contestants were Clara and I.
- **Objective** case is used for direct and indirect objects and objects of prepositions: *Blake, can you help me? Jay bought her a gift.*
- **Possessive** case is used to show that something belongs to a person or thing: *That's her key chain. What is your homework for tonight?*
- The possessive pronouns *my, your, his, her, its, our,* and *their* are used before nouns.

A. Read each sentence. On the line provided, write whether the underlined pronoun is nominative, objective, or possessive.

1. Makayla accidently dropped <u>her</u> coins in the dark theater. _____
2. <u>They</u> must have rolled away. _____
3. Connor helped Makayla look for <u>them</u>. _____
4. <u>He</u> found a quarter under the seats in the front row. _____

B. Read each sentence. Write the possessive pronoun on the line.

5. Makayla found her nickels in the aisle. _____
6. Makayla thanked Connor for his help. _____
7. The two friends put on their coats. _____
8. "Next time, put your change away!" said Connor. _____

Reading/Writing Connection Read the excerpt from "Treasure in the Attic." Is *her* nominative, objective or possessive? Explain on the line below.

"I feel such empathy for Anna Snow and her family. They may have to leave us to find work elsewhere."

_____
_____

Grammar • Stand-Alone Possessive Pronouns

Name _____

- Some possessive pronouns can stand alone and are used in place of nouns. These possessive pronouns are *mine, yours, his, hers, ours,* and *theirs.*
- Most possessive pronouns that can stand on their own are different from possessives that precede nouns. *My* becomes *mine, your* becomes *yours, her* becomes *hers, our* becomes *ours,* and *their* becomes *theirs. His* stays the same: *The notebook is <u>mine</u>. The project is <u>theirs</u>.*

Read each pair of sentences. In the second sentence, choose the correct possessive pronoun in parentheses ( ) and write it on the line.

1. That is her jacket.
   That jacket is (hers, her). _____

2. Mark said this is his backpack.
   Mark said this is (his, him). _____

3. Is this your project?
   Is this project (your, yours)? _____

4. The huge poster belongs to Abigail and Mark.
   The huge poster is (theirs, their). _____

5. If you forget to bring markers, you may borrow my markers.
   If you forget to bring markers, you may borrow (my, mine). _____

6. These are our papers.
   These papers are (theirs, ours). _____

7. I found my homework on the table.
   I found (mine, my) on the table. _____

In your writer's notebook, write about a class trip that you have taken. Reread your work to make sure you used pronouns correctly.

Grammar • Mechanics: Punctuating Dialogue

Name _____

- Use quotation marks to set off a direct quotation from the rest of the sentence: *Rebecca said, "I have softball practice after school."*
- Capitalize the first word in a quotation. Put commas and periods inside quotation marks: *"I love when it snows," said Marcus.*
- Use a comma before the quotation when the speaker's name comes first: *Jasper said, "The movie starts at noon."*
- Use a comma, a question mark, or an exclamation point before the closing quotation mark when the speaker's name comes last:
    "Can we go outside for recess?" asked Dylan.

Rewrite each sentence below, using correct punctuation.

1. is this your sweater asked Father

   _____

2. Carmen answered no it is Chloe's sweater

   _____

3. this is my sweater but these are not my shoes" stated Chloe

   _____

4. Carmen confessed, those shoes are mine.

   _____

5. Father exclaimed to Carmen "put your shoes away!

   _____

> In your writer's notebook, write a dialogue between you and a friend or family member. Check your work to make sure you used quotation marks to show a speaker's exact words.

Name _____

Grammar • Proofreading

- A **possessive pronoun** shows who or what owns something. The possessive pronouns *my, your, his, her, its, our,* and *their* are used before nouns.
- Some possessive pronouns can stand alone and are used in place of nouns. These possessive pronouns are *mine, yours, his, hers, ours,* and *theirs.*
- Use quotation marks to set off a direct quotation from the rest of the sentence.
- Use a comma before the quotation when a speaker's name comes first. Use a comma, a question mark, or an exclamation point before the closing quotation mark when the speaker's name comes last.

Proofread each sentence. Watch for errors in possessive pronouns, punctuation, and capitalization. Rewrite the sentence correctly.

1. is this yours newspaper asked Ms. Ruiz?

   _____

2. she said I found it on mine porch

   _____

3. it must be my answered Mr. Holloway

   _____

4. mine paper was missing this morning, he said

   _____

5. Ms. Ruiz said we picked up ours paper earlier

   _____

6. our was in the driveway. she explained"

   _____

208 Grade 6 • Unit 4 • Week 3

English: Grammar • Apply

Name _____

What was your favorite reading selection or other text you read this week? Write a paragraph describing what you learned from it or why you enjoyed it. When you're done, exchange your writing with a partner. Proofread your partner's writing. Remember to apply the grammar you have learned this week.

Spelling • **Prefixes and Suffixes**

Name _____

Fold back the paper along the dotted line. Use the blanks to write each word as it is read aloud. When you finish the test, unfold the paper. Use the list at the right to correct any spelling mistakes.

1. _____
2. _____
3. _____
4. _____
5. _____
6. _____
7. _____
8. _____
9. _____
10. _____
11. _____
12. _____
13. _____
14. _____
15. _____
16. _____
17. _____
18. _____
19. _____
20. _____

Review Words
21. _____
22. _____
23. _____

Challenge Words
24. _____
25. _____

1. disgraceful
2. unsuccessful
3. outlandish
4. outsider
5. incorrectly
6. enjoyment
7. disappointment
8. discouragement
9. enforcement
10. repayment
11. enclosure
12. unselfish
13. unhappiness
14. disapproval
15. unfairness
16. reminder
17. designer
18. departure
19. delightful
20. unevenly
21. competition
22. national
23. original
24. displeasure
25. informal

Phonics/Spelling • Word Sort

Name _____

Prefixes and **suffixes** are word parts that are added to the beginning or ending of a word. These word parts change the word's meaning. Here are some common prefixes and suffixes and their definitions.

un- "not"   -ful "full of"

dis- "not"   -able "can be done"

in- "not" or   -ment "action; process" or
"opposite of" "result of action or process"

Read the prefixes and suffixes above. Then read the spelling words aloud.

DECODING WORDS

Look at the word *uncomfortable*. The base word is *comfort*. It begins with the prefix *un-*, which means "not." It ends with the suffix *-able*, which means "can be done." Using the prefix and suffix, *uncomfortable* means "not comfortable" or "cannot be comforted."

Write the spelling words that contain the prefix and/or suffix shown.

disgraceful	incorrectly	enforcement	unhappiness	designer
unsuccessful	enjoyment	repayment	disapproval	departure
outlandish	disappointment	enclosure	unfairness	delightful
outsider	discouragement	unselfish	reminder	unevenly

prefix *un-*

1. _____
2. _____
3. _____
4. _____
5. _____

prefix *out-*

6. _____
7. _____

prefix *in-*

8. _____

prefix *de-* **and suffix** *-ful*

9. _____

suffix *-ment*

10. _____
11. _____
12. _____
13. _____
14. _____

suffix *-er*

15. _____
16. _____

suffix *-ure*

17. _____
18. _____

prefix *dis-* **and suffix** *-al* **or** *-ful*

19. _____
20. _____

Grade 6 • Unit 4 • Week 3

Spelling • Word Meaning

Name _____

disgraceful	incorrectly	enforcement	unhappiness	designer
unsuccessful	enjoyment	repayment	disapproval	departure
outlandish	disappointment	enclosure	unfairness	delightful
outsider	discouragement	unselfish	reminder	unevenly

A. Write the spelling word that matches each definition below.

1. sadness; sorrow _____

2. the act of experiencing something pleasurable _____

3. failing to accomplish something _____

4. someone who is not a member of a group _____

5. considerate and generous; not greedy _____

6. joyful or entertaining _____

7. the act of giving back money owed _____

8. the act of ensuring observance or obedience _____

9. loss of hope or courage _____

10. an unjust act; inequality _____

B. Write the spelling word that best completes each sentence.

11. She spelled the difficult word _____ on her spelling test.

12. His flashy green tuxedo for the prom was _____.

13. The _____ was large enough for several small animals.

14. The coat of paint was applied _____, so there were streak marks.

15. The popular dress _____ created a gown for the Queen of England.

16. The look on his face showed his _____ of the concert performance.

17. She looked at the screen to see the _____ time of her flight.

18. The note on the board was a _____ about the test on Monday.

19. I felt _____ after the movie, which was supposed to be good.

20. Their behavior was _____ when they littered the park.

212 Grade 6 • Unit 4 • Week 3

Spelling • Proofreading

Name _____

There are three misspelled words in each paragraph. Underline each one. Then write the words correctly on the lines.

Hugo experienced great unhappyness when he failed his science exam. He failed because he answered most of the questions incorectly. When his friends were discussing how well they had done on the exam, Hugo felt like an outsidder.

Hugo's teacher told him that he should not let his discouragemint defeat him. His teacher felt that if Hugo studied extra hard for the next exam, he would be able to experience the enjoymint of doing well. Although he was unsuccesfull on this exam, Hugo vowed he would try harder next time.

1. _____ 2. _____ 3. _____

4. _____ 5. _____ 6. _____

Writing Connection Write about a piece of schoolwork that made you proud. Use at least four words from the spelling list.

Grade 6 • Unit 4 • Week 3

Phonics/Spelling • **Review**

Name _____

Remember

A **prefix** is a group of letters added to the *beginning* of a word that changes the word's meaning. A **suffix** is a group of letters added to the *end* of a word that changes the word's meaning. Knowing the meanings of the most common prefixes and suffixes can help you figure out the meaning of unfamiliar words.

As you read each spelling word aloud, think about how the prefix or suffix changes the meaning of the base word.

disgraceful	incorrectly	enforcement	unhappiness	designer
unsuccessful	enjoyment	repayment	disapproval	departure
outlandish	disappointment	enclosure	unfairness	delightful
outsider	discouragement	unselfish	reminder	unevenly

Fill in the missing prefix or suffix of each word to form a spelling word. Then write the spelling word and the base word on the line.

1. ____ payment _____
2. ____ appointment _____
3. unfair ____ _____
4. disgrace ____ _____
5. ____ correctly _____
6. ____ joyment _____
7. unhappi ____ _____
8. ____ parture _____
9. ____ selfish _____
10. uneven ____ _____
11. ____ landish _____
12. unsuccess ____ _____
13. ____ signer _____
14. ____ minder _____
15. ____ sider _____
16. discourage ____ _____
17. ____ forcement _____
18. ____ approval _____
19. ____ closure _____
20. delight ____ _____

214 Grade 6 • Unit 4 • Week 3

Vocabulary • Related Words

Name _____

Expand your vocabulary by adding or removing inflectional endings, prefixes, or suffixes to a base word to create different forms of a word.

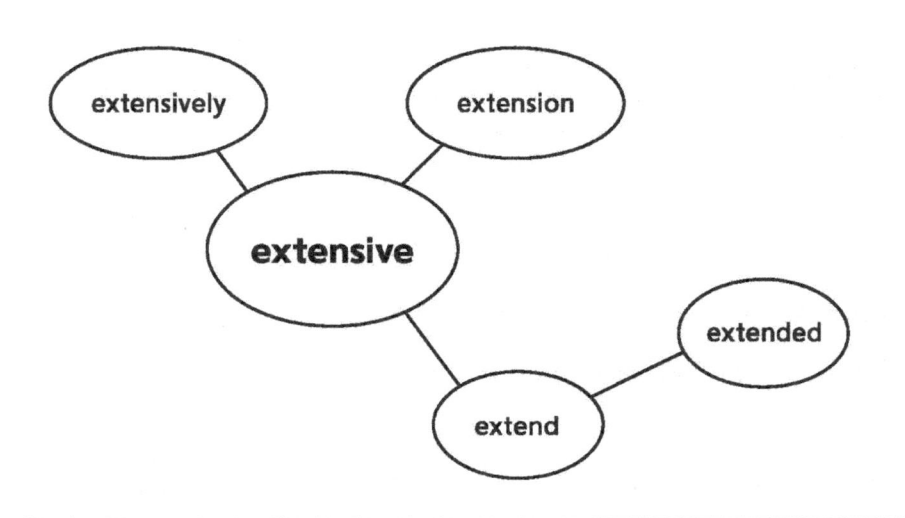

- extensively
- extension
- **extensive**
- extend
- extended

Add or remove inflectional endings, prefixes and suffixes to form related words and write them in the blanks. Use an electronic or print dictionary to help you.

indecision

_____   _____

_____   _____

_____   _____

Grade 6 • Unit 4 • Week 3   **215**

Vocabulary • **Spiral Review**

Name _____

Write the vocabulary word from the box that is a synonym for each group of words below. Use a dictionary to confirm word meanings if you need to.

| commerce | compensate | implement |
| assess | potential | devastating |

1. apply, execute, carry out, perform _____
2. disastrous, destructive, damaging, ruinous _____
3. estimate, judge, evaluate, determine _____
4. business, trade, buying and selling, transactions _____
5. improve, repair, counteract, make up for _____
6. ability, power, possibility, capacity _____

Write the vocabulary word from the box that is an antonym for each group of words below. Use a dictionary to confirm word meanings if you need to.

| forlorn | deteriorated | impoverished |
| summit | peripheral | abundant |

7. base, bottom, low point, foundation _____
8. scarce, rare, lacking, depleted _____
9. joyful, elated, upbeat, cheerful _____
10. rich, wealthy, full, plentiful _____
11. central, interior, internal, inside _____
12. built, strengthened, grew, improved _____

216 Grade 6 • Unit 4 • Week 3

Grammar • Pronoun-Verb Agreement

Name _____

- Subject pronouns and verbs must agree.
- Add -s to regular present-tense verbs when you use the singular pronouns *he, she,* and *it*: She <u>walks</u> her dog every morning. He <u>sleds</u> down the hill.
- Do not add -s to regular present-tense verbs when you use the pronouns *I, we, you,* and *they*: I <u>visit</u> my grandmother every Sunday. We <u>swim</u> in Lake Hopatcong.
- An **indefinite pronoun** does not refer to a specific person, place, or thing. Some indefinite pronouns are singular, such as *anyone* and *everyone*. Others are plural, such as *both* and *several*. Some can be plural or singular, such as *all* and *some*: <u>All</u> of the ice is melted. <u>Some</u> of the baseball players are happy spring is here.

Read each sentence. Choose the verb in parentheses ( ) that correctly completes the sentence. Write the correct verb on the line. Underline the subject pronoun. Circle indefinite pronouns.

1. Jack thinks it (look, looks) like a good day for kickball. _____

2. He (say, says) he will organize a game. _____

3. We (play, plays) on the corner near Claire's house. _____

4. Anyone in the neighborhood (know, knows) where Claire lives. _____

5. Today, everyone (agree, agrees) to play after lunch. _____

6. I (want, wants) to be on Claire's team. _____

7. She (kick, kicks) the ball harder than the other players do. _____

8. Two teams will play; both (hope, hopes) to win. _____

9. All of the players (feel, feels) ready to play. _____

10. You (need, needs) to join our team! _____

In your writer's notebook, write a dialogue between two friends on their way home from school. Then have two classmates read your dialogue aloud. Edit your work for correct punctuation.

Grammar • **Subject Pronoun-Verb Contractions**

Name _____

- A contraction is a shortened form of two words in which the missing letters are replaced by an apostrophe: *They are leaving tomorrow.* *They're* leaving *tomorrow.*
- Subject pronouns can be combined with some verbs to form contractions.

Write the contractions for the following pronoun-verb combinations.

1. I am _____
2. we are _____
3. he is _____
4. they are _____
5. it is _____
6. you will _____
7. I have _____
8. she has _____
9. they have _____
10. we will _____

Reading/Writing Connection Read the excerpt from "Treasure in the Attic." On the lines below, describe the difference in usage of the apostrophe for the words, *We're* and *grandmother's*.

> We're trying to solve a mystery. Our great-grandmother, Flossie Howard, was a good friend of your grandmother's.

_____
_____

218 Grade 6 • Unit 4 • Week 4

Grammar • Mechanics: **Frequently Confused Words**

Name _____

> - Words such as *there, they're,* and *their* are often used incorrectly. *There* refers to a place. *They're* is a contraction of *they are*. *Their* is a possessive pronoun.
> - Other homophones can be confusing, such as *to, too,* and *two*; *it's* and *its*; *who's* and *whose*; and *you're* and *your*. *It's, who's,* and *you're* are contractions of a subject pronoun and a verb.

Read each sentence. Choose the word in parentheses ( ) that correctly completes the sentence. Rewrite the sentence correctly on the line.

1. (They're, There, Their) will be an election for class officers tomorrow.
   _____

2. If you want to run for office, submit (your, you're) name to Mr. Hoang.
   _____

3. (Who's, Whose) going to run for class president?
   _____

4. Victor and Leah are (too, two, to) good candidates for treasurer.
   _____

5. Students who run for election will have (they're, their, there) names on the ballot.
   _____

6. (It's, Its) going to be an interesting race!
   _____

Imagine that you are running for student council or class representative. Write a speech to explain why you are the best for the role. Be sure to edit your work for frequently confused words.

Grammar • Proofreading

Name _____

- Subject pronouns and verbs must agree.

- Add *-s* to regular present-tense verbs when you use the singular pronouns *he, she,* and *it*. Do not add *-s* to regular present-tense verbs when you use the pronouns *I, we, you,* and *they*.

- An **indefinite pronoun** does not refer to a specific person, place, or thing. Some indefinite pronouns are singular, such as *anyone* and *everyone*. Others are plural, such as *both* and *several*. Some can be plural or singular, such as *all* and *some*.

- Subject pronouns can be combined with some verbs to form contractions. Do not confuse words such as *there, they're,* and *their; to, too,* and *two; it's* and *its; who's* and *whose;* or *you're* and *your*.

Rewrite each sentence, correcting mistakes in subject-verb agreement and in spelling and punctuation.

1. Our dog Scout likes to chase squirrels when we goes too the park

   _____

2. She bark and chase them until they runs up a tree.

   _____

3. No matter how fast Scout run, she never catch them?

   _____

4. once their safe in the trees, Scout sit and barks at the squirrels.

   _____

5. Everyone think its the chase that interests Scout,

   _____

220   Grade 6 • Unit 4 • Week 4

English: Grammar • **Apply**

Name _____

What was your favorite reading selection or other text you read this week? Write a paragraph describing what you learned from it or why you enjoyed it. When you're done, exchange your writing with a partner. Proofread your partner's writing. Remember to apply the grammar you have learned this week.

_____
_____
_____
_____
_____
_____
_____
_____
_____
_____
_____
_____
_____
_____

Spelling • **Greek and Latin Prefixes**

Name _____

Fold back the paper along the dotted line. Use the blanks to write each word as it is read aloud. When you finish the test, unfold the paper. Use the list at the right to correct any spelling mistakes.

1. _____
2. _____
3. _____
4. _____
5. _____
6. _____
7. _____
8. _____
9. _____
10. _____
11. _____
12. _____
13. _____
14. _____
15. _____
16. _____
17. _____
18. _____
19. _____
20. _____

Review Words
21. _____
22. _____
23. _____

Challenge Words
24. _____
25. _____

1. co-worker
2. commission
3. profession
4. proportion
5. companion
6. intersection
7. postwar
8. transparent
9. submit
10. interrupt
11. postpone
12. cooperate
13. submarine
14. transformation
15. transform
16. suburb
17. combine
18. interfere
19. transfer
20. copilot
21. reminder
22. unhappiness
23. delightful
24. profound
25. subscribe

222 Grade 6 • Unit 4 • Week 4

Phonics/Spelling • Word Sort

Name _____

Prefixes are word parts that are added to the beginning of a word to change its meaning. Many English words have prefixes that come from ancient Greek and Latin. You can use a Greek or Latin prefix as a clue to the meaning of unfamiliar words. Here are some common Greek and Latin prefixes:

co-/com- "with"   **trans-** "across"

post- "after"   **pro-** "forward; in favor of"

inter- "between"   **sub-** "below, almost"

DECODING WORDS

Look at the word *postwar*. The base word is *war*. The word *war* means "a state of conflict or hostility." The Latin prefix *post-* means "after." Using the prefix, you can determine that the meaning of the word *postwar* is "after a war."

Write the spelling words that contain the matching prefix.

co-worker	companion	submit	submarine	combine
commission	intersection	interrupt	transformation	interfere
profession	postwar	postpone	transform	transfer
proportion	transparent	cooperate	suburb	copilot

co-
1. _____
2. _____
3. _____

trans-
4. _____
5. _____
6. _____
7. _____

pro-
8. _____
9. _____

sub-
10. _____
11. _____
12. _____

inter-
13. _____

14. _____
15. _____

com-
16. _____
17. _____
18. _____

post-
19. _____
20. _____

Look through this week's selections for more words with Greek and Latin prefixes to sort. Create a word sort in your writer's notebook.

Spelling • Word Meaning

Name _____

co-worker	companion	submit	submarine	combine
commission	intersection	interrupt	transformation	interfere
profession	postwar	postpone	transform	transfer
proportion	transparent	cooperate	suburb	copilot

A. Look at each Greek or Latin root and its meaning. Write the spelling word that contains each root.

1. *sect:* "to cut apart" _____
2. *pan:* "all" or "everyone" _____
3. *urb:* "city" _____
4. *mar:* "sea" _____
5. *fer:* "to bring" _____
6. *bin:* "to join" _____

B. Write the spelling word that best completes each sentence.

7. The _____ took over flying the plane when the pilot needed rest.
8. The _____ of people who voted in the city election is quite high.
9. She is considering nursing as a _____.
10. The curtain fabric was light-colored and _____.
11. The referee did not _____ and she let the players continue.
12. The architect will _____ a proposal for the football stadium.
13. We need to _____ with each other to get the project done.
14. Please don't _____ the performance!
15. My _____ was a big help in preparing for the presentation.
16. Let's _____ this barren field into a lush garden.
17. We need to _____ the meeting because three people are sick.
18. Each employee gets a _____ for selling toys and books.
19. For history, I'm writing a paper about the _____ economy.
20. His _____ from an ordinary boy to a rock star was amazing.

Spelling • Proofreading

Name _____

There are seven misspelled words in the paragraphs below. Underline each misspelled word. Then write the words correctly on the lines.

Luisa and Marco's school was holding a design competition. They decided to work together to design a playground for Calabasas, a suberb of Los Angeles. They knew if they could cooperrate and combin their talents, they would have a good chance of winning. Both students were eager to submitt their design.

The students went to the site of the proposed playground. It was just a barren, rock-filled lot. Luisa and Marco got to work. What a transfermation they made! Their design included playground equipment surrounded by trees and colorful plants. On the day of the competition, it was very cloudy. Each co-werker was secretly hoping the officials wouldn't pospone the event. Luckily, the competition was held and Luisa and Marco came in first!

1. _____ 2. _____ 3. _____ 4. _____

5. _____ 6. _____ 7. _____

Writing Connection

Suppose you found out that you had won something. Write a letter to a friend, explaining how you felt when you won. Use at least four words from the spelling list.

_____
_____
_____
_____
_____
_____
_____
_____

Phonics/Spelling • Review

Name _____

Remember

A **prefix** is a group of letters added to the *beginning* of a word that changes the word's meaning. Knowing the meanings of the most common Greek and Latin prefixes can help you figure out the meaning of unfamiliar words.
Review these common Greek and Latin prefixes:

co-/con- "with"   **post-** "after"   **pro-** "before; in favor of"
sub- "below, almost"   **trans-** "across"   **inter-** "between"

co-worker	companion	submit	submarine	combine
commission	intersection	interrupt	transformation	interfere
profession	postwar	postpone	transform	transfer
proportion	transparent	cooperate	suburb	copilot

Write the missing prefix to complete the spelling word. Then write the spelling word on the line.

1. _____ section   _____   11. _____ form   _____

2. _____ mit   _____   12. _____ urb   _____

3. _____ pilot   _____   13. _____ operate   _____

4. _____ fer   _____   14. _____ formation _____

5. _____ rupt   _____   15. _____ bine   _____

6. _____ fession   _____   16. _____ worker   _____

7. _____ war   _____   17. _____ fere   _____

8. _____ marine   _____   18. _____ panion   _____

9. _____ parent   _____   19. _____ portion   _____

10. _____ mission   _____   20. _____ pone   _____

226   Grade 6 • Unit 4 • Week 4

Vocabulary Strategy • Sound Devices

Name _____

> Writers often use words with particular sounds to convey a certain tone or feeling. These **sound devices** include:
>
> **onomatopoeia:** words that sound like the thing or action they name (*buzz, hiss*)
>
> **assonance:** the repetition of a certain vowel sound in nearby syllables and words (*H*ow *does the br*ow*n c*ow *s*ou*nd?*)
>
> **consonance:** the repetition of a certain consonant sound in nearby syllables and at the middles and ends of words (*Chuck likes the ducks on the lake.*)
>
> **alliteration:** the repetition of a consonant sound at the beginnings of words (*Make the most of every moment.*)

Read each line of poetry below. Write whether it contains onomatopoeia, assonance, consonance, or alliteration. Then use that sound device to write the next line. Your line does not have to rhyme with the first one.

1. Run, oh raging river, run. _____
   _____

2. The thunder came with a clap, bang, boom. _____
   _____

3. The hill was yellow with daffodils. _____
   _____

4. Waving, weeping willows filled me with woe. _____
   _____

5. I do not mind the silence of the night. _____
   _____

6. Twigs snapped and leaves rustled under our feet. _____
   _____

Grade 6 • Unit 4 • Week 4   227

Vocabulary Strategy • Homophones

Name _____

A. Write the definition for each word below. Then provide a homophone for each word.

1. bawl _____

2. wail _____

3. night _____

4. stairs _____

5. groan _____

B. Finish each sentence two ways, once for each of the homophones provided.

6. (right/write) I will _____

   I will _____

7. (sight/site) The new school will _____

   The new school will _____

8. (your/you're) I love to dance _____

   I love to dance _____

9. (great/grate) Last night, my mom _____

   Last night, my mom _____

Grammar • Relative and Interrogative Pronouns

Name _____

- A **relative pronoun** links a clause to another noun or pronoun.
  The girls performed a song that they had chosen.
- An **interrogative pronoun** asks a question when a noun in the sentence is not known: *What happened on the bus yesterday?*
- *Who, whom, whose,* and *which* can be used as either relative or interrogative pronouns. *That* is a relative pronoun, and *what* is an interrogative pronoun. *Whose* is only used to show possession.

A. Choose the correct relative pronoun in parentheses ( ) to complete each sentence. Write the corrected sentence on the line provided.

1. This is the magazine (what, that) I told you about.

   _____

2. She is the artist (whose, which) work I like best.

   _____

3. He is the boy (who, which) lives downstairs from me.

   _____

B. Turn the following statements into questions using the interrogative pronoun in parentheses ( ). Write the question on the line.

4. These books are due back to the library today. (which)

   _____

5. I will have a sandwich for lunch today. (what)

   _____

6. These are Rebecca's rain boots. (whose)

   _____

Write a paragraph about a place you want to visit. Include and underline the relative and interrogative pronouns.

Grade 6 • Unit 4 • Week 5   **229**

Grammar • **Demonstrative and Indefinite Pronouns**

Name _____

- **Demonstrative pronouns** tell whether something is here or there.
- *This* and *that* are singular demonstrative pronouns; *these* and *those* are plural: *These are the plates for dinner.*
- **Indefinite pronouns** do not refer to a specific person, place, or thing.
    Anyone can join the Ecology Club!
- Indefinite pronouns include *everyone, both, few, no one,* and *many.*

A. Choose the correct demonstrative pronoun to complete each sentence. Write the corrected sentence on the line provided.

1. (This, These) is where the bicycle race starts.

_____

2. (That, Those) are the riders registered for the race.

_____

3. (That, Those) will be the most difficult stretch of road.

_____

B. Underline the indefinite pronoun in each sentence.

4. Everyone agrees it is a perfect day for cycling.
5. Each of the riders is ready for the race.
6. Everybody riding in the race must wear a helmet.

Reading/Writing Connection

Read the stanza from "Hey Nilda." Write Rachel's response to Nilda's text. Use demonstrative and indefinite pronouns in your answer.

> I've got two tickets to Friday's concert, and I don't want to go by myself.

_____

_____

230 Grade 6 • Unit 4 • Week 5

Grammar • Mechanics: Who/Whom; Pronoun/Verb Agreement

Name _____

- Use *who* as a subject.
- Use *whom* as an object.
- Use singular indefinite pronouns with singular verbs.
- Use plural indefinite pronouns with plural verbs.
- The indefinite pronouns *some, any, none, all,* and *most* can be singular or plural.

A. Correctly complete each sentence with *who* or *whom*. Then rewrite the entire sentence.

1. Jasmine is the lifeguard _____ worked at the pool last summer.
   _____

2. Dr. Gillespie is the physician _____ my neighbors recommend.
   _____

3. _____ plans to attend the meeting?
   _____

4. Mateo is the person with _____ you should study.
   _____

B. Read each sentence. Choose the verb in parentheses ( ) that correctly completes the sentence and write it on the line.

5. Everybody (is, are) ready to take the math test. _____

6. No one (deny, denies) that Geraldo is the best actor in the play. _____

7. Both of the scientists (work, works) at a major university. _____

8. A few of the volunteers (is, are) students at our school. _____

In your writer's notebook write an interview between two people. Use *who* and *whom* three times in your dialogue.

Grammar • Proofreading

Name _____

> - A **relative pronoun** links a clause to another noun or pronoun.
> - An **interrogative pronoun** asks a question when a noun in the sentence is not known.
> - **Demonstrative pronouns** tell whether something is here or there. *This* and *that* are singular; *these* and *those* are plural.
> - **Indefinite pronouns** do not refer to any specific person, place, or thing. Use singular indefinite pronouns with singular verbs; use plural indefinite pronouns with plural verbs.
> - Use *who* as a subject; use *whom* as an object.

Proofread each sentence. Rewrite the sentence, correcting errors in pronoun use and punctuation.

1. Everyone know that I like to watch movies.

   _____

2. Whom doesn't love the excitement of watching action on the big screen?

   _____

3. I like comedies and adventure films; that are my favorites

   _____

4. I do not enjoy scary or sad films, because both gives me bad dreams

   _____

5. Here we are at the Grand Theater, that is my favorite place to watch a movie.

   _____

6. These is the theater which I go to when I have saved up enough money for a ticket.

   _____

   _____

232   Grade 6 • Unit 4 • Week 5

English: Grammar • **Apply**

Name _____

What was your favorite reading selection or other text you read this week? Write a paragraph describing what you learned from it or why you enjoyed it. When you're done, exchange your writing with a partner. Proofread your partner's writing. Remember to apply the grammar you have learned this week.

_____
_____
_____
_____
_____
_____
_____
_____
_____
_____
_____
_____
_____

Spelling • **Consonant Alternation**

Name _____

Fold back the paper along the dotted line. Use the blanks to write each word as it is read aloud. When you finish the test, unfold the paper. Use the list at the right to correct any spelling mistakes.

1. _____ 1. crumb
2. _____ 2. crumble
3. _____ 3. design
4. _____ 4. designate
5. _____ 5. solemn
6. _____ 6. solemnity
7. _____ 7. muscle
8. _____ 8. muscular
9. _____ 9. reject
10. _____ 10. rejection
11. _____ 11. create
12. _____ 12. creation
13. _____ 13. public
14. _____ 14. publicity
15. _____ 15. prejudice
16. _____ 16. prejudicial
17. _____ 17. magic
18. _____ 18. magician
19. _____ 19. office
20. _____ 20. official

Review Words
21. _____ 21. cooperate
22. _____ 22. submit
23. _____ 23. suburb

Challenge Words
24. _____ 24. complicate
25. _____ 25. complication

Phonics/Spelling • Word Sort

Name _____

Adding a suffix to the end of a word sometimes changes the consonant sound in the original word. This change in the consonant sound is called consonant alternation.

| sign | muscle | decorate |
| signal | muscular | decoration |

Read each pair of words and notice how the consonant sound in each word changes when the suffix is added.

DECODING WORDS

Adding a suffix may change the sound of the consonant in the base word. For example, in the word *crumb*, the *b* is silent. When you add the suffix *-le* to make *crumble*, the *b* is no longer silent.

Write the pairs of spelling words according to their pattern.

crumb	create	prejudice	muscle	design
crumble	creation	prejudicial	muscular	designate
magic	solemn	office	reject	public
magician	solemnity	official	rejection	publicity

silent consonant to sounded consonant

1. _____ _____
2. _____ _____
3. _____ _____
4. _____ _____

/k/ to /sh/

5. _____ _____

/k/ to /s/

6. _____ _____

/t/ to /sh/

7. _____ _____
8. _____ _____

/s/ to /sh/

9. _____ _____
10. _____ _____

Look through this week's selections for more words with vowel alternations. Record each word and a related word in your writer's notebook. Underline the vowel sound changes.

Grade 6 • Unit 4 • Week 5   235

Spelling • Word Meaning

Name _____

crumb	solemn	reject	public	magic
crumble	solemnity	rejection	publicity	magician
design	muscle	create	prejudice	office
designate	muscular	creation	prejudicial	official

A. Write the spelling word that best completes each analogy.

1. *Paint* is to *painting* as *create* is to _____.
2. *Open* is to *closed* as _____ is to *private*.
3. *Tolerance* is to *fairness* as _____ is to *discrimination*.
4. *Cheerfulness* is to *happiness* as _____ is to *sadness*.
5. *Manage* is to *manager* as _____ is to *magician*.

B. Write the spelling word that best completes each sentence.

6. A memorial service can be a _____ occasion.
7. The latest fashion _____ was featured in this month's magazine.
8. The cake might _____ if you use the wrong knife to cut it.
9. The club president will _____ three members to help.
10. He didn't leave a _____ on his dessert plate!
11. The decision was _____ and terribly unfair.
12. My uncle may _____ the job offer.
13. My calf _____ hurts because I didn't stretch before running.
14. I think everyone experiences _____ at some point in life.
15. The athlete is _____ because she lifts weights.
16. The _____ performed many convincing tricks.
17. Independence Day is one of several _____ US holidays.
18. The court case got a lot of _____ in the media.
19. I hope the young children don't _____ a mess during lunch!
20. The _____ was closed over the weekend.

Spelling • Proofreading

Name _____

There are three misspelled words in the first paragraph and four in the second. Underline each misspelled word. Then write the words correctly on the lines.

   In the next election, my friends and I want to be informed about the candidates who are running for offise. We will learn about each candidate's position on important issues. If a candidate expresses any pregudice toward a group of people, we will rejeckt the candidate immediately.

1. _____   2. _____   3. _____

   I've always wondered what it might it be like to desine a monument that honors soldiers who have served our country. It must be a challenge to creeate a building or sculpture that everyone likes. I'm sure it is a solem occasion for everyone at the offishal unveiling of such a monument.

4. _____   5. _____   6. _____

7. _____

Writing Connection Write about your community. Use at least four words from the spelling list.

_____
_____
_____
_____
_____
_____
_____
_____
_____

Phonics/Spelling • Review

Name _____

Remember

Adding a suffix to the end of a word sometimes changes the consonant sound in the original word. This change in the consonant sound is called consonant alternation.

sign	muscle	decorate
signal	muscular	decoration

Read each pair of words and notice how the consonant sound in each word changes when the suffix is added. For example, the *silent g* in *sign* changes to /g/ when -al is added (*signal*)

crumb	create	prejudice	muscle	design
crumble	creation	prejudicial	muscular	designate
magic	solemn	office	reject	public
magician	solemnity	official	rejection	publicity

Fill in the missing letters of each word to form a spelling word. Then write the spelling word on the line.

1. mus ___ ___ ___ _____
2. prejudi ___ ___ ___ l _____
3. ma ___ ___ ___ _____
4. muscu ___ ___ ___ _____
5. solem ___ ___ ___ y _____
6. des ___ ___ ___ _____
7. re ___ ___ ___ t _____
8. creat ___ ___ ___ _____
9. pre ___ ___ ___ ice _____
10. magi ___ ___ ___ n _____

11. crum ___ ___ ___ _____
12. pub ___ ___ ___ _____
13. office ___ ___ ___ _____
14. publi ___ ___ ___ y _____
15. desi ___ ___ ___ te _____
16. off ___ ___ ___ _____
17. cr ___ ___ ___ e _____
18. cr ___ ___ ___ _____
19. rejec ___ ___ ___ n _____
20. sol ___ ___ ___ _____

238 Grade 6 • Unit 4 • Week 5

Vocabulary • **Related Words**

Name _____

Expand your vocabulary by adding or removing inflectional endings, prefixes, or suffixes to a base word to create different forms of a word.

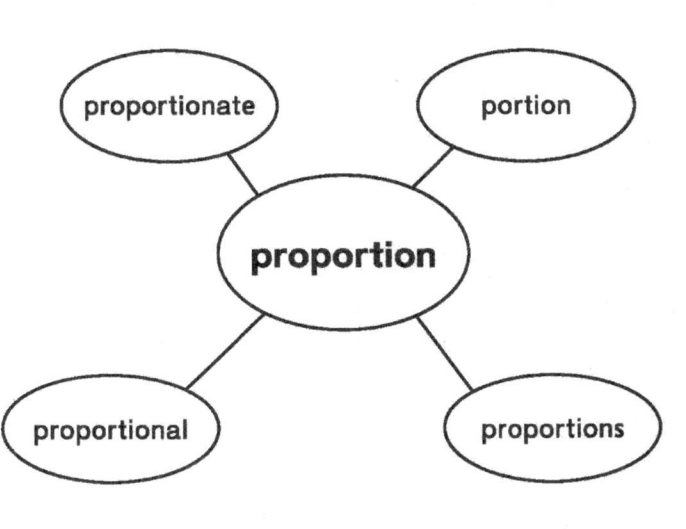

- proportionate
- portion
- **proportion**
- proportional
- proportions

Read the word below. Add or remove inflectional endings, prefixes, or suffixes to form related words and write them in the blanks. Use a print or electronic dictionary to help you.

Answerable

_____   _____

_____   _____

Grade 6 • Unit 4 • Week 5   239

Vocabulary Strategy • Figurative Language

Name _____

Read each passage from "Dear Lola" and "Dear Carolyn." Use context clues to help you figure out the meaning of each idiom in bold. Then write the idiom's meaning on the line.

1. It's been a full day since you've gone missing and I've been **a bundle of nerves**.

   _____

2. Or see your face as you come **barreling** down the street.

   _____

3. I've put up posters and **pounded the pavement** for hours, wishing I had gotten that back gate fixed faster.

   _____

4. You won't believe the adventure I've been having! It's been **a wild ride!**

   _____

5. I was **scared stiff** at first, but then a nice woman took me in.

   _____

6. She smiled and said that big changes will be **just around the corner**.

   _____

Grammar • **Adjectives**

Name _____

- An **adjective** describes a person, place, thing, or idea. Adjectives modify nouns or pronouns.
- An adjective may tell what kind, which one, or how many.
- A **predicate adjective** follows a linking verb and tells about the subject of a sentence: *The soap smelled floral.*
- A **proper adjective** is formed from a proper noun: I hung an American flag outside my house.

A. Write the adjectives in the following sentences. (Some sentences have more than one adjective.)

1. Anja and her mother visit the animal shelter every Saturday. _____

2. They bring pet supplies and dog treats when they visit. _____

3. Anja walks the small dogs, and her mom walks the big ones. _____

4. Anja likes to play with the cute cats. _____

5. She especially likes the Siamese kittens. _____

B. Write the predicate adjectives in the following sentences. (Some sentences have more than one predicate adjective.)

6. Most of the animals at the shelter are friendly, but some are shy. _____

7. The bulldog barks at visitors, but he is nice. _____

8. The terrier seems sweet and playful. _____

9. The kittens are frisky too. _____

10. All the animals seem happy to have visitors. _____

In your writer's notebook, write a short paragraph describing a park scene. Underline each adjective. Check your work for correct grammar.

Grammar • Order of Adjectives

Name _____

- When more than one adjective is used to describe something, the adjectives follow a particular order.
- Opinion adjectives come before size adjectives.
- Size adjectives come before age adjectives.
- Age adjectives come before color adjectives.
- Color adjectives come before material adjectives.
- Try to use no more than three adjectives to describe: Her beautiful young black horse won the jumping competition.

Write a sentence using each group of adjectives. Make sure to put the adjectives in the proper order.

1. red, new

   _____

2. young, tiny

   _____

3. pretty, yellow

   _____

4. big, cardboard, brown

   _____

5. marble, interesting, white

   _____

Reading/Writing Connection — Read this sentence from "The Science of Silk." Circle the adjectives that describe the products. Then write a new sentence about another fabric. Use adjectives in the correct order in your sentences.

> As a result, fine silk products were soon available at prices that more people could afford.

_____

242 Grade 6 • Unit 5 • Week 1

Grammar • Mechanics: **Capitalizing Proper Nouns and Adjectives**

Name _____

- A **proper noun** names a specific person, place, or thing, and it always should be capitalized: *Dr. Robinson, Pacific Ocean, Hillcrest Middle School.*
- **Proper adjectives** always should be capitalized, too. Many proper adjectives describe where someone or something is from. They may refer to languages, races, or nationalities.
- Some proper adjectives describe a time period or holiday: *Thanksgiving Day parades, Renaissance paintings.*

Rewrite each sentence, using capital letters for any proper nouns.

1. Many people in japan study the english language.

   _____

2. japanese students sometimes learn english from american teachers.

   _____

3. Cities like tokyo and osaka are modern and busy but still observe traditional customs.

   _____

   _____

4. many japanese traditions have been influenced by years of history.

   _____

5. It might surprise you to know that beethoven's music is traditionally performed during the japanese new year celebration.

   _____

   _____

In your writer's notebook, create a menu with three dishes from different countries. On your menu, describe each dish in detail using adjectives.

Grade 6 • Unit 5 • Week 1   **243**

Grammar • Proofreading

Name _____

- An **adjective** describes a person, place, thing, or idea. Adjectives modify nouns or pronouns and tell what kind, how many, or which one.
- A **predicate adjective** follows a linking verb and describes the subject.
- A **proper adjective** is formed from a proper noun.
- When more than one adjective is used to describe something, the adjectives follow a particular order: opinion, size, age, color, material.
- Proper nouns and proper adjectives always should be capitalized.

Proofread the paragraph. Then rewrite it, correcting any errors in the capitalization of proper nouns and proper adjectives. When more than one adjective is used to describe something, make sure the adjectives are in the correct order.

Hernando de Soto was a spanish explorer who led the first european expedition into the area that became the southern part of the united states. In 1539, he sailed from cuba to florida in search of gold and other riches. Two years later, the expedition crossed the mississippi river into what is now the state of arkansas. de soto and his army met many obstacles. It was a long hard winter, and many died. The army found none of the splendid riches they had imagined. De Soto became ill and died before the expedition returned to mexico in 1543.

English: Grammar • **Apply**

Name _____

What was your favorite reading selection or other text you read this week? Write a paragraph describing what you learned from it or why you enjoyed it. When you're done, exchange your writing with a partner. Proofread your partner's writing. Remember to apply the grammar you have learned this week.

Spelling • **Homophones**

Name _____

Fold back the paper along the dotted line. Use the blanks to write each word as it is read aloud. When you finish the test, unfold the paper. Use the list at the right to correct any spelling mistakes.

1. _____
2. _____
3. _____
4. _____
5. _____
6. _____
7. _____
8. _____
9. _____
10. _____
11. _____
12. _____
13. _____
14. _____
15. _____
16. _____
17. _____
18. _____
19. _____
20. _____

Review Words
21. _____
22. _____
23. _____

Challenge Words
24. _____
25. _____

1. lesson
2. lessen
3. aisle
4. isle
5. I'll
6. navel
7. naval
8. pane
9. pain
10. miner
11. minor
12. vain
13. vane
14. vein
15. principal
16. principle
17. idle
18. idol
19. sheer
20. shear
21. crumble
22. rejection
23. publicity
24. hanger
25. hangar

Phonics/Spelling • Word Sort

Name _____

Homophones are words that sound the same but have different spellings and meanings. They are often commonly used and confused words. Context clues or a dictionary can help you determine the meaning or correct use of a homophone. Read the examples below:

steak/stake   *tall/tale*
flour/flower   *you're/your*

COMMON ERRORS

Some contractions form homophones with other words, such as *it's* and *its*. The apostrophe tells you that *it's* is a contraction that stands for *it is*. The word *its* shows possession: *The cat licked its paw.*

Write the words that contain the matching spelling patterns.

lesson	I'll	pain	vane	idle
lessen	navel	miner	vein	idol
aisle	naval	minor	principal	sheer
isle	pane	vain	principle	shear

one-syllable words, long *a* sound

1. _____
2. _____
3. _____
4. _____
5. _____

one-syllable words, long *i* sound

6. _____
7. _____
8. _____

one-syllable words, *r*-controlled vowels

9. _____
10. _____

more than one syllable, ə sound in last syllable

11. _____
12. _____
13. _____
14. _____
15. _____
16. _____
17. _____
18. _____
19. _____
20. _____

Look through this week's selections for more homophones to sort. Read the words aloud and create a word sort for a partner in your writer's notebook.

Name _____

Spelling • Word Meaning

lesson	I'll	pain	vane	idle
lessen	navel	miner	vein	idol
aisle	naval	minor	principal	sheer
isle	pane	vain	principle	shear

A. Write the spelling word that best fits the analogy, or comparison.

1. *Coach* is to *team* as _____ is to *school*.

2. *Cook* is to *cooking* as _____ is to *mining*.

3. *Small* is to *large* as _____ is to *increase*.

4. *Door* is to *wood* as _____ is to *glass*.

5. *Path* is to *woods* as _____ is to *theater*.

B. Write the spelling word that best completes each sentence.

6. After we complete the spelling _____, there will be a quiz.

7. What math _____ did you use to solve the problem?

8. A _____ is different from an artery.

9. He placed the weather _____ on the roof of the house.

10. It is time for the farmer to _____ the sheeps' wool.

11. You will enjoy the sandy beaches on the tropical _____.

12. The baby's _____ showed just above his diaper.

13. He felt a sharp _____ when he cut his finger.

14. The machines at the site sat _____ during the holidays.

15. She couldn't see the movie because she is a _____.

16. The guitarist is an _____ to many teenagers.

17. The _____ base was crowded with sailors.

18. The thin drapery fabric is very _____.

19. The team tried in _____ to win the game.

20. _____ be the first person in the cafeteria line.

248   Grade 6 • Unit 5 • Week 1

Spelling • Proofreading

Name _____

There are six misspelled words in the paragraphs below. Underline each misspelled word. Then write the words correctly on the lines.

Of all the important people in Dana's life, her elementary school principle, Mr. Reiner, was one of the most influential. Mr. Reiner taught Dana one very important lessen in life—the importance of working hard and not being idel.

Mr. Reiner explained to Dana that life can be difficult and pane is inevitable. But he encouraged her to remain focused on her goals. "Hard work will not be in vein," he always said. Dana will always remember Mr. Reiner's advice. In many ways, she considers him her idle.

1. _____ 2. _____ 3. _____

4. _____ 5. _____ 6. _____

Writing Connection Write about an important person who has influenced your life. Use at least four words from the spelling list.

_____
_____
_____
_____
_____
_____
_____
_____
_____
_____
_____
_____

Phonics/Spelling · **Review**

Name _____

> **Remember**
>
> Words that sound the same when spoken but have different meanings and spellings are called **homophones**. Using context clues or a dictionary can help you determine the meaning or correct use of a homophone. Read the examples below:
>
> *pair/pear*   *sun/son*   *hole/whole*   *Sunday/sundae*

lesson	I'll	pain	vane	idle
lessen	navel	miner	vein	idol
aisle	naval	minor	principal	sheer
isle	pane	vain	principle	shear

A. Write a word that sounds the same but has a different spelling and meaning. For some items, there may be more than one answer.

1. pane _____
2. lesson _____
3. navel _____
4. minor _____
5. vain _____
6. sheer _____
7. principal _____
8. idle _____
9. aisle _____

B. Circle the spelling word in each row that rhymes with the word in bold type. Write the spelling word on the line.

10. **style** cry I'll fire _____
11. **crane** vain great when _____
12. **fear** quite earn sheer _____
13. **delicatessen** mitten lesson written _____
14. **file** pilot tiles aisle _____
15. **refrain** pain tame hair _____
16. **diner** shine crime minor _____
17. **invincible** principal mince full _____
18. **bridal** doll idol cradle _____
19. **stain** vein deem air _____
20. **tidal** bell while idle _____

Vocabulary • Related Words

Name _____

Expand your vocabulary by adding or removing inflectional endings, prefixes, or suffixes to a base word to create different forms of a word.

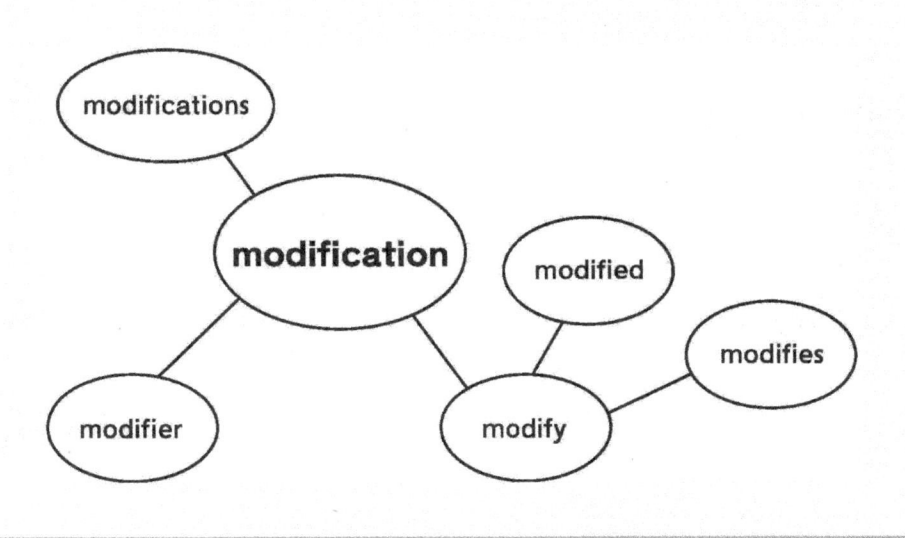

- modifications
- **modification**
- modified
- modifies
- modifier
- modify

Read the word below. Add or remove inflectional endings, prefixes, or suffixes to form related words and write them in the blanks. Use a print or online dictionary to help you.

Nutrients

_____   _____

_____   _____

_____   _____

Vocabulary • Spiral Review

Name _____

Slam dunk! Match the vocabulary words on the left with the definitions on the right. Use a dictionary if you need to.

1. unearthed — referring to the outer edge

2. windswept — act of sharing feelings

3. answerable — room for relaxing

4. productivity — proper relationship between things

5. potential — not protected from a breeze

6. tentatively — serious attempt

7. lounge — moral or legal duty

8. peripheral — rate at which a person does something

9. obligation — discovered or dug up

10. empathy — needing to explain actions

11. proportion — with hesitation

12. endeavor — possibility

252 Grade 6 • Unit 5 • Week 1

Grammar • Articles

Name _____

- An **article** is a kind of adjective. There are three articles: *a, an,* and *the*.
- *A* and *an* are **indefinite articles** because they refer to a noun in general. Use *a* before a noun that begins with a consonant. Use *an* before a noun that begins with a vowel: *a desk, an eagle*.
- *The* is a definite article because it refers to a specific noun: <u>*The*</u> *blue chair is comfortable.*

Read the sentences. Circle the article that correctly completes the sentence.

1. (The, A) Sun is the center of our solar system.
2. (The, An) Earth and seven other planets orbit the Sun in circular paths.
3. Pluto also orbits the Sun, but it is no longer called (a, an) planet.
4. Pluto is classified as (a, an) dwarf planet.
5. Pluto's orbit is shaped like (a, an) oval.
6. The solar system has other dwarf planets and (a, an) number of smaller bodies.
7. (A, An) asteroid is a small rocky body that travels through space.
8. Most asteroids are found in a region between Mars and Jupiter called (a, the) asteroid belt.

Reading/Writing Connection

Read this excerpt from "The Science of Silk." Underline the articles. Then write a paragraph about something you created. Explain why you're proud of what you made.

> A single raw silk filament is too thin to use for weaving. So the next common step in the process, called *throwing*, involves twisting several filaments together to form a thread.

_____

_____

_____

Grade 6 • Unit 5 • Week 2 253

Grammar • Demonstrative Adjectives

Name _____

> - *That, this, these,* and *those* are **demonstrative adjectives**. They point out people, places, things, or ideas: Put *those* plates in the sink.
> - Demonstrative adjectives can also take the place of nouns. When they do, they become **demonstrative pronouns**: *This* is Jessica's lunch bag.

A. Choose the demonstrative adjective that correctly completes each sentence. Write it on the line provided.

1. The school principal keeps lost items in _____ box. (this, these)

2. _____ gloves might belong to Matthew. (That, Those)

3. Samantha lost a hat just like _____ one. (this, these)

4. Ask William if _____ sweater is his. (that, those)

B. Complete each sentence with an appropriate demonstrative pronoun.

5. Lee said _____ are his baseball cards in the lost and found box.

6. A water bottle was left on the bus. _____ might be mine.

7. I found a ball. Could _____ be the ball missing from the gym?

8. The books on the table go back to the library. _____ on the desk are for the students.

In your writer's notebook, write about a hobby that you have or a hobby that interests you. Use demonstrative adjectives and pronouns in your writing. Then edit your work.

Grammar • Mechanics: **Using Colons and Semicolons**

Name _____

- Use a **colon** after the salutation in a business letter.
- Use a **colon** to introduce a list of items.
   Purchase these supplies: pencils, paper, markers, and pens.
- Use a **semicolon** to join together two independent clauses—that is, two clauses that could be sentences on their own. The semicolon takes the place of a comma and conjunction.
   The sixth graders will visit the planetarium; they will learn about constellations.

Read the letter. Correct errors with colons and semicolons.

3100 Olive Street
Pico Rivera, CA 90060
December 15, 2019

Dear Ms. Newman,

   I am sending the additional information you need for the choir program. The event begins at 7:00 P.M. The girls' chorus will perform first the mixed choir will perform last. Please add the following names to the list of choir members Abby Stein, Hannah Wilbanks, Windom Merrill, and Paul Stanley.

   If you need any other information, please let me know.

Sincerely,
Lachandra Newman

Connect to Community

Talk to a parent or another trusted adult about a business that you would like to start in your community or a business that you would like to learn more about in your community. Use the library's resources or the internet to help you learn more about your selected business. Then write a paragraph about why this business interests you. Edit your paragraph to make sure you used correct spelling and punctuation.

_____
_____
_____
_____

Grammar • Proofreading

Name _____

- An **article** is a kind of adjective. There are three articles: *a, an,* and *the. A* and *an* are **indefinite articles**. *The* is a definite article.
- *That, this, these,* and *those* are **demonstrative adjectives**. They point out people, places, things, or ideas. When **demonstrative adjectives** take the place of nouns, they become demonstrative pronouns.
- Use a **colon** after the salutation in a business letter and to introduce a list of items. Use a **semicolon** to join together two independent clauses.

Proofread the announcement. Watch for errors in articles, in demonstrative adjectives and demonstrative pronouns, and in punctuation. Rewrite the passage correctly.

To all students

The school assembly will take place these afternoon at 2:00 P.M. in a school gymnasium. All students must be seated in a gym no later than 1:50.

Principal Davis will recognize the following students for their top achievements in an state science fair Cody Massenelli, Sheree Jones, and Nikki Tagupa. This students should sit with me by a stage.

A principal will also recognize students who won honorable mention at a fair. That students should remain with their class they should stand when their names are called.

Sincerely,
Mrs. Pringle

English: Grammar • **Apply**

Name _____

What was your favorite reading selection or other text you read this week? Write a paragraph describing what you learned from it or why you enjoyed it. When you're done, exchange your writing with a partner. Proofread your partner's writing. Remember to apply the grammar you have learned this week.

Spelling • **Words from Around the World**

Name _____

Fold back the paper along the dotted line. Use the blanks to write each word as it is read aloud. When you finish the test, unfold the paper. Use the list at the right to correct any spelling mistakes.

1. _____ 1. bazaar
2. _____ 2. bronco
3. _____ 3. sombrero
4. _____ 4. caribou
5. _____ 5. chocolate
6. _____ 6. pajamas
7. _____ 7. plaza
8. _____ 8. igloo
9. _____ 9. pizza
10. _____ 10. barbecue
11. _____ 11. canoe
12. _____ 12. denim
13. _____ 13. gong
14. _____ 14. plateau
15. _____ 15. poodle
16. _____ 16. apricot
17. _____ 17. balcony
18. _____ 18. yacht
19. _____ 19. cruise
20. _____ 20. ballet

Review Words
21. _____ 21. lesson
22. _____ 22. minor
23. _____ 23. idol

Challenge Words
24. _____ 24. gondola
25. _____ 25. kindergarten

258   Grade 6 • Unit 5 • Week 2

Phonics/Spelling • Word Sort

Name _____

Many English words originate from other languages around the world.

- The word *origami* is a Japanese loanword that means "fold paper."
- *Salsa* is a word borrowed from the Spanish language that means "sauce"

Understanding where words originate can help you say, spell, and determine the meaning of unfamiliar words.

DECODING WORDS

Say each word syllable by syllable. Try to remember any unusual sounds or spellings. Write the word down, sounding out each syllable. Confirm the spelling, pronunciation, and word origin using a dictionary.

Read the words in the box. Write the spelling words that fit the category.

bazaar	chocolate	pizza	gong	balcony
bronco	pajamas	barbecue	plateau	yacht
sombrero	plaza	canoe	poodle	cruise
caribou	igloo	denim	apricot	ballet

related to clothing

1. _____
2. _____
3. _____

related to animals

4. _____
5. _____
6. _____

related to food

7. _____

8. _____
9. _____
10. _____

related to transportation

11. _____
12. _____
13. _____

related to dance and music

14. _____

15. _____

related to places

16. _____
17. _____
18. _____
19. _____
20. _____

Work with a partner to find more words from around the world. Record the words you find in your writer's notebook.

Grade 6 • Unit 5 • Week 2   259

Spelling • Word Meaning

Name _____

bazaar	chocolate	pizza	gong	balcony
bronco	pajamas	barbecue	plateau	yacht
sombrero	plaza	canoe	poodle	cruise
caribou	igloo	denim	apricot	ballet

A. Read each word origin and write the matching spelling word.

1. Italian, *balletto* _____
2. Dutch, *kruisen* _____
3. Dutch, *jaght* _____
4. Italian, *balcone* _____
5. Spanish, *canoa* _____
6. German, *pudel* _____
7. Inuit, *iglu* _____
8. Persian, *paejamah* _____
9. French, *plat* _____

B. Write the spelling word that best completes each sentence.

10. The large _____ in the center of town had a pretty fountain.
11. _____ is a sweet dessert.
12. There were many goods to choose from at the _____.
13. Are jeans made out of a fabric called _____?
14. Jonah was hoping to eat _____ for dinner.
15. We will have a _____ on the 4th of July.
16. The cowboy held on tightly as he tamed the _____.
17. The percussionist hit the _____ with his mallet.
18. We made delicious _____ jam from the fresh fruit at the market.
19. Both male and female _____ have antlers.
20. The guitarist wore a _____ as he played in the hot sun.

260 Grade 6 • Unit 5 • Week 2

Spelling • Proofreading

Name _____

There are seven misspelled words in the paragraphs below. Underline each misspelled word. Then write the words correctly on the lines.

My family and I were excited because there was a bazzar being held in the town's plasa. I brought my own money so I could buy some things. There were many goods to choose from. First, I bought a pair of denum jeans. Then I saw a colorful pair of pajames and decided to buy them, too.

There were also many delicious foods to eat. I bought a slice of pitza for lunch and a tiny bar of chocolit for dessert. Then I bought a jar of apprikot jam. I know that my mother will serve it when she makes French toast in the morning!

1. _____   2. _____   3. _____

4. _____   5. _____   6. _____

7. _____

Writing Connection Write about things you would like to buy if you went to a bazaar. Use at least four words from the spelling list.

_____
_____
_____
_____
_____
_____
_____
_____
_____

Phonics/Spelling • Review

Name _____

Remember

Many English words have been borrowed from other languages around the world.

- The word *delicatessen* (often abbreviated as deli) is a German loanword that means "fine/fancy foods." Delis in the United States often serve sandwiches.
- *Cul-de-sac* is a word borrowed from the French language that means "bottom of the bag." In English, it refers to a street that is closed at one end.

Understanding where words originate can help you say, spell, and determine the meaning of unfamiliar words.

bazaar	chocolate	pizza	gong	balcony
bronco	pajamas	barbecue	plateau	yacht
sombrero	plaza	canoe	poodle	cruise
caribou	igloo	denim	apricot	ballet

A. Fill in the missing letters to form a spelling word. Then write the spelling word.

1. g ___ ___ ___   _____
2. sombr ___ ___ ___   _____
3. barbe ___ ___ e   _____
4. p ___ ___ ___ a   _____
5. br ___ ___ ___ o   _____
6. car ___ ___ ___ u   _____
7. apri ___ ___ ___   _____
8. chocol ___ ___ ___   _____
9. plat ___ ___ ___   _____
10. pl ___ ___ ___   _____
11. balc ___ ___ ___   _____
12. ig ___ ___ ___   _____
13. paja ___ ___ ___   _____

B. Circle the word that rhymes with the word in bold type. Write the spelling word.

14. **car** park hard bazaar _____
15. **news** rose cruise froze _____
16. **venom** home denim whim _____
17. **noodle** cradle ladle poodle _____
18. **weigh** ballet crate height _____
19. **drew** canoe flown shoot _____
20. **blot** yacht hop tote _____

Vocabulary Strategy • Homographs

Name _____

Homographs are words that are spelled the same but have different meanings and origins. Some homographs have different pronunciations and syllable breaks as well. They have separate, numbered entries in the dictionary:

min•ute¹ (min' it) *noun* 1. a unit of time equal to 60 seconds. 2. a short period of time; moment: *Can I speak to you for a minute?* [Old French *minute*, fr. Late Latin *minuta* small section, fr. Latin *minuere* to make smaller.]

mi•nute² (mī nōōt') *adjective* 1. very small; tiny: *A minute particle of dust floated in the air.* 2. of small importance: *I will take care of the minute details.* [Latin *minutus.*]

Minute has a different meaning, pronunciation, and syllable break depending on whether it is used as a noun or an adjective. Context clues will tell you which homograph you are reading.

Study the dictionary entries for homographs. Then answer the questions that follow.

in•va•lid¹ (in' və lid) *noun.* a person who is disabled by disease or injury: *The invalid could not leave the house.* [French *invalide* sick, disabled, fr. Latin *invalidus* weak, infirm.]

in•val•id² (in val' id) *adjective.* without force, basis, or authority: *The contract was found to be invalid.* [Latin, fr. *in-* not + *validus* strong and powerful.]

1. In which entry is *invalid* an adjective? What is the part of speech in the other entry?

   _____

2. Do the two words have the same pronunciation? Are their syllables divided in the same way? Explain.

   _____
   _____
   _____

3. Write which definition is used in the following sentence: An invalid driver's license will not be accepted. How do you know?

   _____

Grade 6 • Unit 5 • Week 2   263

Vocabulary Strategy • Context Clues

Name _____

Read each passage below from, "Something to Write On, Please." Determine the cause-and-effect relationship described in each passage. Write the missing cause or effect on the line provided. Then, thinking about the cause and effect, define the word in bold in each passage.

1. To make papyrus paper, the Egyptians cut thin strips of grass and soaked them in water, which softened them. To make a flat surface, they laid the strips at right angles to each other and **pounded** them into a thin sheet.

   cause: _____

   effect: making papyrus paper with a flat surface

   definition of **pounded**: _____

2. The end of a reed made a wedge-shaped **impression** in the wet clay.

   cause: end of reed pushed into clay

   effect: _____

   definition of **impression**: _____

3. The drying of the clay made the writing harden and become **permanent**, but it could still be carried from one place to another.

   cause: drying of the clay

   effect: _____

   definition of **permanent**: _____

4. Silk was also used to make books, but it made them **costly**.

   cause: using silk, an expensive material, to make books

   effect: _____

   definition of **costly**: _____

264 Grade 6 • Unit 5 • Week 2

Grammar • Comparative Adjectives

Name _____

- **Comparative adjectives** compare two people, places, or things.
- Form comparative adjectives by adding -er to most one-syllable and some two-syllable words: *large/larger; quick/quicker.*
- If an adjective ends in -e, drop the e before adding -er. If it ends in a consonant preceded by a single vowel, double the consonant. If it ends in -y, change the y to i: *steady/steadier; busy/busier.*

A. Read each sentence. On the lines provided, write the correct comparative form of the adjective in parentheses ( ).

1. Ian's house is close to mine, and Dev's house is even _____. (close)

2. Jackson Street is busy, but Jefferson Street is _____. (busy)

3. The weather is hot today, but it will be even _____ tomorrow. (hot)

B. Rewrite the sentence using the correct comparative form of the adjective in parentheses ( ).

4. My dog was (big) than Jung's dog.

_____

5. The leaves are (pretty) today than they were last week.

_____

Writing Connection

Write a paragraph using comparative adjectives describing parts of your school. You may use a dictionary when you edit and proofread your work.

_____
_____
_____
_____

Grammar • Superlative Adjectives

Name _____

- **Superlative adjectives** compare more than two people, places, or things.
- Form superlative adjectives by adding -*est* to most one-syllable and some two-syllable adjectives.
- If an adjective ends in -*e*, drop the e before adding -*est*. If it ends in a consonant preceded by a single vowel, double the consonant. If it ends in -*y*, change the y to *i*.

Complete each sentence with the correct superlative form of the adjective in parentheses ( ). Write the correct form on the line.

1. John is the (young) _____ member of our large family.

2. Brianna is the (old) _____ girl.

3. Even though James is only twelve, he is the (tall) _____ boy.

4. I am the (short) _____ girl in the family.

5. Mom says John was the (large) _____ baby of all.

6. Now that John is talking, he is the (noisy) _____ member of the family.

7. James has the (big) _____ bedroom.

8. Brianna and James are the (close) _____ in age.

9. The mornings at our house are (busy) _____ around 8:00.

10. That is the (lively) _____ time of our day.

In your writer's notebook, compare yourself with your favorite characters from a book. Use superlative adjectives to show how you are alike and different.

266 Grade 6 • Unit 5 • Week 3

Grammar • Mechanics: **Hyphenated Words**

Name _____

- Compound words can be written as one word (*homework*), as two words (*paper clip*), or with a hyphen (*all-American*).
- Hyphens are often used in compound numbers and fractions, with prefixes such as *ex-* or *self-* or the suffix *-elect,* and with prefixes before proper nouns and adjectives: *self-made, ex-football player.*
- A compound adjective that precedes the word it modifies should be hyphenated: *up-to-date maps.*

Read each sentence. Decide whether the words in parentheses ( ) should be one word, two words, or a hyphenated word. Write the word correctly on the line. If the word is correct, write C on the line. Use a dictionary if necessary.

1. We are having (left overs) for dinner. _____

2. Roberto finished (twenty five) problems before recess. _____

3. My brother is a (self taught) tennis player. _____

4. We watch his tennis matches from the (fourth floor) window. _____

5. My brother will graduate from (high school) next year. _____

6. The (president elect) received a warm welcome from the theater club members. _____

Reading/Writing connection

Read this sentence from "Journey to Freedom." Circle the hyphenated word. Then write a new sentence about a talent you have. Include a hyphenated word.

> But I lack Mother's know-how for curing, I whispered.

_____

_____

_____

Name _____

Grammar • Proofreading

> - **Comparative adjectives** compare two people, places, or things.
> - **Superlative adjectives** compare more than two people, places, or things.
> - Compound words can be written as one word (*homework*), as two words (*paper clip*), or with a hyphen (*all-American*).

Proofread each sentence. Watch for errors in comparative and superlative adjectives and in compound words. Also correct errors in capitalization and the use of hyphens and other punctuation. Use a dictionary if necessary.

1. Florence Griffith Joyner made history in the 1980s when she became the world's faster woman

   _____

   _____

2. She won three-gold medals at the 1988 Olympic games?

   _____

3. Her colorful outfits and six inch finger nails made her a standout on the track,

   _____

4. last night? I stayed up latest than I will tonight.

   _____

5. Tonight will be the early bedtime of all for me this week.

   _____

6. The weather reports, say that Tonight will be the cold night of the year,"

   _____

268 Grade 6 • Unit 5 • Week 3

English: Grammar • Apply

Name _____

What was your favorite reading selection or other text you read this week? Write a paragraph describing what you learned from it or why you enjoyed it. When you're done, exchange your writing with a partner. Proofread your partner's writing. Remember to apply the grammar you have learned this week.

Spelling • Latin Roots

Name _____

Fold back the paper along the dotted line. Use the blanks to write each word as it is read aloud. When you finish the test, unfold the paper. Use the list at the right to correct any spelling mistakes.

1. _____ 1. audience
2. _____ 2. benefit
3. _____ 3. factory
4. _____ 4. flexible
5. _____ 5. reduce
6. _____ 6. section
7. _____ 7. inject
8. _____ 8. insect
9. _____ 9. incredible
10. _____ 10. structure
11. _____ 11. reflection
12. _____ 12. objection
13. _____ 13. dejected
14. _____ 14. prediction
15. _____ 15. introduce
16. _____ 16. education
17. _____ 17. dictionary
18. _____ 18. destruction
19. _____ 19. audio
20. _____ 20. credit

Review Words
21. _____ 21. denim
22. _____ 22. barbecue
23. _____ 23. ballet

Challenge Words
24. _____ 24. manufacture
25. _____ 25. dictate

Grade 6 • Unit 5 • Week 3

Phonics/Spelling • Word Sort

Name _____

Many English words are of Latin origin. Recognizing Latin roots can help you remember a word's spelling and meaning.

Some Latin roots include: *ject* (throw), *bene* (well), *struct* (put together), *aud* (hear), *fac* (make), *dict* (speak), *duc* (lead), *sect* (cut), *cred* (believe), and *flect* (end).

Read each spelling word aloud. Do you notice any patterns?

DECODING WORDS

Many verbs end with the Latin root *ject*, such as *object, eject,* and *inject.* When these words become nouns, the final consonant sound changes. For example, the /t/ in *eject* changes to /sh/ in *ejection.*

Write the spelling words that contain the Latin roots.

audience	reduce	incredible	dejected	dictionary
benefit	section	structure	prediction	destruction
factory	inject	reflection	introduce	audio
flexible	insect	objection	education	credit

ject
1. _____
2. _____
3. _____

bene
4. _____

struct
5. _____
6. _____

aud
7. _____

8. _____

dict
9. _____
10. _____

fac
11. _____

duc
12. _____
13. _____
14. _____

sect
15. _____
16. _____

cred
17. _____
18. _____

flect
19. _____
20. _____

Look through this week's selections for more words with Latin roots to sort. Create a word sort in your writer's notebook.

Spelling • Word Meaning

Name _____

audience	reduce	incredible	dejected	dictionary
benefit	section	structure	prediction	destruction
factory	inject	reflection	introduce	audio
flexible	insect	objection	education	credit

A. Write the spelling word that matches the definition.

1. recognition that a class has been successfully completed _____
2. to put medicine into the body through a needle; to insert _____
3. development of knowledge or skill _____
4. a statement made about the future _____
5. the act of protesting _____
6. something that is built _____
7. great damage _____
8. to come to know personally; to make known _____
9. able to bend easily _____
10. to do good for _____

B. Write the spelling word that best completes each sentence.

11. The _____ gave the orchestra a standing ovation.
12. Would you look up these words in the _____?
13. The _____ specializes in making wooden toys.
14. We need to _____ the amount of water we use every day.
15. The _____ fireworks display excited the crowd.
16. The baby saw her _____ in the mirror and giggled!
17. He felt _____ until he heard the good news.
18. Vanessa enjoys reading the arts _____ of the Sunday newspaper.
19. That _____ is crawling up the wall now.
20. I turned up the volume on the _____ so we could hear better.

272 Grade 6 • Unit 5 • Week 3

Spelling • Proofreading

Name _____

There are six misspelled words in the paragraphs below. Underline each misspelled word. Then write the words correctly on the lines.

When a city is awarded the honor of holding the Olympics, a strukchur is built to house a large awdience. Because the Olympic events are televised live across the world, the producers make sure the audeo is working effectively before the telecast.

Many people contribute to the success of the Olympics and should be given credet for their efforts. No one should feel dejekted during this incredable series of events, most of all, the participating athletes.

1. _____ 2. _____ 3. _____

4. _____ 5. _____ 6. _____

Writing Connection — Write about a special event you've been to or seen on television. Use at least four words from the spelling list.

_____
_____
_____
_____
_____
_____
_____
_____
_____
_____
_____

Phonics/Spelling • Review

Name _____

Remember

Recognizing that many English words have Latin roots can help you remember a word's spelling and meaning. For example, if you know the Latin root *aud* (to hear), you should be able to determine the spelling and meaning of *auditorium*.

Read each spelling word aloud. Which words share the same Latin roots?

audience	reduce	incredible	dejected	dictionary
benefit	section	structure	prediction	destruction
factory	inject	reflection	introduce	audio
flexible	insect	objection	education	credit

Fill in the missing letters of each word to form a spelling word. Then write the spelling word on the line.

1. cr _ _ _ t _____
2. in _ _ _ t _____
3. _ _ dience _____
4. a _ _ _ o _____
5. des _ _ _ ction _____
6. obj _ _ _ ion _____
7. _ _ _ efit _____
8. pre _ _ _ tion _____
9. _ _ _ tion _____
10. in _ _ _ dible _____
11. _ _ _ ucture _____
12. re _ _ _ ction _____
13. inj _ _ _ _____
14. _ _ _ tionary _____
15. educa _ _ _ n _____
16. de _ _ _ ted _____
17. red _ _ _ _____
18. _ _ _ xible _____
19. intro _ _ _ e _____
20. _ _ _ tory _____

274 Grade 6 • Unit 5 • Week 3

Vocabulary • **Related Words**

Name _____

Expand your vocabulary by adding or removing inflectional endings, prefixes, or suffixes to a base word to create different forms of a word.

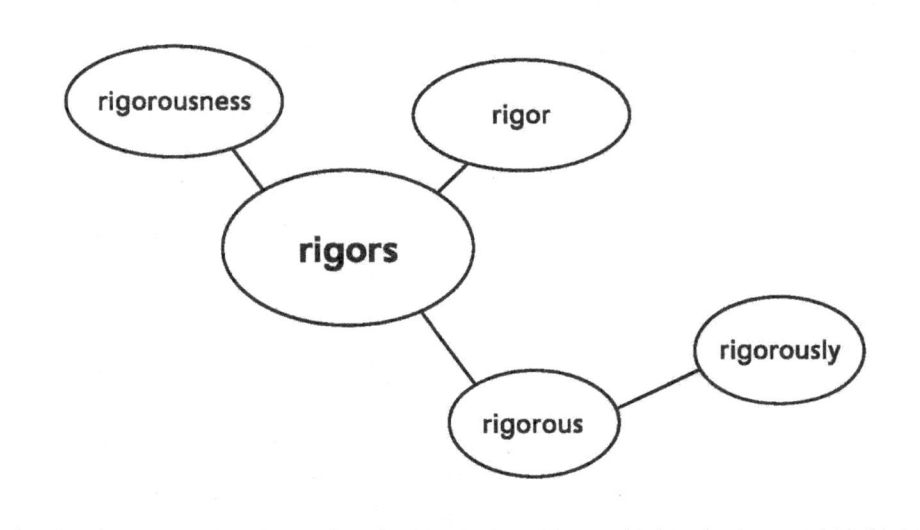

- rigorousness
- rigor
- **rigors**
- rigorous
- rigorously

Read the word below. Add or remove inflectional endings, prefixes, or suffixes to form related words and write them in the blanks. Use a print or online dictionary to help you.

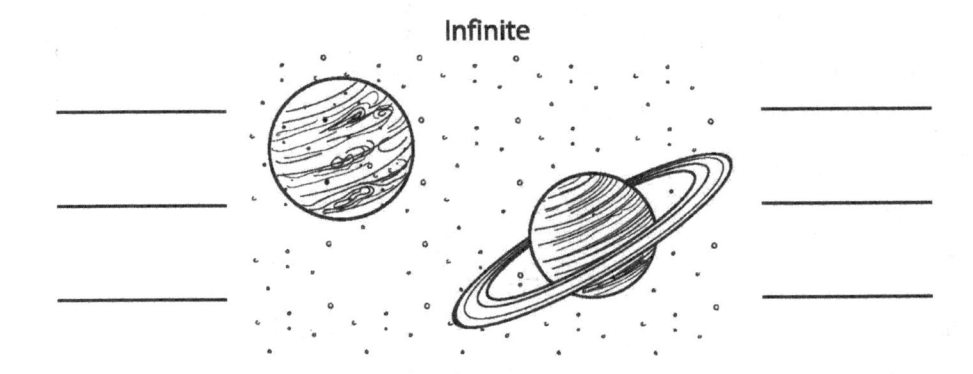

Infinite

_____   _____

_____   _____

_____   _____

Vocabulary • Spiral Review

Name _____

Use the words in the box and the clues below to help you solve the crossword puzzle.

implement	manipulation	nutrients	glimmer
industrial	indispensable	domestic	sparse
mutated	inefficient	surplus	exotic

Across
1. home-related
5. clever control
6. unusual
7. nourishing substances
11. put into effect

Down
2. machine-related
3. not effective
4. essential
5. changed form
8. an over-amount
9. faint sign
10. thin

276 Grade 6 • Unit 5 • Week 3

Grammar • Comparing with *More*

Name _____

- Form the **comparative** of most one- and some two-syllable adjectives by adding -er to the word: *softer, quieter, harder*
- For adjectives of more than two syllables, form the comparative by adding *more* in front of the adjective: *more emotional, more colorful, more common*

Underline the word or words in parentheses that form the correct comparative adjective.

1. This basketball game is (excitinger, more exciting) than last week's game.
2. Our team is (more enthusiastic, enthusiasticer) than the other team is.
3. This week's crowd is (bigger, more big) than last week's.
4. Our offense is (effectiver, more effective) than our defense.
5. The point guard on our team is (more fast, faster) than their point guard.
6. Games are (more enjoyable, enjoyabler) in the new gym than they were in the old gym.
7. The new gym is (spaciousser, more spacious) than the old one was.
8. These padded seats are (comforabler, more comfortable) than the old wooden ones.
9. The score of this game is (closer, more close) than the score of Wednesday's game.
10. A close game is (more satisfying, satisfyinger) than an easy victory.

Reading/Writing Connection

Read this sentence from "Journey to Freedom" and underline the adjectives. Then rewrite the sentence using a comparative adjective.

Mother often said, "Patience is bitter, but its fruit is sweet."

_____

_____

Grade 6 • Unit 5 Week 4 277

Grammar • Comparing with *Most*

Name _____

> - Form the **superlative** of most one- and some two-syllable adjectives by adding *-est* to the word: *coziest, warmest, toughest*
> - Form the superlative of many adjectives with two or more syllables by adding *most* in front of the adjective: *most effective, most talented, most athletic*

A. Choose the superlative adjective that correctly completes each sentence. Write it on the line provided.

1. That movie was one of the (entertainingest, most entertaining) films of the year.

   _____

2. The special effects were among the (incrediblest, most incredible) I have ever seen.

   _____

3. Science fiction is the (most fascinating, fascinatingest) type of movie to me.

   _____

B. Complete each sentence with the correct superlative form of the adjective in parentheses. Write the correct form on the line.

4. My other favorite film this year had the _____ script. (amusing)

5. It was one of the _____ movies I've seen in a while. (funny)

6. The comical ice skating scene made me laugh the _____. (hard)

> In your writer's notebook, write about a genre of books that you enjoy reading. Review your work to make sure that you used the correct forms of the adjectives.

278 Grade 6 • Unit 5 Week 4

Grammar • Mechanics: Using *More* and *Most*

Name _____

> - When using the comparative form in a sentence, do not add *-er* and *more* to the same adjective: *more creativer (incorrect); more creative (correct)*
> - When using the superlative form to compare more than two things, do not add *-est* and *most* to the same adjective: *most helpfulest (incorrect); most helpful (correct)*

Read each sentence. Put brackets [ ] around incorrect comparative or superlative adjectives. Rewrite the sentence correctly on the lines. If the sentence is correct, write *C*.

1. San Antonio is one of the most interestingest cities in Texas.

   _____

2. It is also one of the most largest cities in the state.

   _____

3. Houston is the only city in Texas larger than San Antonio.

   _____

4. It is one of the most oldest cities in the United States.

   _____

5. San Antonio has one of the largest concentrations of Spanish missions.

   _____

6. The Alamo is the city's most old mission.

   _____

7. One of the most famous battles was fought at the Alamo.

   _____

In your writer's notebook, write about a time when you had to be brave. Edit your work for spelling and correct comparative adjectives.

Grammar • Proofreading

Name _____

> - Form the **comparative** of most one- and some two-syllable adjectives by adding -*er* to the word. For adjectives of more than two syllables, add *more* in front of the adjective.
> - Form the **superlative** of most one- and some two-syllable adjectives by adding -*est* to the word. For adjectives of more than two syllables, add *most* in front of the adjective.
> - When using the comparative form in a sentence, do not add -*er* and *more* to the same adjective.
> - When using the superlative form, do not add -*est* and *most* to the same adjective.

Proofread each sentence. On the lines, rewrite the sentence. Correct mistakes in comparative and superlative adjectives. Change articles if you need to.

1. I heard the most excitingest news today!

   _____

2. My most oldest friend, Maya, is coming for a visit.

   _____

3. Maya has always been my most close friend, too.

   _____

4. She lived in my neighborhood when we were more young, but she moved away.

   _____

5. We had the amazingest times together.

   _____

280 Grade 6 • Unit 5 Week 4

English: Grammar • **Apply**

Name _____

What was your favorite reading selection or other text you read this week? Write a paragraph describing what you learned from it or why you enjoyed it. When you're done, exchange your writing with a partner. Proofread your partner's writing. Remember to apply the grammar you have learned this week.

_____
_____
_____
_____
_____
_____
_____
_____
_____
_____
_____
_____
_____
_____

Spelling • Greek Roots

Name _____

Fold back the paper along the dotted line. Use the blanks to write each word as it is read aloud. When you finish the test, unfold the paper. Use the list at the right to correct any spelling mistakes.

1. _____ 1. thermometer
2. _____ 2. aerospace
3. _____ 3. diagram
4. _____ 4. paragraph
5. _____ 5. biography
6. _____ 6. microscope
7. _____ 7. autobiography
8. _____ 8. microwave
9. _____ 9. hydrant
10. _____ 10. grammar
11. _____ 11. catalog
12. _____ 12. thermal
13. _____ 13. symphony
14. _____ 14. microphone
15. _____ 15. chronic
16. _____ 16. program
17. _____ 17. hydrogen
18. _____ 18. dialogue
19. _____ 19. aerial
20. _____ 20. biology

Review Words
21. _____ 21. credit
22. _____ 22. dictionary
23. _____ 23. education

Challenge Words
24. _____ 24. graphic
25. _____ 25. logical

282 Grade 6 • Unit 5 • Week 4

Phonics/Spelling • Word Sort

Name _____

Many English words are of Greek origin. Recognizing Greek roots can help you remember a word's spelling and meaning.

Some common Greek roots include: *aer* (air), *bio* (life), *chron* (time), *gram/graph* (written), *hydr* (water), *log* (word), *micro* (small), *phon* (sound), *scope* (see), and *therm* (heat).

SPELLING TIP

Many Greek roots include the spelling pattern *ph*, which makes the sound /f/. Say the following words: *symphony; microphone*. Can you think of any other words that have the *ph* spelling pattern?

Write the spelling words that contain the Greek root. You will use some words more than once.

thermometer	biography	hydrant	symphony	hydrogen
aerospace	microscope	grammar	microphone	dialogue
diagram	autobiography	catalog	chronic	aerial
paragraph	microwave	thermal	program	biology

graph
1. _____
2. _____
3. _____

aer
4. _____
5. _____

bio
6. _____
7. _____

chron
8. _____

scope
9. _____

gram
10. _____
11. _____
12. _____

log
13. _____
14. _____
15. _____

micro
16. _____

17. _____
18. _____

phon
19. _____
20. _____

hydr
21. _____
22. _____

therm
23. _____
24. _____

Grade 6 • Unit 5 • Week 4 283

Name _____

Spelling • Word Meaning

thermometer	biography	hydrant	symphony	hydrogen
aerospace	microscope	grammar	microphone	dialogue
diagram	autobiography	catalog	chronic	aerial
paragraph	microwave	thermal	program	biology

A. Solve each riddle by writing the correct spelling word.

1. We are a group of people who play musical instruments. _____
2. Scientists use me to see tiny organisms. _____
3. I am something that is written about a famous person. _____
4. People use me when they want to speak to a large audience. _____
5. I heat up food very quickly, but I'm not a large oven. _____
6. I am the study of living things. _____
7. I am a book about me! _____
8. I am a few sentences long and I express a main idea. _____
9. People use me to take their temperature. _____
10. I am given to audience members at a play or concert. _____

B. Write the spelling word that best completes each sentence.

11. With her interest in flight, studying _____ seemed natural.
12. This is a _____ showing how the Statue of Liberty was built.
13. I hope you don't suffer from _____ migraine headaches.
14. We ordered clothing from a _____.
15. The _____ lesson is about adjectives.
16. This play's _____ is superb!
17. The _____ supplies water in case of a fire.
18. People traveling in jets get an _____ view of the country.
19. Our main source of _____ energy is the sun.
20. Did you know that _____ weighs less than other chemical elements?

284 Grade 6 • Unit 5 • Week 4

Spelling • Proofreading

Name _____

There are six misspelled words in the paragraphs below. Underline each misspelled word. Then write the words correctly on the lines.

When you are accepted to college, you will receive a catolog that contains a list of classes you can take. For example, if you are interested in science and technology, you may want to take a biologie class, or one pertaining to the airospace industry.

If you're interested in writing and reading, you could take a literature class. You might study plays and read dialoge with classmates. You might also read a biografie or an audobiografy about a well-known person in history.

1. _____ 2. _____ 3. _____

4. _____ 5. _____ 6. _____

Writing Connection Think about the subjects you would like to study when you go to college. Write about at least two of them. Use four or more words from the spelling list.

_____
_____
_____
_____
_____
_____
_____
_____
_____
_____
_____
_____

Phonics/Spelling • Review

Name _____

Remember

Many English words are of Greek origin. Recognizing Greek roots can help you remember a word's spelling and meaning. For example, if you know the roots *acro* (top; first) and *phobia* (fear), you should be able to determine the spelling and meaning of words like *acrophobia*.

Read the spelling words aloud. Which words share the same Greek roots?

thermometer	biography	hydrant	symphony	hydrogen
aerospace	microscope	grammar	microphone	dialogue
diagram	autobiography	catalog	chronic	aerial
paragraph	microwave	thermal	program	biology

A. Write the missing Greek root to complete the spelling word. Then write the spelling word on the line.

1. cata _____   _____
2. _____ mar   _____
3. _____ ant   _____
4. _____ wave   _____
5. _____ ospace   _____
6. _____ ial   _____
7. dia _____   _____
8. _____ phone   _____
9. _____ ometer   _____
10. para _____   _____
11. _____ al   _____
12. _____ logy   _____
13. dia _____ ue   _____
14. _____ ic   _____
15. _____ ogen   _____
16. sym _____ y   _____
17. pro _____   _____
18. bio _____ y   _____
19. autobio _____ y   _____
20. micro _____   _____

286   Grade 6 • Unit 5 • Week 4

Vocabulary Strategy • Puns and Humor

Name _____

> Writers often use plays on words to introduce humor into stories and other texts. A common example is the **pun**. This device contains homophones, words with different spellings and meanings that sound alike, or homographs, words with the same spelling but different meanings. The similar-sounding words with different meanings create the humor. Here's an example:
>
> The library is incredibly tall—it has many, many stories!
>
> This statement is clever and funny because the homograph *stories* refers to levels of a building, but also to the books that fill the library.

Each sentence below contains a pun. Circle the homograph or homophone that makes the sentence humorous. Sentences may contain a homograph and a homophone.

1. "I'm a little board," said the carpenter.

2. The pony tried to neigh, but it was a little hoarse.

3. My watch was so hungry that it went back four seconds!

4. "You'll have to bear with me," said the Grizzly.

5. The butcher refused to grab the meat on the top shelf; he said the steaks were too high.

6. The garbage can wouldn't take my trash. "I refuse!" it said.

Grade 6 • Unit 5 • Week 4 287

Vocabulary Strategy • Adages and Proverbs

Name _____

Read each passage below from "Following a Star." Using context clues to help you, write a definition of each adage or proverb in bold.

1. Henry walked carefully through the dark woods. He wished he could progress faster, but he recalled his mother's words, **haste makes waste**. It would be dangerous to draw attention to himself.

   _____

2. Suddenly, a twig snapped nearby, and Henry jumped. "Oh, no!" he thought, his heart pounding within his chest. He squeezed his eyes shut tight and told himself, **"A coward dies a thousand deaths; a brave man dies but once."** He turned around, anticipating an angry slave catcher, but instead he saw the worried but friendly face of a boy not much older than himself.

   _____

3. "Follow the North Star, and always be remembering—stay alert, and understand that your very life depends on your actions. Didn't your mama ever tell you **danger foreseen is half avoided?**"

   _____

4. Unsure of what to do, Henry hung his head, and with a heavy sigh he thought of something else his mama used to say, **nothing ventured, nothing gained**. Henry had the experience of being a slave his whole life, and he knew that he just HAD to be free!

   _____

5. Henry looked up at the sky and searched until he found the North Star shining down on him like a ray of promise. **Fortune favors the bold**, thought Henry, and he took off to follow the North Star to freedom.

   _____

Grammar • Comparing With *Good*

Name _____

> Some adjectives form **irregular comparisons**. These are not formed by adding *-er* and *-est* to the end of words or by preceding words with *more* and *most*.
>
> - The adjective *good* is an irregular comparison.
> - The comparative of *good* is *better*. Use *better* to compare two things.
> - The superlative of good is *best*. Use *best* to compare three or more things: *I think Gino's is the best pizza parlor in Springfield, Illinois.*

Rewrite each sentence using the correct comparative or superlative form of the adjective in parentheses ( ).

1. Sometimes the (best, goodest) thing to do is to stand up for what is right.

   _____

2. Mrs. Acosta wants to get a (gooder, better) job.

   _____

3. She also wants the (best, most good) working conditions possible at her workplace.

   _____

4. Mrs. Acosta knows there is a (better, more good) way to manage the business.

   _____

5. She wants the (best, most good) possible work environment for everyone.

   _____

Writing Connection In your writer's notebook, write about your favorite author. Use comparative adjectives to explain why you like his or her books best.

_____

_____

_____

Grammar • Comparing with *Bad*

Name _____

- The adjective *bad* is another irregular comparison.
- The comparative of *bad* is *worse*. Use *worse* to compare two things.
- The superlative of *bad* is *worst*. Use *worst* to compare three or more things.

Read each sentence. Complete the sentence with the correct comparative or superlative form of the adjective *bad*. Then rewrite the sentence correctly.

1. The television program we saw last week was bad, but this one is _____ .

   _____

2. Marina expected it to be bad, but it was much _____ than she expected.

   _____

3. I don't know which was _____, the script or the plot.

   _____

4. In my opinion there is nothing _____ than wasting time on a bad TV show.

   _____

5. Marina thinks it's _____ to spend money on a terrible movie.

   _____

Reading/Writing Connection

Read the sentence from "Tools of the Explorer's Trade" about Polaris. Then compare today's navigation technology with those of the past.

> First, it can only be seen on clear nights, so attempting to navigate through unknown waters on a cloudy night could be catastrophic.

_____

_____

_____

290 Grade 6 • Unit 5 • Week 5

Name _____

Grammar • Mechanics: Irregular Comparative Forms

- The adjectives *good, well, bad, many, much,* and *less* all form irregular comparisons.
- *Good* and *well* have the same comparative and superlative forms: *better* and *best.*
- *Many* and *much* have the same comparative and superlative forms: *more* and *most.*
- The comparative and superlative forms of *bad* are *worse* and *worst.* The comparative and superlative forms of *less* are *lesser* and *least.*

Rewrite each sentence below using the correct comparative or superlative form in parentheses ( ).

1. Kai has not been feeling well, but she hopes to feel (best, better) soon.

   _____

2. Cameron has many rocks in his collection, but Audrey has (more, most).

   _____

3. Elliot has the (least, less) experience of any of the players on the team.

   _____

4. I have very little time to play today, but tomorrow I have even (less, least) time.

   _____

5. Yesterday's game was bad, but today's is (worse, worst).

   _____

6. After a good night's sleep, Rodrigo always feels his (better, best).

   _____

In your writer's notebook write about a class that you would like to take. Think about a new topic that is not offered at your school. Explain why you would like to take this class.

Grammar • Proofreading

Name _____

> - Some adjectives form **irregular comparisons**. These are not formed by adding *-er* and *-est* to the end of words or by preceding words with *more* and *most*.
> - The adjectives *good, well, bad, many,* and *much* all form irregular comparisons.
> - The comparative and superlative forms of *good* and *well* are *better* and *best*. The comparative and superlative forms of *bad* are *worse* and *worst*.
> - The comparative and superlative forms of *many* and *much* are *more* and *most*. The comparative and superlative forms of *less* are *lesser* and *least*.

Proofread each sentence of the dialogue below. Then rewrite the sentence correctly. Watch for errors in comparative and superlative adjectives and in punctuation.

1. "Are you feeling gooder today, Jody? asked Mother.

   _____

2. I'm still not feeling my wellest, but I felt much badder yesterday. answered Jody

   _____

3. I hope you got manier hours of sleep last night than the night before, said Mother.

   _____
   _____

4. I did Jody said, I got much gooder sleep last night.

   _____

5. get the muchest rest you can, and tomorrow you will feel weller, said Mother

   _____

English: Grammar • **Apply**

Name _____

What was your favorite reading selection or other text you read this week? Write a paragraph describing what you learned from it or why you enjoyed it. When you're done, exchange your writing with a partner. Proofread your partner's writing. Remember to apply the grammar you have learned this week.

Spelling • Suffixes *-ive*, *-age*, and *-ize*

Name _____

Fold back the paper along the dotted line. Use the blanks to write each word as it is read aloud. When you finish the test, unfold the paper. Use the list at the right to correct any spelling mistakes.

1. _____ 1. percentage
2. _____ 2. explosive
3. _____ 3. recognize
4. _____ 4. passage
5. _____ 5. sympathize
6. _____ 6. modernize
7. _____ 7. positive
8. _____ 8. vocalize
9. _____ 9. emphasize
10. _____ 10. organize
11. _____ 11. creative
12. _____ 12. storage
13. _____ 13. advantage
14. _____ 14. attractive
15. _____ 15. negative
16. _____ 16. criticize
17. _____ 17. wreckage
18. _____ 18. specialize
19. _____ 19. realize
20. _____ 20. secretive

Review Words
21. _____ 21. paragraph
22. _____ 22. grammar
23. _____ 23. microscope

Challenge Words
24. _____ 24. progressive
25. _____ 25. scrutinize

Phonics/Spelling • **Word Sort**

Name _____

A suffix is a group of letters added to the end of a word that changes the word's meaning or part of speech. Knowing the meanings of the most common suffixes can help you to understand new words.

- The suffix *-ive* means **having the nature of** (*secretive*). The suffix *-ize* means **become** (*modernize*).

- The suffix *-age* can mean **collective** (*percentage*), **action/process** (*manage*), **result of** (*damage*), or **house/place** of (*cottage*).

Read the words with suffixes below.

SPELLING TIP

Before the suffix *-ive* or *-ize* can be added to a word that ends in *-e* or *-y*, that letter must be dropped. For example, in the word *creative*, the *-e* was dropped from the word *create* in order to add the suffix. In the word *sympathize*, the *-y* in *sympathy* had to be dropped before adding the suffix.

Write the spelling words that contain the suffix.

percentage	sympathize	emphasize	advantage	wreckage
explosive	modernize	organize	attractive	specialize
recognize	positive	creative	negative	realize
passage	vocalize	storage	criticize	secretive

-ive

1. _____
2. _____
3. _____
4. _____
5. _____
6. _____

-age

7. _____
8. _____
9. _____
10. _____
11. _____

-ize

12. _____

13. _____
14. _____
15. _____
16. _____
17. _____
18. _____
19. _____
20. _____

Grade 6 • Unit 5 • Week 5   295

Spelling • Word Meaning

Name _____

percentage	sympathize	emphasize	advantage	wreckage
explosive	modernize	organize	attractive	specialize
recognize	positive	creative	negative	realize
passage	vocalize	storage	criticize	secretive

A. Write the spelling word that goes with each word history.

1. *kritikos*: Greek; "able to judge" _____

2. *réaliser*: French; "to bring into existence" _____

3. *positivus*: Latin; "certain" _____

4. *explodere*: Latin; "scare off; drive offstage by clapping" _____

B. Write the spelling word that best completes each sentence.

5. Jamie's friends were very _____ about his surprise party.

6. I _____ with Ana about the loss of her cat.

7. The _____ from the accident was extensive.

8. The manager will _____ the importance of the sale tomorrow.

9. A _____ of what the company makes will go to charity.

10. One _____ our team has is that every player is strong.

11. We were asked to be _____ when writing our stories.

12. The film star wore a very _____ dress to the awards ceremony.

13. The architect will _____ the building to fit its new purpose.

14. I will _____ the books alphabetically by author's last name.

15. No one likes to receive _____ comments.

16. Does the doctor _____ in treating ear, nose, and throat problems?

17. Each spring, we put our winter clothing in _____.

18. The _____ is brightly lit and safe to walk through at night.

19. I didn't _____ my long-lost friend until I heard her voice.

20. The singer will _____ to prepare for this evening's performance.

296 Grade 6 • Unit 5 • Week 5

Spelling • Proofreading

Name _____

There are five misspelled words in the paragraphs below. Underline each misspelled word. Then write the words correctly on the lines.

Some children have the advantige of learning a skill or craft from their parents. For example, if a parent is creatave and works as a singer or actor, the parent may teach the child how to vocalise or act at an early age.

For some children, this posative experience can turn into a career when they grow up. In other cases, an acting coach or music teacher may recugnise that a child has talent and recommend to the parent that the child take acting or voice lessons.

1. _____ 2. _____ 3. _____

4. _____ 5. _____

Writing Connection — **Write about something you might like to do as a career. Use at least four words from the spelling list.**

_____
_____
_____
_____
_____
_____
_____
_____
_____
_____
_____

Phonics/Spelling • Review

Name _____

> **Remember**
>
> A suffix is a group of letters added to the end of a word. It changes the base word's meaning or part of speech. Knowing the meanings of the most common suffixes can help you to understand new words.
>
> - The suffix **-ive** means **having the nature of** (*perspective*).
> - The suffix **-ize** means **become** (*specialize*).
> - The suffix **-age** can mean **collective** (*package*), **action/process** (*salvage*), **result of** (*breakage*), or **house/place of** (*cottage*).
>
> Read these words aloud. Then determine their meaning using your knowledge of suffixes.

Fill in the missing suffix to form a spelling word. Then write the spelling word on the line.

1. secre _____   _____
2. sympath _____   _____
3. wreck _____   _____
4. emphas _____   _____
5. special _____   _____
6. percent _____   _____
8. real _____   _____
7. vocal _____   _____
9. organ _____   _____
10. advant _____   _____

11. creat _____   _____
12. modern _____   _____
13. critic _____   _____
14. posit _____   _____
15. stor _____   _____
16. recogn _____   _____
17. attract _____   _____
18. explos _____   _____
19. negat _____   _____
20. pass _____   _____

Grade 6 • Unit 5 • Week 5

Vocabulary • Content Words

Name _____

Content words are words that are specific to a field of study. For example, words such as *technology* and *latitude* are social studies content words.

Authors use content words to explain a concept or idea. Sometimes you can figure out what a content word means by using context clues. You can also use a dictionary to help you find the meaning of unfamiliar content words.

Go on a word hunt with a partner through "Tools of the Explorer's Trade." Find content words related to social studies and exploration. Write them on the lines below.

CONNECT TO CONTENT

"Tools of the Explorer's Trade" teaches the reader about technology used for navigation in the past and present. Some technology from the past is obsolete now. However, tools such as the sextant, wheel, and compass are still used today. Improvements to these technologies have been made, but the original use for the tool remains the same.

Pick two words that you were able to define by using context clues. Write the words and what they mean on the lines.

_____
_____
_____
_____
_____

Grade 6 • Unit 5 • Week 5   299

Vocabulary Strategy • Connotations and Denotations

Name _____

Read each sentence from "Hurtling Through Space from Home." Then explain how the tone of the sentence would change if the words in bold were replaced with the words in parentheses.

1. Other programs let you **soar** through the universe from home like an astronaut. (fly)

   _____
   _____

2. From the world's largest map to flight simulations, this space **exploration** can be a lot of fun. (research)

   _____
   _____

3. They want to know how it feels to guide a spacecraft through our **vast** solar system. (big)

   _____
   _____

4. Celestia is another piece of free software that provides the **experience** of exploring our galaxy but will not be in the cockpit for this virtual adventure. (activity)

   _____
   _____

5. Bruce Irving is one of NASA's Solar System **Ambassadors**. (Representatives)

   _____
   _____

Grammar • **Adverbs**

Name _____

- An **adverb** modifies a verb, an adjective, or another adverb.

    He walked _slowly_.
- Adverbs can come before or after the verbs they modify.
- Adverbs can tell when, where, how, or to what extent.
- Many adverbs are formed by adding –ly to adjectives. However, not all words ending in –ly are adverbs, and some adverbs do not end in –ly.

    Yesterday our family _excitedly_ moved to a new home. _Now_ we can _easily_ walk to school.

Underline the adverb in each sentence below.

1. The alarm clock by Jonathan's bed rang loudly.

2. Jonathan immediately silenced the alarm.

3. He hurriedly threw back the covers and jumped to his feet.

4. Jonathan was especially eager to start the day.

5. The morning of the school spelling bee had finally arrived.

6. Jonathan dressed quickly and joined his family for breakfast.

7. They talked excitedly about the day ahead.

8. Jonathan said he was very prepared for the competition.

9. He said he had studied the spelling words thoroughly.

10. Jonathan's family warmly wished him luck in the spelling bee.

In your writer's notebook finish the story about Jonathan and the spelling bee. Use adverbs to describe what happened during his day at school. Proofread your work for correct adverb usage.

Grammar • Intensifiers

Name _____

> - When an adverb modifies an adjective or another adverb, it is often used for emphasis or intensity. Such adverbs are called **intensifiers**.
> - Intensifiers such as *very, just, quite, rather, so, too,* and *somewhat* clarify the extent of something. Intensifiers are positions before words they modify.
>
>   *New York City is <u>very</u> busy with <u>so</u> many tourists visiting each day.*

Read each sentence. Underline the intensifier. Write the adverb or adjective it modifies on the line provided.

1. Maura knows Alexandra quite well. _____

2. They have been friends for a very long time. _____

3. Alexandra lives just down the street from Maura. _____

4. The girls walk to school together rather often. _____

5. Maura is always so happy to see Alexandra again after school. _____

6. The two friends have an extremely good time together. _____

Reading/Writing Connection — Read the paragraph from "The Fortunes of Fragrance." Underline the adverbs. Then use one of the adverbs in your own sentence.

> Synthetic fragrance chemicals are derived primarily from petroleum. They are usually less expensive than natural materials, because supplies are not affected by weather conditions or crop yields.

_____
_____
_____

302 Grade 6 • Unit 6 • Week 1

Grammar • Mechanics: **Adjectives vs. Adverbs**

Name _____

- *Good* is used as an adjective to describe nouns.
- *Well* can be used as an adjective or adverb.
- *Well* is an adverb when it tells how ably something is done.
- *Well* is an adjective when it means "in good health."

Read the sentences below. Fill in the blank using good or well correctly.

1. The students have a _____ idea for a mural in the school cafeteria.

2. They want to show how important it is to eat as _____ as possible.

3. Eating a variety of nutritious foods is a _____ way to stay healthy.

4. Fresh fruits and vegetables are always _____ choices.

5. Most people don't feel _____ when they eat poorly.

6. It is a _____ idea to avoid non-nutritious snack foods.

7. This wall looks like a _____ spot for the mural.

8. You can see it quite _____ when you walk into the cafeteria.

9. The mural will help remind people to eat _____ and choose wisely.

In your writer's notebook, write a short passage about something you do really well and something you want to do better. Edit your work for the correct use of *good* and *well*.

Grammar • Proofreading

Name _____

- An **adverb** modifies a verb, an adjective, or another adverb.
- Adverbs can tell when, where, how, or to what extent.
- Many adverbs are formed by adding *–ly* to adjectives.
- Not all words ending in *–ly* are adverbs, and some adverbs do not end in *–ly*.
- When an adverb modifies an adjective or another adverb, it is often used to emphasize or intensify the meaning. Such adverbs are called **intensifiers**.
- Intensifiers such as *very, just, quite, rather, so, too,* and *somewhat* clarify the extent of something.
- *Good* is used as an adjective. *Well* can be used as an adjective or adverb.

The writer of the directions below did not proofread for errors. Read the directions. Then rewrite the directions, correcting any errors in the use of adverbs and in the use of *good* and *well*.

How to make a fruit smoothie:

- First, pour careful one-half cup of very cold milk into a blender.
- Next, add one ripely banana and one cup of any frozen fruit. Blackberries, raspberries, and strawberries are well choices.
- Blend the ingredients good.
- When your smoothie is mixed together thorough, pour it into a tall glass and enjoy!

_____
_____
_____
_____
_____

304 Grade 6 • Unit 6 • Week 1

English: Grammar • **Apply**

Name _____

What was your favorite reading selection or other text you read this week? Write a paragraph describing what you learned from it or why you enjoyed it. When you're done, exchange your writing with a partner. Proofread your partner's writing. Remember to apply the grammar you have learned this week.

Spelling • Suffixes -ible and -able

Name _____

Fold back the paper along the dotted line. Use the blanks to write each word as it is read aloud. When you finish the test, unfold the paper. Use the list at the right to correct any spelling mistakes.

1. _____
2. _____
3. _____
4. _____
5. _____
6. _____
7. _____
8. _____
9. _____
10. _____
11. _____
12. _____
13. _____
14. _____
15. _____
16. _____
17. _____
18. _____
19. _____
20. _____

Review Words
21. _____
22. _____
23. _____

Challenge Words
24. _____
25. _____

1. terrible
2. audible
3. valuable
4. reliable
5. lovable
6. available
7. horrible
8. believable
9. impossible
10. predictable
11. remarkable
12. reversible
13. changeable
14. noticeable
15. acceptable
16. probable
17. admirable
18. dependable
19. profitable
20. considerable
21. recognize
22. positive
23. percentage
24. eligible
25. legible

Phonics/Spelling • Word Sort

Name _____

A suffix is a group of letters added to the end of a word that changes the word's meaning or part of speech. The suffixes *-ible* and *-able* mean "can be done."

- collect + ible = collectible: can be collected
- depend + able = dependable: can be depended on

Read the spelling words aloud. Listen carefully to each syllable.

SPELLING TIP BOX

When *-ible* or *-able* is added to a word that ends in *e*, the *e* is usually dropped before the suffix is added: *reverse/reversible, believe/believable*. Some exceptions to this rule are *noticeable* and *changeable*.

Read the words in the box. Write the spelling words that contain the suffix.

terrible	lovable	impossible	changeable	admirable
audible	available	predictable	noticeable	dependable
valuable	horrible	remarkable	acceptable	profitable
reliable	believable	reversible	probable	considerable

-ible

1. _____
2. _____
3. _____
4. _____
5. _____

-able

6. _____
7. _____
8. _____
9. _____
10. _____
11. _____
12. _____
13. _____
14. _____
15. _____
16. _____
17. _____
18. _____
19. _____
20. _____

Look through this week's selections for more words with the suffixes *-ible* and *-able*. Create a word sort for a partner in your writer's notebook.

Spelling • Word Meaning

Name _____

terrible	lovable	impossible	changeable	admirable
audible	available	predictable	noticeable	dependable
valuable	horrible	remarkable	acceptable	profitable
reliable	believable	reversible	probable	considerable

A. Write the spelling word that is an antonym of the word listed.

1. constant _____
2. untrustworthy _____
3. inconspicuous _____
4. ordinary _____
5. inaccessible _____
6. unconvincing _____
7. insignificant _____
8. achievable _____
9. unlikely _____
10. worthless _____

B. Write the spelling word that best completes each sentence.

11. The adjective form of the noun *terror* is _____.
12. Sophie proved she was _____ when she babysat each weekend.
13. The recording was not _____ until he turned up the volume.
14. Jake spent a _____ Thursday night studying for his weekly test.
15. He bought the _____ coat because he liked both sides of it.
16. After the school clean-up, did the gym look _____ to the principal?
17. The neighbors' efforts to help after the hurricane were _____.
18. It was a _____ drive home in the ice storm.
19. The family thought the puppy was so cute and _____!
20. The company was _____, so the owner felt confident.

Spelling • Proofreading

Name _____

There are four misspelled words in the first paragraph and three in the second. Underline each one. Then write the words correctly on the lines.

There are many people who spend a considerable amount of time collecting objects. For example, some car enthusiasts have remarckable collections of antique vehicles. Other people search for valueable rare stamps and coins. Many of these stamps and coins would be extremely profetable if sold. However, collectors seldom want to break up their collections.

1. _____ 2. _____ 3. _____

4. _____

Yesterday, the principal announced that my poem was eligable for the Milford County Young Poets prize. Only a small percentidge of students from my school were nominated for the prize. My poem is about my loveable golden retriever. I hope I win!

5. _____ 6. _____ 7. _____

Writing Connection Write about something you have read about in the newspaper or seen on a television news show. Use at least four words from the spelling list.

_____
_____
_____
_____
_____
_____
_____
_____

Phonics/Spelling • **Review**

Name _____

> **Remember**
>
> The suffixes *-ible* and *-able* mean "can be done."
> - *collapse + ible = collapsible* (drop the *e*): *can be collapsed*
> - *favor + able = favorable: can be favored*
>
> As you read each spelling word aloud, think about how the suffix changes the meaning of the base word.

terrible	lovable	impossible	changeable	admirable
audible	available	predictable	noticeable	dependable
valuable	horrible	remarkable	acceptable	profitable
reliable	believable	reversible	probable	considerable

Fill in the missing letters of each word to form a spelling word. Then write the spelling word on the line.

1. lov ___ ___ le _____
2. avai ___ ___ ble _____
3. val ___ ___ ___ le _____
4. rever ___ ___ ble _____
5. ter ___ ___ ble _____
6. chang ___ ab ___ e _____
7. consid ___ r ___ ble _____
8. remark ___ b ___ e _____
9. impos ___ ___ ble _____
10. predi ___ ___ ___ ble _____
11. accept ___ ___ le _____
12. noti ___ e ___ ble _____
13. relia ___ l ___ _____
14. prob ___ bl ___ _____
15. aud ___ bl ___ _____
16. admi ___ ___ ble _____
17. depend ___ b ___ e _____
18. belie ___ ___ ble _____
19. profita ___ ___ e _____
20. hor ___ ib ___ e _____

310 Grade 6 • Unit 6 • Week 1

Vocabulary • Content Words

Name _____

Content words are words that are specific to a field of study. For example, words like *chemicals*, *identify*, and *fragrance* are science content words.

Authors use content words to explain a concept or idea. Sometimes you can figure out what a content word means by using context clues. You can also use a dictionary to help you find the meaning of unfamiliar content words.

Go on a word hunt with a partner through "The Fortunes of Fragrance." Find content words related to science. Write them in the chart.

_____ _____ _____

_____ _____ _____

_____ _____ _____

CONNECT TO CONTENT

"The Fortunes of Fragrance" gives facts about the history of capturing fragrance across the world. The author writes chronologically to show how the business of perfume has changed. It is important to understand that perfume and other fragrances are just as popular in the past as today.

Circle two words that you were able to figure out the meaning of using context clues. Write the words and what they mean on the lines.

_____
_____
_____
_____
_____

Grade 6 • Unit 6 • Week 1   311

Vocabulary • Spiral Review

Name _____

Read the clues. Complete the puzzle with the vocabulary words. Then write the letters in the boxes to solve the riddle. Use a dictionary if you need help.

undaunted	elevating	application	disposed
obsolete	deployed	retaliation	computations
fortitude	catastrophic	subsequently	magnetic

1. sudden and disastrous
2. distributed for a specific purpose
3. not afraid
4. act of putting something to use
5. striking back to get even
6. following in time or order
7. mathematic calculations
8. raising higher
9. inclined to do something
10. mental strength
11. attracting metal objects
12. out of date

What was the first food eaten by an American astronaut in space?

312 Grade 6 • Unit 6 • Week 1

Grammar • Adverbs That Compare

Name _____

- **Comparative adverbs** compare two actions.
- Form the comparative by adding *-er* to most one-syllable adverbs and some two-syllable adverbs: *louder, wilder, earlier.*
- For most adverbs of two or more syllables, add *more* to form the comparative: *more thoughtfully, more gracefully, more delicately.*

    Alexis spelled the words more carefully than all the other students in the spelling bee.

Write the comparative of each of the following adverbs.

1. soon _____ 4. safely _____

2. quietly _____ 5. straight _____

3. easily _____ 6. calmly _____

Underline the comparative form of the adverb that correctly completes each sentence.

7. The pole-vaulter from our school jumped (higher, more highly) than anyone else jumped at the track meet.

8. The person who can sprint (more fast, faster) than Yosef can, will probably win the race.

9. The crowd cheers (more enthusiastically, enthusiasticer) every time Selena comes around the track.

10. Jed throws the discus (powerfuller, more powerfully) than Henry does.

Write a paragraph in your writer's notebook about a superhero power you wish you could have. Include at least three comparison adverbs. Edit your work for correct adverb usage.

Grade 6 • Unit 6 • Week 2   313

Grammar • Superlative Adverbs

Name _____

> - The **superlative** of an adverb compares more than two actions. It is formed by adding *-est* to most adverbs of one syllable and some adverbs of two syllables.
> - Add *most* or *the most* to adverbs of two or more syllables.
>   *Of all the gymnasts on the team, Abigail performs the <u>most</u> <u>artistically</u>.*

Write the superlative form of each of the following adverbs.

1. loud _____
2. gracefully _____
3. happily _____
4. certainly _____

Rewrite each sentence using the correct superlative form of the adverbs in parentheses.

5. Of all the choir members, Sergio sings (naturally).
   _____

6. Quinten may not be the best singer, but he performs (energetically).
   _____

7. Tyrell sings (low) of all the baritones.
   _____

8. Heidi projects her voice (powerfully).
   _____

Reading/Writing Connection

Read this sentence from "The Not-So-Golden Touch." Underline the adverbs. Then write your own sentence using one of the words you underlined.

> Midas raised one finger, tentatively reached over to touch the small table beside his bed, and miraculously it turned to gold!

_____
_____

314 Grade 6 • Unit 6 • Week 2

Grammar • Mechanics: **Comparative and Superlatives**

Name _____

- When using the comparative form of an adverb in a sentence, be sure that two actions are being compared.
- Be sure that your sentence is comparing more than two actions when you use the superlative form of an adverb.
- To form a negative comparison, use the adverbs *less* and *least*.
   This puppy barks less loudly than that one. But this one barks the least loudly of all the puppies in the litter.

A. Read each pair of sentences. Draw an X by the one that uses a comparative or superlative adjective correctly.

1. My sister can swim fastest than her best friend. _____

   My sister can swim faster than her best friend. _____

2. She dives the more skillfully of all her friends, too. _____

   She dives the most skillfully of all her friends, too. _____

3. My brother sleeps more soundly than my sister. _____

   My brother sleeps most soundly than my sister. _____

4. He also snores the loudest of all. _____

   He also snores the louder of all. _____

B. Rewrite each sentence by writing the words in parentheses that form the correct negative comparison.

5. My dog barks (less often, least often) than Zoey's dog.

   _____

6. Zoey's dog is the (less friendly, least friendly) dog in the neighborhood.

   _____

In your writer's notebook, write a short paragraph describing an experience that turned out better than you expected. Include at least five comparative adverbs. Edit your work for correct adverb usage.

Grammar • Proofreading

Name _____

- **Comparative adverbs** compare two actions.
- Form the comparative by adding *-er* to most one-syllable adverbs and some two-syllable adverbs.
- For most adverbs of two or more syllables, add *more* to form the comparative.
- The **superlative** of an adverb compares more than two actions. It is formed by adding *-est* to most adverbs of one syllable and some adverbs of two syllables.
- Add *most,* or *the most* to adverbs of two or more syllables.
- To form a negative comparison, use the adverbs *less* and *least.*

The writer of these survey questions did not check his or her use of adverbs. Rewrite the questions, making sure that comparative and superlative adverbs are used correctly.

1. Of the two classrooms, which one looks largest?

   _____

2. Among the students in our class, who helps others more often?

   _____

3. Which of the two musicals from last year was least memorable?

   _____

4. Which student draws most realistically, Timothy or Bryce?

   _____

5. In your opinion, who is the faster runner in the entire sixth grade?

   _____

English: Grammar • **Apply**

Name _____

What was your favorite reading selection or other text you read this week? Write a paragraph describing what you learned from it or why you enjoyed it. When you're done, exchange your writing with a partner. Proofread your partner's writing. Remember to apply the grammar you have learned this week.

_____
_____
_____
_____
_____
_____
_____
_____
_____
_____
_____
_____
_____
_____

Spelling • Suffixes -ance, -ence, -ant, and -ent

Name _____

Fold back the paper along the dotted line. Use the blanks to write each word as it is read aloud. When you finish the test, unfold the paper. Use the list at the right to correct any spelling mistakes.

1. _____
2. _____
3. _____
4. _____
5. _____
6. _____
7. _____
8. _____
9. _____
10. _____
11. _____
12. _____
13. _____
14. _____
15. _____
16. _____
17. _____
18. _____
19. _____
20. _____

Review Words

21. _____
22. _____
23. _____

Challenge Words

24. _____
25. _____

1. experience
2. conference
3. persistent
4. acquaintance
5. important
6. permanent
7. disappearance
8. fragrance
9. president
10. occurrence
11. intelligent
12. observant
13. constant
14. nuisance
15. violence
16. evident
17. incident
18. defiance
19. excellent
20. hesitant
21. terrible
22. noticeable
23. profitable
24. elegance
25. diligent

Phonics/Spelling • Word Sort

Name _____

The suffixes *-ance* and *-ence* mean "an action or act" or "the state of." Adding these suffixes to a base word or root creates a noun: *disappear + ance = disappearance*.

Sometimes adding *-ance* or *-ence* changes the base word: *defy → defiance* (change *y* to *i*).

The suffixes *-ant* and *-ent* mean "performing a specified action" or "being in a specified condition." Many words that end in *-ance* or *-ence* are related to adjectives that end with *-ant* or *-ent*: *defiance* is related to *defiant*.

SPELLING TIP BOX

Adding suffixes can change the pronunciation of a word. For example, the /t/ in *excellent* changes to /s/ when adding *-ence* to form *excellence*. Use knowledge of adding suffixes to sound out each word.

Read the words in the box. Write the spelling words that contain the suffix.

experience	important	president	constant	incident
conference	permanent	occurrence	nuisance	defiance
persistent	disappearance	intelligent	violence	excellent
acquaintance	fragrance	observant	evident	hesitant

-ance
1. _____
2. _____
3. _____
4. _____
5. _____

-ence
6. _____

7. _____
8. _____
9. _____

-ant
10. _____
11. _____
12. _____
13. _____

-ent
14. _____
15. _____
16. _____
17. _____
18. _____
19. _____
20. _____

Look through this week's selections for more words with suffixes to sort. Record them in your writer's notebook. Make a word sort for a partner. Read the words aloud.

Spelling • Word Meaning

Name _____

experience	important	president	constant	incident
conference	permanent	occurrence	nuisance	defiance
persistent	disappearance	intelligent	violence	excellent
acquaintance	fragrance	observant	evident	hesitant

A. Read the sentence starter below. Then fill in each blank with the correct spelling word.

Another word for

1. *significant* is _____

2. *indecisive* is _____

3. *aroma* is _____

4. *attentive* is _____

5. *annoyance* is _____

Another word for

6. *meeting* is _____

7. *superior* is _____

8. *lasting* is _____

9. *unvarying* is _____

10. *smart* is _____

B. Write the spelling word that best completes each sentence.

11. Did your _____ playing baseball help you run faster?

12. Since the _____ of my gloves, my hands have been cold.

13. Jane is a _____ math student. She never gives up.

14. The jaywalker acted in _____ of the law.

15. My father met an old _____ on the train.

16. This natural _____ in space happens only once a decade.

17. It was _____ that the main street needed repair.

18. There was a traffic _____ on a corner by the school.

19. Unfortunately, the news was filled with too much _____.

20. The _____ scheduled a speech for Tuesday.

320 Grade 6 • Unit 6 • Week 2

Spelling • Proofreading

Name _____

There are eight misspelled words in the student speech. Underline each one. Then write the words correctly on the lines.

To the students of Morris Middle School,

I am running for sixth grade class presidant! To some of you, I might just be an acquaintence, but I hope to become a trusting friend to each student in our grade. I have expereince representing my peers because I was a class representative in fifth grade. I am a diligant student and I am pursistant when I encounter any difficult situation. My hope is to have a confurance with our principal and vice principal monthly to make sure there is constent communication between them and the student government. Make an excelant choice, and vote for me: Milan Johnson!

1. _____   4. _____   7. _____

2. _____   5. _____   8. _____

3. _____   6. _____

Writing Connection — **Write about a time you had to speak or perform in front of a lot of people. Use at least four words from the spelling list.**

_____
_____
_____
_____
_____
_____
_____
_____
_____

Grade 6 • Unit 6 • Week 2

Phonics/Spelling • **Review**

Name _____

Remember

Adding the suffixes -*ance* and -*ence* to a base word or root creates a noun: correspond + *ence* = *correspondence*.

Sometimes adding -*ance* or -*ence* changes the base word: *rely* → *reliance* (change y to i).

Many words that end in -*ance* or -*ence* are related to adjectives that end with -*ant* or -*ent*: *significance* is related to *significant*.

Read each word aloud. Can you think of a related word?

experience	important	president	constant	incident
conference	permanent	occurrence	nuisance	defiance
persistent	disappearance	intelligent	violence	excellent
acquaintance	fragrance	observant	evident	hesitant

Fill in the missing suffix to form a spelling word. Then write the spelling word on the line.

1. persist _____ _____
2. occur _____ _____
3. observ _____ _____
4. nuis _____ _____
5. hesit _____ _____
6. experi _____ _____
7. confer _____ _____
8. presid _____ _____
9. disappear _____ _____
10. excell _____ _____
11. intellig _____ _____
12. fragr _____ _____
13. defi _____ _____
14. const _____ _____
15. evid _____ _____
16. perman _____ _____
17. import _____ _____
18. viol _____ _____
19. incid _____ _____
20. acquaint _____ _____

322 Grade 6 • Unit 6 • Week 2

Vocabulary Strategy • Greek and Latin Affixes

Name _____

> Prefixes and suffixes are added to the beginning or end of a word to change that word's meaning. Many of these affixes, like word roots, come from ancient Greek and Latin. Knowing the meaning of the affix can help you define an unfamiliar word. Here are some common **Greek and Latin affixes**:
>
> *anti-* (Greek) "against"　　　　*-ary* (Latin) "place for"
>
> *equi-* (Latin) "equal"　　　　*-ism* (Latin) "practice or system of"
>
> *mega-* (Greek) "large"　　　　*-ist* (Latin) "one who practices"
>
> *multi-* (Latin) "many"　　　　*-ology* (Greek) "study of"
>
> *neo-* (Greek) "new"　　　　*-ous* (Latin) "full of"
>
> *semi-* (Latin) "half"　　　　*-tion* (Latin) "state or quality of"

Circle the word in parentheses that best completes each sentence below. Then write a definition for the word. Use the meanings of the Greek and Latin affixes above to help you.

1. The library happens to be (multidistant, equidistant, neodistant) from my house and the school.

   _____

2. The three long-separated sisters had a (joyous, joyist, joyary) reunion.

   _____

3. Jill is a (columnism, columnous, columnist) for the local newspaper, so she always knows what's going on around town.

   _____

4. This cheerful painting with colorful shapes is a good example of an artistic style known as (expressionism, expressionary, expressionology).

   _____

5. This unique restaurant has a (semicultural, multicultural, anticultural) menu with foods from all over the world.

   _____

6. The singer sold ten million records and became a (semistar, equistar, megastar) overnight.

   _____

Grade 6 • Unit 6 • Week 2

Vocabulary Strategy • Latin Roots

Name _____

Read each sentence from "Harnessing the Sun's Energy." Use the chart below to help you figure out the meaning of each word in bold. Then write the root of each word and a new sentence using that word.

Latin Root	Meaning
flec, flex	bend, break
ology	study or science of
scrib, scrip	write
vert, vers	turn
sign	sign

1. Many ancient people found ways to harness solar power by **converting**, or turning, sunlight into thermal energy (heat).

   root: _____

   sentence: _____

2. Greeks and Romans used the Sun's **reflection** on mirrors to light torches.

   root: _____

   sentence: _____

3. Solar **technology** is not new, yet we continue to learn ways to harness the sun's power.

   root: _____

   sentence: _____

4. In 1905, Albert Einstein **described** the details of this process.

   root: _____

   sentence: _____

5. New **designs** in windows, skylights, and even roof shingles help homeowners use the Sun's energy directly.

   root: _____

   sentence: _____

324 Grade 6 • Unit 6 • Week 2

Grammar • Negatives

Name _____

- A **negative** is a word that means no.
- A common negative is **not**. Not can appear in contractions as *n't*.
- Other common negatives are *nobody, nowhere, nothing, never,* and *neither*.
I can't go to the carnival because I'm sick. Nobody wants to catch my cold!

Underline each negative, including contractions with *not*, in the sentences below.

1. Mr. Aldoni was not happy with the pot of soup he made.
2. "I don't think the soup is flavorful enough," he said.
3. He tried adding more spices, but nothing made it taste better.
4. "Nowhere can I find the recipe I used the last time I made this soup," he said.
5. Sami tasted his uncle's soup and said, "There is no paprika in it."
6. "I can't believe I forgot the paprika!" cried Mr. Aldoni.
7. "Neither can I!" exclaimed Sami.
8. Sami's uncle added the paprika and said he would never forget it again.
9. They tasted the soup and agreed nobody would recognize the mistake.
10. "No one makes a soup as delicious as you do." said Sami.

Reading/Writing Connection

Read this paragraph from "Messages in Stone and Wood" and underline the negatives. Then write two sentences of your own that each contain a negative.

At first, no one understood the meanings of these mysterious *petroglyphs* (stone carvings) and *dendroglyphs* (tree carvings and paintings). Nor did they know who had created them.

_____

_____

Grade 6 • Unit 6 • Week 3   325

Grammar • Double Negatives

Name _____

> - A **double negative** occurs when two negatives within a clause cancel each other. *I didn't go nowhere. (incorrect) I didn't go anywhere. (correct)*
> - Sentences containing multiple clauses can have more than one negative, so long as they do not cancel each other.
>   *I haven't done anything to prepare for the test. (Or: I have done nothing to prepare for the test.)*

Each sentence below contains more than one negative. Put brackets [ ] around the negative words. If the sentence contains a double negative within a clause, correctly rewrite the sentence by removing one negative. If the negatives do not cancel each other, and the sentence is correct, write C.

1. Cole wants to play baseball but he does not have no time to practice.

   _____

2. Coach Hicks will not let students play if they can't get to practice by 3:30.

   _____

3. Coach says it's a school rule, and he can't do nothing about it.

   _____

4. Cole cannot get there until 4:30, so he won't be able to play.

   _____

5. Cole doesn't not know what to do.

   _____

6. He might not never get to play baseball this year.

   _____

> In your writer's notebook, write a recipe for a food you like to make. Try to use three negatives in your instructions. Then read your recipe to a friend.

326 Grade 6 • Unit 6 • Week 3

Grammar • Mechanics: Correcting Double Negatives

Name _____

- Fix a double negative by changing one of the negatives to its positive equivalent.
- Some negatives and their positive equivalents are never/ever and no/any.
- The words hardly, scarcely, and barely are also negatives.
- If no precedes a noun, you often can change it to *a* or *an*.

   It is not never good to be unprepared for class. (incorrect)

   It is never good to be unprepared for class. (correct)

Rewrite each sentence on the line so that it does not contain a double negative. Change or remove words as needed.

1. It was so rainy and foggy we couldn't barely see in front of us.
   _____

2. It is not never safe to travel in the fog.
   _____

3. We couldn't hardly tell if anyone else was on the highway.
   _____

4. Not nobody was more worried than Mother was.
   _____

5. "There is not no exit for miles," she said.
   _____

6. We would not have never left the house if we had heard the weather forecast.
   _____

7. Mother couldn't scarcely believe it when we finally saw an exit.
   _____

Grade 6 • Unit 6 • Week 3   **327**

Grammar • Proofreading

Name _____

> - A **negative** is a word that means no. Common negatives are *not (n't), nobody, nowhere, nothing, never,* and *neither.*
> - A double negative occurs when two negatives within a clause cancel each other. Sentences with multiple clauses can have more than one negative, so long as they do not cancel each other.
> - Fix a double negative by changing one of the negatives to its positive equivalent. Some negatives and their positive equivalents are *never/ever* and *no/any.* The words *hardly, scarcely,* and *barely* are also negatives.
> - If *no* precedes a noun, you often can change it to *a* or *an.*

Proofread the speech below. Rewrite the passage correctly, fixing errors in the use of negatives, capitalization, and punctuation.

In my opinion there is not no better candidate for class president than Charles Ota. charles is one of the best students in our class. he does not have no bad qualities When I have a problem there is not no one I can count on like Charles. I have never known nobody as honest and reliable. Charles never has no shortage of ideas for ways to better the school. not nowhere will we find someone to represent our class as well as Charles can If you want the best class president, please vote for Charles Ota.

_____

_____

_____

_____

_____

_____

_____

English: Grammar • **Apply**

Name _____

What was your favorite reading selection or other text you read this week? Write a paragraph describing what you learned from it or why you enjoyed it. When you're done, exchange your writing with a partner. Proofread your partner's writing. Remember to apply the grammar you have learned this week.

Spelling • Greek Suffixes

Name _____

Fold back the paper along the dotted line. Use the blanks to write each word as it is read aloud. When you finish the test, unfold the paper. Use the list at the right to correct any spelling mistakes.

1. _____
2. _____
3. _____
4. _____
5. _____
6. _____
7. _____
8. _____
9. _____
10. _____
11. _____
12. _____
13. _____
14. _____
15. _____
16. _____
17. _____
18. _____
19. _____
20. _____

Review Words
21. _____
22. _____
23. _____

Challenge Words
24. _____
25. _____

1. democrat
2. democracy
3. physician
4. specialist
5. archaeology
6. sympathy
7. technology
8. biologist
9. pianist
10. geologist
11. musician
12. telegraph
13. technician
14. politician
15. tourist
16. heroism
17. apology
18. novelist
19. ecology
20. zoology
21. experience
22. important
23. excellent
24. electrician
25. mythology

Phonics/Spelling • Word Sort

Name _____

Many words in English have suffixes that come from ancient Greek. You can use the suffix as a clue to the meaning of the word. Some common Greek suffixes include:

- **-ist** and **-ian** refers to a person who studies or practices something: *novelist, physician*
- **-ology** means the study or practice of something: *zoology*
- **-graph** refers to something written or drawn: *telegraph*
- **-ism** refers to an action or characteristic of a person or thing: *heroism*
- **-cracy** refers to government: *democracy*
- **-pathy** means feeling or suffering: *empathy*

SPELLING TIP

Before adding the suffix *-ist* to the words *biology* and *geology*, be sure to drop the *y*. Which other words in the box drop a letter in order to add the suffix?

Read the words in the box. Write the spelling words that contain the suffix.

democrat	archaeology	pianist	technician	apology
democracy	sympathy	geologist	politician	novelist
physician	technology	musician	tourist	ecology
specialist	biologist	telegraph	heroism	zoology

-ist

1. _____
2. _____
3. _____
4. _____
5. _____
6. _____

-ian

7. _____
8. _____

9. _____
10. _____

-graph

11. _____

-ism

12. _____

-ology

13. _____
14. _____

15. _____
16. _____
17. _____

-crat

18. _____

-cracy

19. _____

-pathy

20. _____

Grade 6 • Unit 6 • Week 3

Spelling • Word Meaning

Name _____

democrat	archaeology	pianist	technician	apology
democracy	sympathy	geologist	politician	novelist
physician	technology	musician	tourist	ecology
specialist	biologist	telegraph	heroism	zoology

A. Write the spelling word that matches each word origin.

1. Greek *bios*, meaning "life" _____
2. Greek *demokratia*, meaning "popular government" _____
3. Greek *archaiologia*, meaning "study of ancient things" _____
4. Greek *technologia*, meaning "science of mechanical and industrial arts" _____
5. Greek *zoion*, meaning "animal" + *-logia*, meaning "study" _____

B. Write the spelling word that best completes each sentence.

6. Please accept my _____.
7. You will need to call a good _____ to solve the problem.
8. Can the _____ afford to buy a new piano before the concert?
9. The voters must choose whether they will vote republican or _____.
10. The _____ took three years to write her last book.
11. An elected _____ represents all the people in his or her district.
12. I have _____ for the team who will play the world champions.
13. Has the _____ examined you yet?
14. The _____ is visiting European cities next month.
15. The _____ must study the soil samples.
16. Many years ago, the _____ was used to communicate.
17. After studying the trumpet, my father became a professional _____.
18. An act of _____ saved the family during the hurricane.
19. Years of research made the scientist a _____ in her field.
20. Students in the _____ club learn about the environment.

332 Grade 6 • Unit 6 • Week 3

Spelling • Proofreading

Name _____

There are six misspelled words in the paragraphs below. Underline each misspelled word. Then write the words correctly on the lines.

There are many college courses for students interested in pursuing a career in science. Zoologie and biollogy courses focus on life science. Gealogy focuses on earth science, specifically, the study of soil and rocks. Many college students enjoy taking arkeology courses. They find learning about prehistoric people and their cultures fascinating.

Some students enter college determined to become a physishun. This career path takes several years to complete. Although a doctor can become a generalist and open a family practice after completing his or her residency, he or she can choose to become a speshalist. Becoming an expert in a specific area of the human anatomy, such as the heart, feet, or ears, nose, and throat, can be very rewarding.

1. _____   2. _____   3. _____

4. _____   5. _____   6. _____

Writing Connection — Write about the subjects you might like to study in college or a career that sounds interesting to you. Use four or more words from the spelling list.

_____
_____
_____
_____
_____
_____
_____
_____
_____

Phonics/Spelling · Review

Name _____

> **Remember**
>
> Many words in English have suffixes that come from ancient Greek. Below are some common Greek suffixes and their meanings.
> - *-ist* and *-ian* refers to a person who studies or practices something
> - *-ology* means the study or practice of something
> - *-graph* refers to something written or drawn
> - *-ism* refers to an action or characteristic of a person or thing
> - *-cracy* refers to a form of government
> - *-pathy* means feeling or suffering

democrat	archaeology	pianist	technician	apology
democracy	sympathy	geologist	politician	novelist
physician	technology	musician	tourist	ecology
specialist	biologist	telegraph	heroism	zoology

Fill in the missing letters of each word to form a spelling word. Then write the spelling word on the line.

1. symp ___ ___ ___ y _____
2. ge ___ ___ ___ gist _____
3. apol ___ ___ y _____
4. musi ___ ___ ___ n _____
5. techno ___ ___ ___ y _____
6. arch ___ ___ ___ logy _____
7. bi ___ ___ ___ gist _____
8. demo ___ ___ ___ t _____
9. zo ___ ___ ___ gy _____
10. pian ___ ___ ___ _____
11. democ ___ ___ ___ y _____
12. teleg ___ ___ ___ h _____
13. to ___ ___ ___ st _____
14. physi ___ ___ ___ n _____
15. tech ___ ___ ___ ian _____
16. her ___ ___ ___ m _____
17. ec ___ ___ ___ gy _____
18. politi ___ ___ ___ n _____
19. nov ___ ___ ___ st _____
20. spe ___ ___ ___ list _____

334 Grade 6 · Unit 6 · Week 3

Vocabulary • Related Words

Name _____

Expand your vocabulary by adding or removing inflectional endings, prefixes, or suffixes to a base word to create different forms of a word.

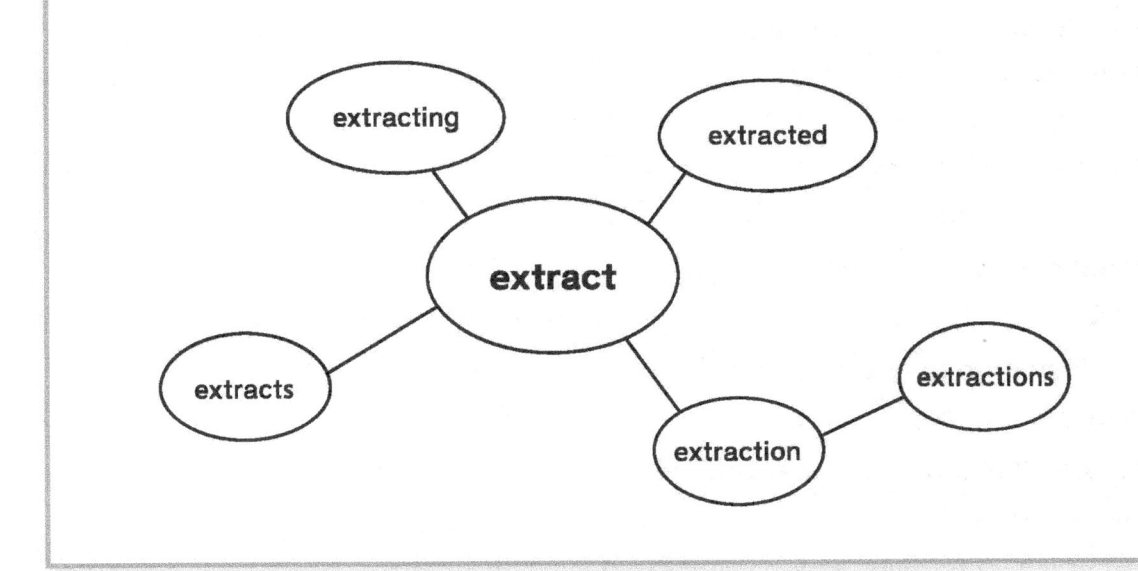

- extracting
- extracted
- **extract**
- extracts
- extraction
- extractions

Read the word below. Add or remove inflectional endings, prefixes, or suffixes to form related words and write them in the blanks. Use a print or online dictionary to help you.

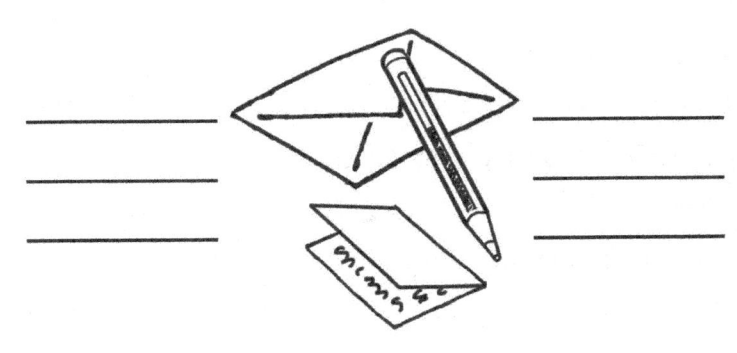

Correspond

_____   _____
_____   _____
_____   _____

Vocabulary • Spiral Review

Name _____

Write the vocabulary word from the box that completes each rhyming couplet below. Use a dictionary to confirm word meanings if you need to.

vastness	impenetrable	benefactor	abundant
multitude	dominant	commodity	distribution
significant	edible	skewed	replenished

1. Fair-minded readers are not in the mood
   For a newspaper article that is _____.

2. Need more work, support, and pay?
   Find a _____ right away!

3. Is this strange food even credible?
   Why yes, it is quite _____

4. Look at that moat, and that towering wall!
   The fortress is _____ after all.

5. What is that faraway look on your face?
   I'm considering the _____ of outer space.

6. It's a Thanksgiving feast, and the food is _____
   All these pale, starchy dishes seem, in fact, quite redundant.

7. Be sure to wear your sturdiest hats.
   This cave contains a _____ of bats!

8. The crops in the fields will flourish once again.
   The dry, dusty soil has been _____ by rain.

9. They rushed to California, the young and the old,
   To find and sell a new _____—a nugget of gold.

10. In history class, we learn important information
    About _____ events that have shaped our nation.

11. On the court, this winning player is a real menace,
    The most _____ force in the sport of tennis.

12. The siblings demand a _____ that's fair:
    "Divide the dessert, Dad, and do it with care."

336 Grade 6 • Unit 6 • Week 3

Grammar • Prepositions

Name _____

- A preposition is a word that shows how a noun or pronoun relates to some other word in a sentence.
- Some common prepositions are *about, above, across, at, before, behind, but, by, down, during, except, for, from, in, into, like, near, of, over, past, since, through, to, toward, under,* and *with*.

  I always put my books <u>in</u> my locker.

Put brackets [ ] around the prepositions in each of the following sentences. Some sentences have more than one preposition.

1. Rafael's mom helped him make space in his bedroom for his new bookcase.
2. They put his chest of drawers in the corner by the closet.
3. They moved his bed to the other side of the room.
4. They put the bookcase against the wall near the window.
5. Rafael moved his table beside the bed and put the lamp on it.
6. He put the chair near the bookcase.
7. Then Rafael moved all his books to the shelf and organized them by author.
8. When he was done, he had space for some other special things.
9. His mom suggested that he put his basketball trophies on the top shelf.
10. Rafael likes the way his room looks with the addition of the new bookcase.

Reading/Writing Connection

Read the excerpt from "Messages in the Stone and Wood." Circle the prepositions in the excerpt below. Then write two sentences of your own. Circle the prepositions in your writing.

> These spots are often outcroppings of bedrock that have been covered over by soil or moss.

_____

_____

Grade 6 • Unit 6 • Week 4   337

Grammar • Prepositional Phrases

Name _____

> - A **prepositional phrase** consists of a preposition and the object of the preposition (a noun or pronoun) and any words that modify it.
> - Prepositional phrases can function as adjectives and adverbs.
>
>   *The owl was perched <u>on the branch</u>.*

A. Read each sentence below. Underline each prepositional phrase and write the object of the preposition on the line provided.

1. Yesterday, Lena's class took a field trip to the nature center. _____

2. The first thing they saw was the colorful butterfly garden in front. _____

3. Inside, they watched a film about an earthquake. _____

4. Lena and Tasha were most interested in the wildlife exhibit. _____

5. Tasha took a picture of the huge brown bear. _____

B. Read each sentence. Underline each prepositional phrase. On the line, write whether the prepositional phrase functions as an adverb or adjective.

6. The observation tower provides a good view of the landscape. _____

7. Habitat trails wind around the grounds. _____

8. The class took a hike before lunch. _____

9. We saw many ducks with dark green heads. _____

10. Everyone was hungry after the long hike. _____

Writing Connection   On the lines below, describe a room in your house. Use prepositions in your writing to add detail. Edit your work for correct punctuation.

_____

_____

_____

338   Grade 6 • Unit 6 • Week 4

Grammar: Mechanics • **Commas, Dashes, and Parentheses**

Name _____

- Use a comma after an introductory prepositional phrase, after a long introductory phrase, and to show a pause after an introductory word.
- Use a comma to make the meaning clear.
- Use commas, dashes, or parentheses before and after a phrase that acts as an interrupter.

  In the end, the weather—finally—cleared up and we were able to ride the roller coaster.

On the lines provided, rewrite the sentences correctly by inserting commas, dashes, or parentheses in the appropriate places.

1. "After high school I want to study to be a veterinarian," said Mallory.

   _____
   _____

2. "Patrick, what job if you could choose anything do you think you would pick?" asked Mallory.

   _____
   _____

3. "Well I think I would like to become an oceanographer I love the ocean or a dentist." Patrick said.

   _____
   _____

4. "With either of those jobs you will need to do well in science" said Mallory.

   _____
   _____

5. "I am lucky to have Mrs. Kline the best teacher ever for science," said Patrick.

   _____
   _____

In your writer's notebook, describe your favorite science topic. When you're done, check that you used commas, dashes and parentheses correctly.

Grammar • Proofreading

Name _____

- A preposition is a word that shows how a noun or pronoun relates to some other word in a sentence.
- A prepositional phrase consists of a preposition and the object of the preposition (a noun or pronoun) and any words that modify it.
- Use a comma after an introductory prepositional phrase, a long introductory phrase, and an introductory word.
- Use a comma to make the meaning clear.
- Use commas, dashes, or parentheses before and after a phrase that acts as an interrupter.

Proofread the following sentences. Correct mistakes in the use of prepositional phrases, capitalization, or punctuation. Then rewrite the sentences correctly.

1. If you want to do well on a test you should follow my plan.

2. first and most importantly pay attention in class and always do your homework.

3. when you don't understand something ask questions.

4. Don't wait, until the night, before the test, to start studying

5. On the morning, of the test you should eat—a healthy breakfast with good protein.

English: Grammar • **Apply**

Name _____

What was your favorite reading selection or other text you read this week? Write a paragraph describing what you learned from it or why you enjoyed it. When you're done, exchange your writing with a partner. Proofread your partner's writing. Remember to apply the grammar you have learned this week.

Spelling • **Absorbed Prefixes**

Name _____

Fold back the paper along the dotted line. Use the blanks to write each word as it is read aloud. When you finish the test, unfold the paper. Use the list at the right to correct any spelling mistakes.

1. _____ 1. immigrate
2. _____ 2. illuminate
3. _____ 3. accompany
4. _____ 4. announce
5. _____ 5. impatiently
6. _____ 6. immature
7. _____ 7. immigration
8. _____ 8. irregular
9. _____ 9. correspond
10. _____ 10. illogical
11. _____ 11. collaborate
12. _____ 12. suppress
13. _____ 13. assembly
14. _____ 14. accommodate
15. _____ 15. arrest
16. _____ 16. arrive
17. _____ 17. illegal
18. _____ 18. support
19. _____ 19. suffix
20. _____ 20. collect

Review Words
21. _____ 21. musician
22. _____ 22. democracy
23. _____ 23. sympathy

Challenge Words
24. _____ 24. impractical
25. _____ 25. suffocate

342   Grade 6 • Unit 6 • Week 4

Phonics/Spelling • Word Sort

Name _____

A prefix is a word part that is added to the beginning of a base word or root and changes its meaning. Sometimes when a prefix is added to a word, the last letter of the prefix is "absorbed" by the base word or root. This means the last letter of the prefix changes to match the first letter of the base word or root. Here are some examples:

- **ad-** "to, toward" = *accompany (ad + company)* means "to go with someone"
- **con-** "together, with" = *correspond (con + respond)* means "to communicate with"
- **in-** "not, the opposite of" = *irregular (im + regular)* means "not regular"
- **sub-** "under, below" = *suppress (sub + press)* means "to push down"

SPELLING TIP

Usually, words with absorbed prefixes **in-, im-, ir-, il-** follow these spelling patterns:

Add **im-** to words that begin with *m* (immature) or *p* (impatiently)

Add **ir-** to words that begin with *r* (irrational)

Add **il-** to words that begin with *l* (illegible)

Read the words in the box. Write the spelling words that contain the absorbed prefix.

immigrate	impatiently	correspond	assembly	illegal
accompany	immature	illogical	accommodate	support
illuminate	collaborate	immigration	suffix	arrest
announce	irregular	suppress	arrive	collect

ad-

1. _____
2. _____
3. _____
4. _____
5. _____
6. _____

con-

7. _____

8. _____
9. _____

in-

10. _____
11. _____
12. _____
13. _____
14. _____
15. _____

16. _____
17. _____

sub-

18. _____
19. _____
20. _____

Grade 6 • Unit 6 • Week 4   343

Spelling • Word Meaning

Name _____

immigrate	impatiently	correspond	assembly	illegal
illuminate	immature	illogical	accommodate	support
accompany	immigration	collaborate	arrest	suffix
announce	irregular	suppress	arrive	collect

A. Write the spelling word that matches each definition.

1. come to a new country _____
2. reach a destination _____
3. gather or pull together _____
4. light up _____
5. go with or keep company _____
6. work together _____
7. not coherent _____
8. unlawful _____
9. hold up or sustain _____
10. gathering or meeting _____

B. Write the spelling word that best completes each sentence.

11. We can _____ by writing letters or e-mails.
12. I tried to _____ a cough during the concert.
13. _____ to the United States was high in the early 1900s.
14. A kitten is an _____ cat.
15. The _____ -able is at the end of the word *valuable*.
16. If you have an _____ heartbeat, your doctor might order tests.
17. Will the police officer _____ the burglary suspect?
18. The couple will _____ their engagement on Sunday.
19. The hotel will be able to _____ the large party this weekend.
20. He was _____ awaiting the results of his science test.

Spelling • Proofreading

Name _____

There are three misspelled words in the first paragraph and four misspelled words in the second. Underline each misspelled word. Then write the words correctly on the lines.

Many people imigrate to the United States. They are often seeking basic rights, such as freedom of asembly and freedom of speech. Going through the imigrashun process, many are filled with hope for a better life.

When people arive, they frequently look for jobs. Sometimes, they send money back home to loved ones who didn't acompanie them on their journey. Immigrants can coresspond with loved ones by sending letters calling and sending emails. Many wait inpatiently to speak with their loved ones.

1. _____ 2. _____ 3. _____

4. _____ 5. _____ 6. _____

7. _____

Writing Connection Write about the reasons that people might immigrate to the United States. Use at least four words from the spelling list.

_____
_____
_____
_____
_____
_____
_____
_____
_____
_____
_____

Phonics/Spelling • Review

Name _____

Remember

An absorbed prefix is one that has been absorbed into the base or root word. Sometimes when a prefix is added to a word, the last letter of the prefix is "absorbed" into the base word or root. The last letter of the prefix changes to match the first letter of the base word or root.

- *ad-* "to, toward" = *accompany (ad + company)* means "to go with someone"
- *con-* "together, with" = *correspond (con + respond)* means "to communicate with"
- *in-* "not, the opposite of" = *irregular (im + regular)* means "not regular"
- *sub-* "under, below" = *support (sub + press)* means "to push down"

Use a dictionary to help you identify and confirm word origins.

immigrate	impatiently	correspond	assembly	illegal
illuminate	immature	illogical	accommodate	support
accompany	immigration	collaborate	arrest	suffix
announce	irregular	suppress	arrive	collect

Write the missing letters to complete the spelling word. Then write each spelling word on the line.

1. _____ company   _____   11. _____ nounce   _____
2. _____ mature   _____   12. _____ rest   _____
3. _____ laborate   _____   13. _____ port   _____
4. _____ patiently   _____   14. _____ respond   _____
5. _____ fix   _____   15. _____ sembly   _____
6. _____ logical   _____   16. _____ lect   _____
7. _____ migrate   _____   17. _____ regular   _____
8. _____ commodate   _____   18. _____ luminate   _____
9. _____ press   _____   19. _____ rive   _____
10. _____ legal   _____   20. _____ migration   _____

Vocabulary Strategy • Literal and Figurative Language

Name _____

> Most of the text you read every day contains **literal language**. Consider the denotations, or dictionary definitions, of the words, and you will understand the meaning. For example, *It snowed six inches overnight.*
>
> **Figurative language** is not meant to be taken literally. It relies more on the connotations, or feelings and ideas, that readers associate with certain words. Through devices such as similes, metaphors, and personification, figurative language makes creative comparisons. Here are some examples:
>
> **Metaphor:** *A fresh, white blanket had been laid on the ugly brown landscape.*
>
> **Simile:** *The snow-covered woods were as quiet as the library's reading room.*
>
> **Personification:** *A falling snowflake gently kissed my cheek.*

Read each sentence. Write whether it contains literal or figurative language. If the statement is not literal, explain its figurative meaning.

1. The old car wheezed, made one last gasp, and died.
   _____

2. It was October, and the leaves on the aspens were turning bright yellow.
   _____

3. Kelsey shivered and tightened her wool scarf around her neck.
   _____

4. The skater moved on the ice like a high-speed train gliding down a track.
   _____

5. The sun was a giant peach slipping below the horizon.
   _____

6. "It feels like I'm standing on the sun!" Zach said, as he brushed the sweat from his forehead.
   _____
   _____

Vocabulary Strategy • Greek Roots

Name _____

A. Read each passage from "Ancient Threads Reveal Early Weavers." Look at the meanings of the word parts. Then write a definition for the word in bold.

1. For many years, **archaeologists** did not have a good way to tell how old their finds were.

   archaeo = ancient, old; *logos* = study

   _____

2. Then in 1947 a scientist named Willard Libby was trying to find out the age of fossils for a **paleontology** study.

   paleo = prehistoric; *logos* = study

   _____

3. Finally, in 2011, a more advanced method of carbon dating was used on the bits of fabric. This **technique** can tell the age of even one hair.

   tech = skill

   _____

4. Carbon dating has given scientists a way to peer into the past—sort of like having a **telescope** on long ago.

   tele = far; *scope* = see

   _____

B. Write another word that has each of the following roots. Use a dictionary if necessary.

1. tele _____

2. tech _____

3. ology _____

Grammar • Combining Sentences With Adjectives and Adverbs

Name _____

- To avoid short, choppy sentences, **combine sentences** using words, phrases, or clauses.
- You can use an **adjective**, an **adverb**, an **adverbial phrase**, or an **adjectival clause** to combine sentences.

  AJ is a baseball player. He scored the most home runs.
  AJ is the baseball player who scored the most runs.

A. Read each pair of sentences. Combine the two sentences into one sentence with an adjective or adjectival clause. Write the new sentence on the line provided.

1. Lydia is a photographer. She takes great pictures.

   _____

2. Lydia took this photograph of a phone booth. The phone booth was old.

   _____

3. Lydia takes photos with a film camera. The camera belonged to her grandfather.

   _____

B. Read each pair of sentences. Combine the two sentences into one sentence with an adverb or adverbial phrase.

4. Matthew also takes pictures. He takes them constantly.

   _____

5. Matthew uses a digital camera. He uses it exclusively.

   _____

6. Matthew can print his own photos. He can print them from his computer.

   _____

Look back through your writer's notebook for a paragraph you wrote. Look for sentences you can combine to make your writing better. Edit your paragraph for correct punctuation and check for any spelling mistakes.

Grade 6 • Unit 6 • Week 5   349

Grammar • Combining Sentences With Prepositional Phrases

Name _____

> - A **prepositional phrase** consists of a preposition and its object and any words that modify the object.
> - **Prepositional phrases** show how nouns and pronouns relate to something else in a sentence.
> - Use prepositional phrases to combine sentences.
>   Alix got on the bus. She was in a hurry. Alix got on the bus <u>in a hurry</u>.

Read each pair of sentences. Combine the two sentences into one sentence by using a prepositional phrase. Write the new sentence on the line.

1. My aunt is a scientist. She works in Hawaii.

   _____

2. My aunt is a specialist. She is a specialist in volcanic activity.

   _____

3. One of the most active volcanoes is Kilauea. Kilauea is on the island of Hawaii.

   _____

4. Kilauea has been in a state of continuous eruption. It has been that way for many years.

   _____

Connect to Community — Talk to a trusted adult about the different landforms and regions of your state. Use online or print resources to learn about the land in your state. Then choose a land form or region to write about on the lines below. Edit your writing for correct sentences and punctuation.

_____

_____

_____

_____

350 Grade 6 • Unit 6 • Week 5

Grammar • Mechanics: Punctuation Marks: Semicolons, Colons, and Quotation Marks

Name _____

- Use a semicolon to separate two independent clauses that are closely related in meaning: *I love to read mysteries; others prefer fantasy.*
- Use a colon to introduce a list within a sentence: *We need: oatmeal, milk, raisins, and dates.*
- Use quotation marks to set off a person's exact words: *"Go Wildcats!" cheered James.*

Read each sentence. Rewrite the sentence using correct punctuation.

1. Kristi is having a sleepover her new friend Amelia will be there.

   _____

2. You should come over right after school, said Kristi.

   _____

3. I will come as soon as I can, said Amelia.

   _____

4. Amelia packed the things she needed a toothbrush, toothpaste, and pajamas.

   _____

5. You girls have a good time, but don't stay up too late! said Mrs. Diaz.

   _____

Reading/Writing Connection

Read the excerpt from "How Many Seconds?" Turn the sentences into a dialogue between you and a friend. Be sure to edit your work for correct punctuation.

> How many seconds in a minute?
> Sixty, and no more in it.
>
> How many minutes in an hour?
> Sixty for sun and shower.

_____

_____

Grade 6 • Unit 6 • Week 5   351

Grammar • **Proofreading**

Name _____

> - To avoid short, choppy sentences, **combine sentences** using words, phrases, or clauses.
> - You can use an **adjective**, an **adverb**, an **adjectival clause**, an **adverb phrase**, or a **prepositional phrase** to combine sentences.
> - Use a semicolon to separate two independent clauses that are closely related in meaning. Use a colon to introduce a list within a sentence. Use quotation marks to set off a person's exact words.

Proofread each paragraph. Then rewrite each paragraph. Combine short, choppy sentences and correct the punctuation.

1. The staff and students at Main Middle School paid tribute to retiring teacher Clifford Lutz. They paid tribute to him today. They honored him at a ceremony; the ceremony was in the school auditorium.

   _____

   _____

   _____

2. Mr. Lutz spent forty years teaching at Main. He taught English. The school principal, Mary Moore, presented Mr. Lutz with a plaque. The plaque honors his years as a fine teacher.

   _____

   _____

   _____

3. Mr. Lutz thanked everyone at Main Middle School. He thanked them sincerely. "If I could spend another forty years working, I would spend it here," he said.

   _____

   _____

   _____

352   Grade 6 • Unit 6 • Week 5

English: Grammar • **Apply**

Name _____

What was your favorite reading selection or other text you read this week? Write a paragraph describing what you learned from it or why you enjoyed it. When you're done, exchange your writing with a partner. Proofread your partner's writing. Remember to apply the grammar you have learned this week.

Spelling • Words from Mythology

Name _____

Fold back the paper along the dotted line. Use the blanks to write each word as it is read aloud. When you finish the test, unfold the paper. Use the list at the right to correct any spelling mistakes.

1. _____ 1. iris
2. _____ 2. nectar
3. _____ 3. cosmetics
4. _____ 4. chaos
5. _____ 5. solar
6. _____ 6. psychology
7. _____ 7. mania
8. _____ 8. titanic
9. _____ 9. romance
10. _____ 10. geometry
11. _____ 11. helicopter
12. _____ 12. nocturnal
13. _____ 13. geography
14. _____ 14. phobia
15. _____ 15. terrain
16. _____ 16. amnesia
17. _____ 17. tantalize
18. _____ 18. hygiene
19. _____ 19. mercury
20. _____ 20. marathon

Review Words
21. _____ 21. announce
22. _____ 22. collect
23. _____ 23. illegal

Challenge Words
24. _____ 24. lethal
25. _____ 25. hypnotize

354 Grade 6 • Unit 6 • Week 5

Name _____

Phonics/Spelling • Word Sort

Many English words have origins in mythology.

- *Mercury* has its origins in Roman mythology. It comes from the Roman God, Mercury. He was a messenger of the gods and a god of trade.

- *Marathon* has its origins in Greek mythology. In the legend, a Greek soldier named Pheidippides raced from the town of Marathon to Athens with news that the Persians had been defeated in battle.

Recognizing these relationships can help you determine the meaning of unfamiliar words.

SPELLING TIP BOX

In words of Greek origin like *psychology*, the *ps* makes an /s/ sound. The *p* is silent. Try saying the following words: *psyche, psychic, and psychological.*

Read the words in the box. Write the spelling words according to their parts of speech.

iris	solar	romance	geography	tantalize
nectar	psychology	geometry	phobia	hygiene
cosmetics	mania	helicopter	terrain	mercury
chaos	titanic	nocturnal	amnesia	marathon

adjective

1. _____
2. _____
3. _____

verb

4. _____

noun, adjective, or verb

5. _____

noun

6. _____
7. _____
8. _____
9. _____
10. _____
11. _____
12. _____
13. _____
14. _____
15. _____
16. _____
17. _____
18. _____
19. _____
20. _____

Grade 6 • Unit 6 • Week 5 355

Spelling • Word Meaning

Name _____

iris	solar	romance	geography	tantalize
nectar	psychology	geometry	phobia	hygiene
cosmetics	mania	helicopter	terrain	mercury
chaos	titanic	nocturnal	amnesia	marathon

A. Write the spelling word that matches each definition below.

1. a cross-country foot race of about 26 miles _____
2. the practice of promoting sanitary conditions _____
3. an area of land _____
4. great disorder or confusion _____
5. having great stature or enormous strength _____
6. a sweet liquid that comes from flowers _____
7. the science of the mind _____
8. relating to the sun's energy _____
9. preparations for beautifying the skin _____
10. brightly colored flower with sword-like leaves _____

B. Write the spelling word that best completes each sentence.

11. When we studied _____, we learned to measure angles.
12. Excessive excitement and overactivity can be signs of _____.
13. I like to read a _____ novel occasionally.
14. We took a _____ ride along the eastern coast of the island.
15. Besides owls, what other _____ animals can you name?
16. The aroma of pizza would _____ almost anyone!
17. We are learning mapmaking techniques in _____.
18. He has a _____ about climbing ladders.
19. She suffered a mild case of _____ after the car accident.
20. Many thermometers use _____ to show what temperature it is.

356 Grade 6 • Unit 6 • Week 5

Spelling • Proofreading

Name _____

There are four misspelled words in the first paragraph and three misspelled words in the second paragraph. Underline each misspelled word. Then write the words correctly on the lines.

 Mr. Sanchez asked his students to write essays on important technological developments of the last one hundred years. Sol wrote about the helicoptar even though he had never ridden in one. Jen wrote about cosmetiks even though she was not allowed to wear any. Peter thought that advances in personal higene were important, especially because he had a germ fobia!

1. _____ 2. _____ 3. _____

4. _____

 Tonya has different interests than some of her friends. For example, she doesn't enjoy reading romanse novels like Jamie does. She prefers mysteries. Instead of trying out for the cheerleading squad like Ana, Tonya is training for a half-marathon. One of her friends, Lisa, wants to be a teacher when she grows up. Tonya is interested in psycholagy because she'd like to help troubled teens some day.

5. _____ 6. _____ 7. _____

Writing Connection   Write about interests that you have. Use at least four words from the spelling list.

_____
_____
_____
_____
_____
_____
_____
_____

Phonics/Spelling • Review

Name _____

Remember

Many English words are connected to mythology.

- *Atlas* has its origins in Greek mythology. He was a Titan who carried the heavens on his shoulders as a punishment for leading the Titans into battle against the gods.
- *Floral* has its origins in Roman mythology. Flora is the Roman goddess of flowers.

Identifying an unfamiliar word's origin can help you determine its meaning.

iris	solar	romance	geography	tantalize
nectar	psychology	geometry	phobia	hygiene
cosmetics	mania	helicopter	terrain	mercury
chaos	titanic	nocturnal	amnesia	marathon

Write the missing letters that complete the spelling word. Then write the spelling word on the line.

1. ___ r ___ s _____
2. nect ___ ___ _____
3. cos ___ eti ___ s _____
4. ___ ___ aos _____
5. terr ___ ___ n _____
6. heli ___ ___ pter _____
7. pho ___ ___ a _____
8. so ___ ___ r _____
9. geom ___ t ___ y _____
10. p ___ ___ chology _____
11. tita ___ ___ c _____
12. man ___ ___ _____
13. roman ___ ___ _____
14. mara ___ ___ on _____
15. am ___ es ___ a _____
16. tantal ___ ___ e _____
17. mer ___ ___ ry _____
18. geogra ___ ___ y _____
19. noct ___ ___ nal _____
20. hy ___ i ___ ne _____

358   Grade 6 • Unit 6 • Week 5

Vocabulary • Related Words

Name _____

Expand your vocabulary by adding or removing inflectional endings, prefixes, or suffixes to a base word to create different forms of a word.

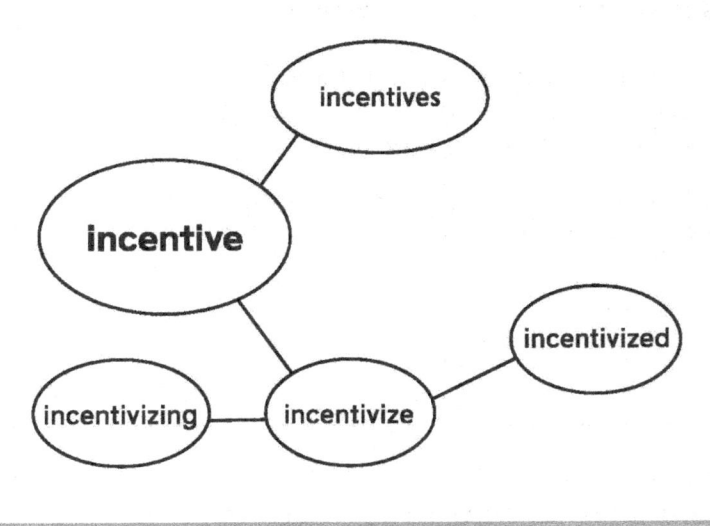

- incentive
  - incentives
  - incentivized
  - incentivize
  - incentivizing

Read the word below. Add or remove inflectional endings, prefixes, and suffixes to form related words and write them on the blanks. Use a print or online dictionary to help you.

Recreation

_____   _____
_____   _____
_____   _____

Grade 6 • Unit 6 • Week 5   **359**

Vocabulary Strategy • Figurative Language

Name _____

Read each passage from "Ode to Mr. Lincoln." Pay special attention to the hyperbole in bold. Then decide whether the statement below the passage expresses the true meaning of the hyperbole. If it does not, write what you think the words in bold are meant to communicate.

1. I see your marble arms and hands, solid and firm
   As the earth itself, and I think to myself those hands
   Once held a whole country together.

   Because Abraham Lincoln was president during the Civil War, he used his hands to help bring the country together.

   ☐ True   ☐ False

   _____
   _____

2. You followed the path you chose for yourself
   As surely as the stars follow their paths across the sky.

   Abraham Lincoln was extremely sure and steady in his beliefs and actions.

   ☐ True   ☐ False

   _____
   _____

3. The worries of your life are behind you, Mr. Lincoln,
   Though once they lay heavy on your heart—
   As weighty as mountains of stone on the horizon,
   As numerous as snowflakes covering a burial ground.

   Abraham Lincoln had millions of worries that weighed many tons.

   ☐ True   ☐ False

   _____
   _____

HANDWRITING

Table of Contents

Left- and Right-Handed Writers	362
The Cursive Alphabet	363
Size and Shape	364
Letters i t	365
Letters e l	366
Letters o a	367
Letters c d	368
Letters n m	369
Connectives	370
Letters u w	371
Letters b f	372
Letters h k	373
Letters g q	374
Letters j p	375
Letters r s	376
Letters y z	377
Letters v x	378
Size and Shape	379
Letters A O	380
Letters C E	381
Letters L D	382
Letters B R	383
Letters T F	384
Letters S G	385
Letters I J	386
Spacing Letters and Words	387
Letters N M	388
Letters H K	389
Letters P Q	390
Letters V U	391
Letters W X	392
Letters Y Z	393
Transition to Two Lines	394
Practice with Small Letters	395
Practice with Tall Letters	396

Name _____ Date _____

Cursive Writing Position

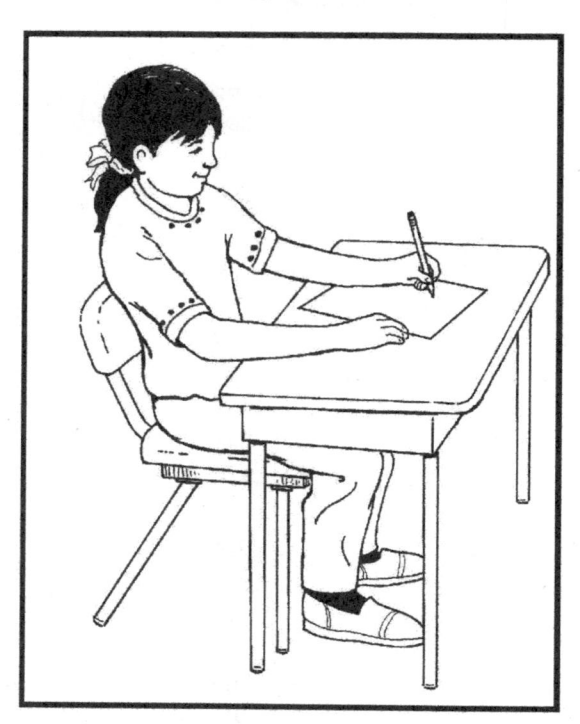

Left-Handed Writers

Sit tall. Place both arms on the table.

Keep your feet flat on the floor.

Slant your paper.

Hold your pencil with your first two fingers and your thumb.

Right-Handed Writers

Sit tall. Place both arms on the table.

Keep your feet flat on the floor.

Slant your paper.

Hold your pencil with your first two fingers and your thumb.

Name _____ Date _____

The Cursive Alphabet

Aa Bb Cc Dd
Ee Ff Gg Hh
Ii Jj Kk Ll
Mm Nn Oo Pp
Qq Rr Ss Tt
Uu Vv Ww Xx
Yy Zz

Name _____ Date _____

Size and Shape

Tall letters touch the top line.

Make your writing easy to read.

h d l t

Short letters touch the middle line.

o a n m c u w

These letters go below the bottom line.

g f z j p y

Circle the letters that are the right size and shape and sit on the bottom line.

a w h n d

g P e b l

q o f m d

364 Handwriting

Name _____ Date _____

i t

Trace and write the letters. Then trace and write the word.

i i i i i i i

t t t t t t t

it it it it it

Handwriting 365

Name _____ Date _____

e l

Trace and write the letters. Then write the words.

e e e e e e e

l l l l l l l

ill lit tie tile

366 Handwriting

Name _____ Date _____

o a

Trace and write the letters. Then write the words.

o o o o o o o

a a a a a a a

toe toll tail ate

tote oil oat lot

Handwriting **367**

Name _____ Date _____

c d

Trace and write the letters. Then write the words and the phrases.

c c c c c c c

d d d d d d d

coat deed code

dime dance time

Name _____ Date _____

n m

Trace and write the letters. Then write the words.

n   n   n   n   n   n

m   m   m   m   m   m

name   note   moat

mitten   tame   nine

Handwriting **369**

Name _____ **Date** _____

Connectives

Trace the connectives.

air tie her like

an and end sand

glad just yell

zebra you yarn

gap lazy game

five pick jam

feel plan quite

Name _____ Date _____

u w

Trace and write the letters. Then write the words.

u u u u u u u

w w w w w w w

wait wit would

undo uncle lute

Handwriting **371**

Name _____ Date _____

b f

Trace and write the letters. Then write the words and the phrases.

b b b b b b b

f f f f f f f

boat fall bubble

fine food bat ball

Name _____ Date _____

h k

Trace and write the letters. Then write the words.

h h h h h h

k k k k k k

chick hatch hook

kilt luck kite

Name _____ Date _____

g q

Trace and write the letters. Then write the phrases.

g g g g g g g g

q q q q q q q q

quacked good game

quite a fog

Name _____ Date _____

j p

Trace and write the letters. Then write the phrases.

j j j j j j j j

p p p p p p p p

jump for joy

picture perfect

Name _____ Date _____

r s

Trace and write the letters. Then write the phrases.

r r r r r r r

s s s s s s s

rose blossom

stars and stripes

Name _____ Date _____

y z

Trace and write the letters. Then write the phrases.

y y y y y y y

z z z z z z z

zip code   zoom in

pretty azaleas

Handwriting **377**

Name _____ Date _____

v x

Trace and write the letters. Then write the phrases.

v v v v v v v v

x x x x x x x x

x marks the spot

vim and vigor

378 Handwriting

Name _____   Date _____

Size and Shape

All uppercase letters are tall letters.
Tall letters should touch the top line.

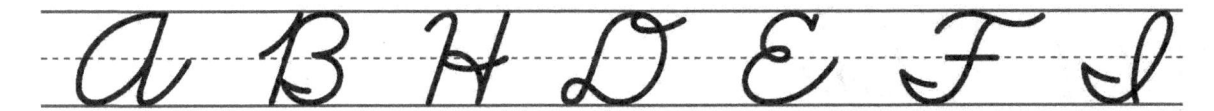

A B H D E F I

Letters with descenders go below the bottom line.

J Z Y

You can make your writing easy to read.

Look at the letters below. Circle the letters that are the correct size and shape.

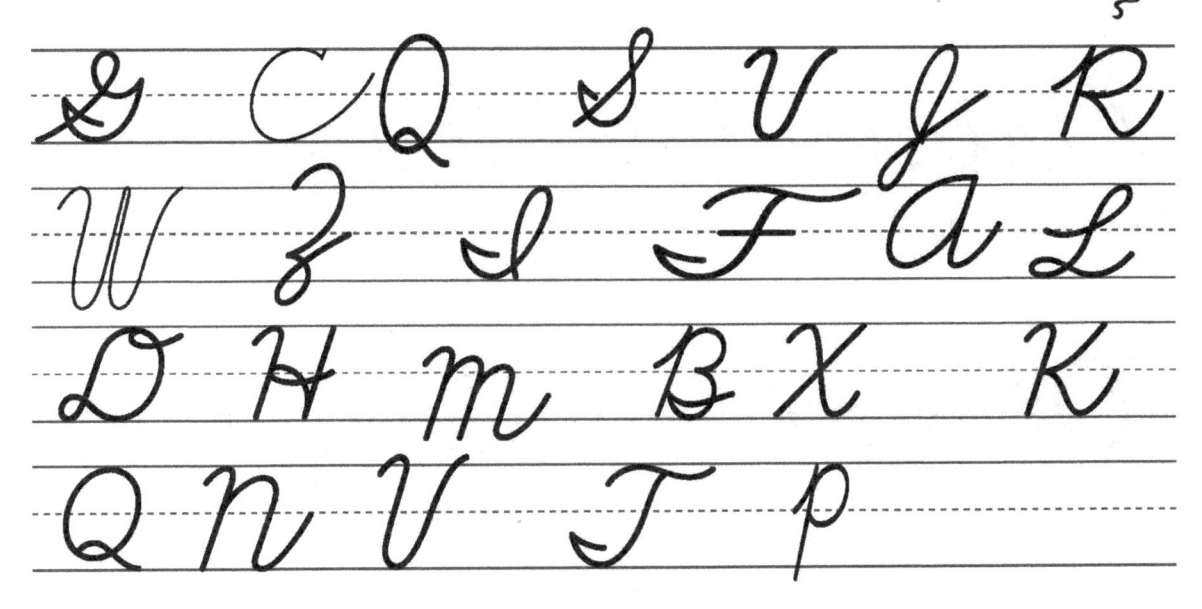

G C Q S V J R
W Z I F A L
D H M B X K
Q N V J P

Handwriting **379**

Name _____ Date _____

A O

Trace and write the letters. Then write the sentences.

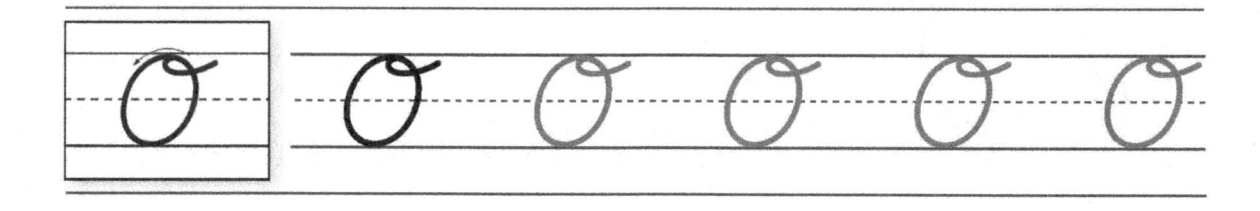

a a a a a a

O O O O O O O

Ari is in Alaska.

Otis is in Oregon.

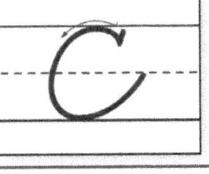

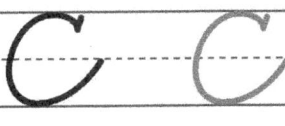

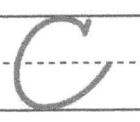

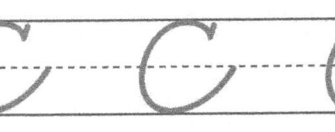

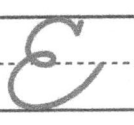

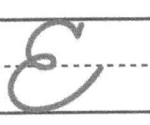

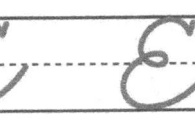

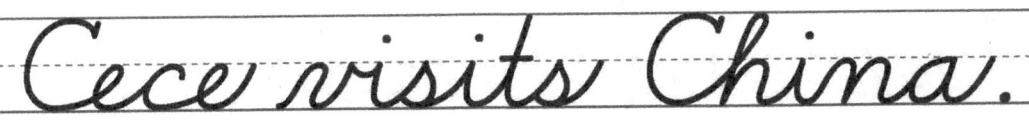

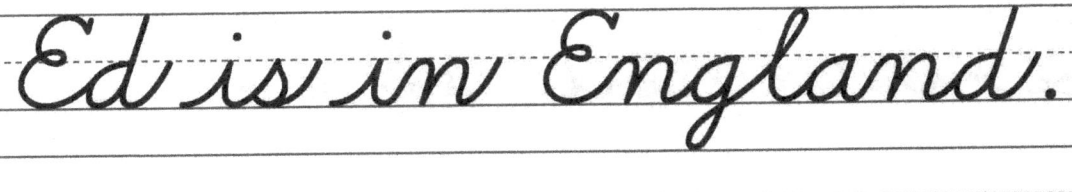

Name _____ Date _____

C E

Trace and write the letters. Then write the sentences.

C C C C C C C

E E E E E E E

Cece visits China.

Ed is in England.

Handwriting **381**

Name _____ Date _____

L D

Trace and write the letters. Then write the sentences.

L L L L L L

D D D D D D D

Dad did a dance.

Leo dined at Del's.

Name _____   Date _____

B R

Trace and write the letters. Then write the sentences.

𝓑 𝓑 𝓑 𝓑 𝓑 𝓑

𝓡 𝓡 𝓡 𝓡 𝓡 𝓡

𝓑𝒾𝓁𝓁 𝒾𝓈 𝒾𝓃 𝓑𝓇𝒶𝓏𝒾𝓁.

𝓡𝑜𝓈𝑒 𝒾𝓈 𝒾𝓃 𝓡𝓊𝓈𝓈𝒾𝒶.

Handwriting 383

Name _____ Date _____

T F

Trace and write the letters. Then write the sentences.

T T T T T T T

F F F F F F F

Theodore Roosevelt won. Friends cheer.

Name _____ Date _____

S G

Trace and write the letters. Then write the sentences.

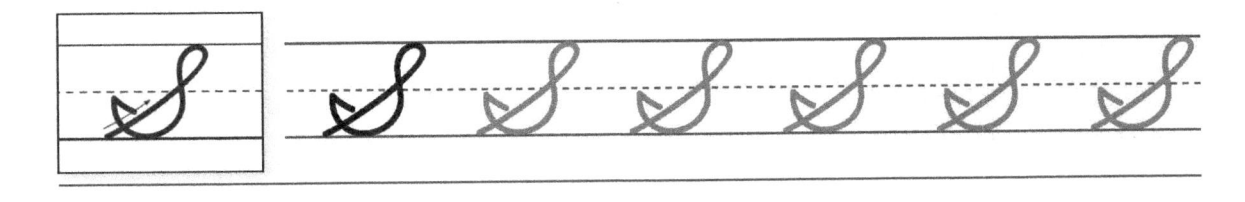

S S S S S S S

G G G G G G G

Sal Sr. met Gail.

Greg is our guest.

Handwriting **385**

Name _____ Date _____

I J

Trace and write the letters. Then write the sentences.

I I I I I I I

J J J J J J J

Ida is in India.

Jack is in Japan.

Name _____ Date _____

Spacing Letters and Words

You can make your writing easy to read. Letters should not be too close or too far apart.

These letters are spaced just right.

Draw a slanted line between these words to check that the spacing is as wide as a small o. Then copy the sentences.

The/flowers/are in/bloom.

Smell the flowers!

Handwriting 387

Name _____ Date _____

N M

Trace and write the letters. Then write the sentences.

n n n n n n

m m m m m m

Nebraska Nevada

Minnesota Maine

Name _____ Date _____

H K

Trace and write the letters. Then write the sentences.

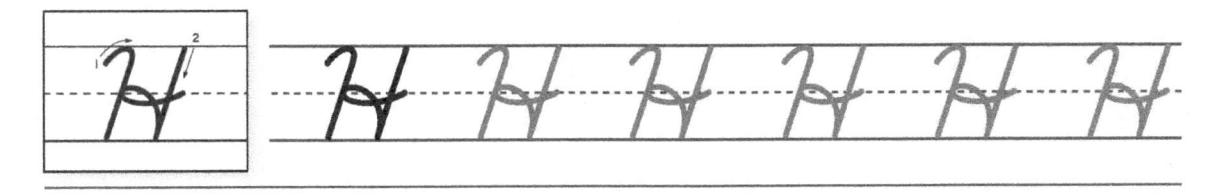

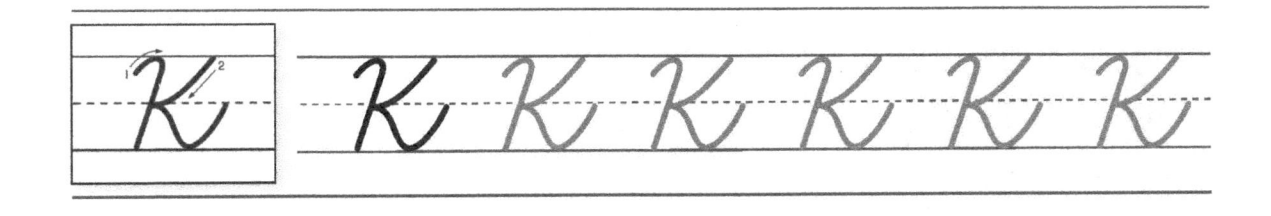

H H H H H H H

K K K K K K K

Hank likes Haiti.

Kai likes Kansas.

Name _____ Date _____

P Q

Trace and write the letters. Then write the sentences.

P P P P P P P

Q Q Q Q Q Q Q

Quebec Quin Quito

Pittsburgh Plano

Name _____ Date _____

V U

Trace and write the letters. Then write the sentences.

V V V V V V V

U U U U U U U

Viv is in Vermont.

Ute lives in Utah.

Name _____ Date _____

W X

Trace and write the letters. Then write the words.

W W W W W W

X X X X X X

Will Waco Wales

Xavier Xia X-axis

Name _____ Date _____

Y Z

Trace and write the letters. Then write the words.

Y Y Y Y Y Y

Z Z Z Z Z Z

Yolanda Yukon

Zena Zen Zachary

Handwriting 393

Name _____ Date _____

Transition to Two Lines

Write the sentences. In the last two rows, write the sentences without the guidelines.

A robin has wings.
Ostriches run fast.
Parrots can talk.
Ducks lay eggs.

Name _____ Date _____

Practice with Small Letters

This is your first complete lesson without a dotted control line. Write your letters and words the same way you have been writing them all year.

e w s r a

i w m n o

see rain mane

Sam was sure

he saw a fox.

Handwriting **395**

Name _____ Date _____

Practice with Tall Letters

Practice writing tall letters and words with tall letters. All tall letters should reach the top line.

t d l k h b f

fit tall doll kit

Tiff is the best.

Jill likes ducks.

Credits

Wonders Practice Book Grade 6 Student Edition: *Chapter from Wonders Practice Book Grade 6 Student Edition by McGraw-Hill, 2020* 1

WB WALKER BOOKSTORE
a Mark My Words Company

Thank you for your order!

We are committed to providing excellent service, consistent quality, and maximum savings.

If you are happy with your order, please leave us a positive review at www.amazon.com/feedback or the marketplace from which you ordered.

To resolve any problems, please contact us through the website on which you ordered with order #, isbn (by the barcode), & an explanation of the problem so we can expedite solving your issue.